토익 Listening 목표 달성기와 함께
목표 점수를 달성해 보세요.

KB132723

나의 토익 Listening 목표 달성기

나의 목표 점수	나의 학습 플랜

나의 목표 점수

_____ 점

나의 학습 플랜

☐ [400점 이상] 2주 완성 학습 플랜

☐ [300~395점] 3주 완성 학습 플랜

☐ [295점 이하] 4주 완성 학습 플랜

* 일 단위의 상세 학습 플랜은 p.20에 있습니다.

각 Test를 마친 후, 해당 Test의 점수를 ● 으로 표시하여 자신의 점수 변화를 확인하세요.

495							토익의 고수!			
450										
				고득점은 이제 시간 문제!					
400										
		토익 감 잡았어!							
350										
토익 초보예요!										
300										

	TEST 01	TEST 02	TEST 03	TEST 04	TEST 05	TEST 06	TEST 07	TEST 08	TEST 09	TEST 10
학습일	/	/	/	/	/	/	/	/	/	/
맞은 개수	개	개	개	개	개	개	개	개	개	개
환산점수	점	점	점	점	점	점	점	점	점	점

* 리스닝 점수 환산표는 p.167에 있습니다.

해커스
토익 LC
실전 **1000**제 **2**
LISTENING

문제집

해커스 어학연구소

최신 토익 경향을 완벽하게 반영한
해커스 토익 실전 1000제 2 LISTENING 문제집을 내면서

해커스 토익이 항상 독보적인 베스트셀러의 자리를 지킬 수 있는 것은 늘 **처음과 같은 마음으로** 더 좋은 책을 만들기 위해 고민하고, **최신 경향을 반영**하기 위해 끊임없이 노력하기 때문입니다.

그리고 이러한 노력 끝에 **최신 토익 경향을 반영**한 《해커스 토익 실전 1000제 2 Listening 문제집》(최신개정판)을 출간하게 되었습니다.

최신 출제 경향 완벽 반영!

최신 출제 경향을 철저히 분석하여 실전과 가장 유사한 지문과 문제 10회분을 수록하였습니다. 수록한 모든 문제는 실전과 동일한 환경에서 풀 수 있도록 실제 토익 문제지와 동일하게 구성하였으며, Answer Sheet를 수록하여 시간 관리 연습과 더불어 실전 감각을 보다 높일 수 있도록 하였습니다.

점수를 올려주는 학습 구성과 학습 자료로 토익 고득점 달성!

모든 문제의 정답과 함께 스크립트를 수록하였으며, 해커스토익(Hackers.co.kr)에서 '문제 해석'을 무료로 제공합니다. 문제의 정확한 이해를 통해 토익 리스닝 점수를 향상할 수 있으며, 토익 고득점 달성이 가능합니다.

《해커스 토익 실전 1000제 2 Listening 문제집》은 별매되는 해설집과 함께 학습할 때 보다 효과적으로 학습할 수 있습니다. 또한, 해커스인강(HackersIngang.com)에서 '온라인 실전모의고사 1회분'과 '단어암기 PDF&MP3'를 무료로 제공하며, 토익 스타 강사의 파트별 해설강의를 수강할 수 있습니다.

《**해커스 토익 실전 1000제 2 Listening 문제집**》이 여러분의 토익 목표 점수 달성에 확실한 해결책이 되고 영어 실력 향상, 나아가 **여러분의 꿈을 향한 길에 믿음직한 동반자**가 되기를 소망합니다.

해커스 어학연구소

CONTENTS

무료 해석 바로 보기

토익, 이렇게 공부하면
확실하게 고득점 잡는다!

01
토익에 완벽하게 대비한다!

최신 토익 출제 경향을 반영한 실전 10회분 수록

시험 경향에 맞지 않는 문제들만 풀면, 실전에서는 연습했던 문제와 달라 당황할 수 있습니다. ≪해커스 토익 실전 1000제 2 Listening 문제집≫에 수록된 모든 문제는 최신 출제 경향과 난이도를 반영하여 실전에 철저하게 대비할 수 있도록 하였습니다.

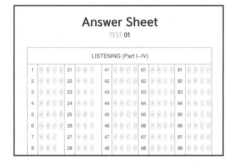

실전과 동일한 구성!

《해커스 토익 실전 1000제 2 Listening 문제집》에 수록된 모든 문제는 실전 문제지와 동일하게 구성되었으며, 미국·캐나다·영국·호주식의 국가별 발음 또한 실전과 동일한 비율로 구성되었습니다. 또한 영국·호주식 실전 버전 MP3로 까다로운 영국·호주식 발음에 확실히 대비할 수 있으며, 고사장/매미 버전 MP3로 실전 감각을 극대화할 수 있습니다. 이와 더불어 교재 뒤에 수록된 Answer Sheet로 실제 시험처럼 답안 마킹을 연습하면서 시간 관리 방법을 익힐 수 있습니다.

02 한 문제를 풀어도, 정확하게 이해하고 푼다!

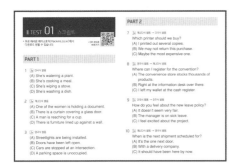

스크립트

수록된 모든 문제에 대한 스크립트를 교재 뒤에 수록하였습니다. 테스트를 마친 후 문제를 풀 때 음성을 정확히 이해하면서 풀었는지, 틀린 문제의 경우 어떤 부분을 놓쳤는지 등을 스크립트를 통해 꼼꼼히 확인하고 다시 듣는 연습을 통해 리스닝 실력을 향상할 수 있도록 하였습니다.

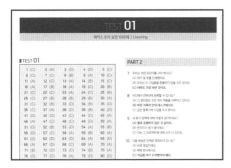

무료 해석 PDF

수록된 모든 지문 및 모든 문제에 대한 정확한 해석을 해커스토익(Hackers.co.kr) 사이트에서 무료로 제공합니다. 이를 통해 테스트를 마친 후, 스크립트를 봐도 잘 이해가 되지 않거나 해석이 어려운 문제를 확인하여 지문과 문제를 보다 정확하게 이해할 수 있도록 하였습니다.

Self 체크 리스트

각 테스트 마지막 페이지에는 Self 체크 리스트를 수록하여 테스트를 마친 후 자신의 문제 풀이 방식과 태도를 스스로 점검할 수 있도록 하였습니다. 이를 통해 효과적인 복습과 더불어 목표 점수를 달성하기 위해 개선해야 할 습관 및 부족한 점을 찾아 보완해나갈 수 있습니다.

03 내 실력을 확실하게 파악한다!

점수 환산표

정답수	리스닝 점수	정답수	리스닝 점수	정답수	리스닝 점수
100	495	66	305	32	135
99	495	65	300	31	130
98	495	64	295	30	125
97	495	63	290	29	120
96	490	62	285	28	115
95	485	61	280	27	110
94	480	60	275	26	105
93	475	59	270	25	100
92	470	58	265	24	95
91	465	57	260	23	90
90	460	56	255	22	85
89	455	55	250	21	80
88	450	54	245	20	75
87	445	53	240	19	70

점수 환산표

교재 부록으로 점수 환산표를 수록하여, 학습자들이 테스트를 마치고 채점을 한 후 바로 점수를 확인하여 **자신의 실력을 정확하게 파악**할 수 있도록 하였습니다. 환산 점수를 교재 첫 장의 목표 달성 그래프에 표시하여 실력의 변화를 확인하고, 학습 계획을 세울 수 있습니다.

무료 온라인 실전모의고사

교재에 수록된 테스트 외에 해커스인강(HackersIngang.com) 사이트에서 온라인 실전모의고사 1회분을 추가로 무료 제공합니다. 이를 통해 토익 시험 전, 학습자들이 자신의 실력을 마지막으로 점검해볼 수 있도록 하였습니다.

인공지능 1:1 토익어플 '빅플'

교재의 문제를 풀고 답안을 입력하기만 하면, 인공지능 어플 '해커스토익 빅플'이 **자동 채점은 물론 성적분석표와 취약 유형 심층 분석까지** 제공합니다. 이를 통해, 자신이 가장 많이 틀리는 취약 유형이 무엇인지 확인하고, 관련 문제들을 추가로 학습하며 취약 유형을 집중 공략하여 약점을 보완할 수 있습니다.

04 다양한 학습 자료를 활용한다!

단어암기 PDF&MP3 / 정답녹음 MP3

해커스인강(HackersIngang.com) 사이트에서 단어암기 PDF와 MP3를 무료로 제공하여, 교재에 수록된 테스트의 중요 단어를 복습하고 암기할 수 있도록 하였습니다. 또한 정답녹음 MP3 파일을 제공하여 학습자들이 보다 편리하게 채점할 수 있도록 하였습니다.

받아쓰기&쉐도잉 워크북 / 받아쓰기&쉐도잉 프로그램

해커스인강(HackersIngang.com) 사이트에서 무료로 제공되는 받아쓰기&쉐도잉 워크북과 MP3를 통해 ≪해커스 토익 실전 1000제 2 Listening 문제집≫ 교재의 파트별 핵심 문장을 반복 학습할 수 있습니다. 동일한 기능의 받아쓰기&쉐도잉 프로그램 또한 무료로 이용 가능하며, 받아쓰기와 쉐도잉을 통해 영어 듣기를 마스터할 수 있게 하였습니다.

방대한 무료 학습 자료(Hackers.co.kr) / 동영상강의(HackersIngang.com)

해커스토익(Hackers.co.kr) 사이트에서는 토익 적중 예상특강을 비롯한 방대하고 유용한 토익 학습 자료를 무료로 이용할 수 있습니다. 또한 온라인 교육 포털 사이트인 해커스인강(HackersIngang.com) 사이트에서 교재 동영상강의를 수강하면, 보다 깊이 있는 학습이 가능합니다.

해설집 미리보기

<해설집 별매>

01 정답과 오답의 이유를 확인하여 Part 1&2 문제 완벽 정복!

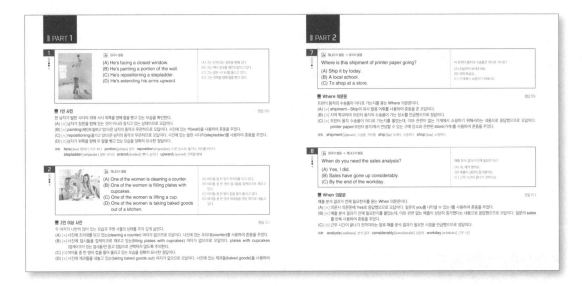

1 문제 및 문제 해석

최신 토익 출제 경향이 반영된 문제를 해설집에도 그대로 수록해, 해설을 보기 전 문제를 다시 한번 풀어보며 자신이 어떤 과정으로 정답을 선택했는지 되짚어 볼 수 있습니다. 함께 수록된 정확한 해석을 보며 문장 구조를 꼼꼼하게 파악하여 문제를 완벽하게 이해할 수 있습니다.

2 문제 유형 및 난이도

모든 문제마다 문제 유형을 제시하여 자주 틀리는 문제 유형을 쉽게 파악할 수 있고, 사전 테스트를 거쳐 검증된 문제별 난이도를 확인하여 자신의 실력과 학습 목표에 따라 학습할 수 있습니다. 문제 유형은 모두 《해커스 토익 Listening》의 목차 목록과 동일하여, 보완 학습이 필요할 경우 쉽게 참고할 수 있습니다.

3 상세한 해설 및 어휘

문제 유형별로 가장 효과적인 해결 방법을 제시하며, 오답 보기가 오답이 되는 이유까지 상세하게 설명하여 틀린 문제의 원인을 파악하고 보완할 수 있습니다. 또한, 영국·호주식 발음으로 들려준 지문문제에서 어휘의 국가별 발음이 다를 경우, 미국·영국식 발음 기호를 모두 수록하여 국가별 발음 차이까지 익힐 수 있도록 하였습니다.

02 효율적인 Part 3&4 문제풀이 전략으로 고득점 달성!

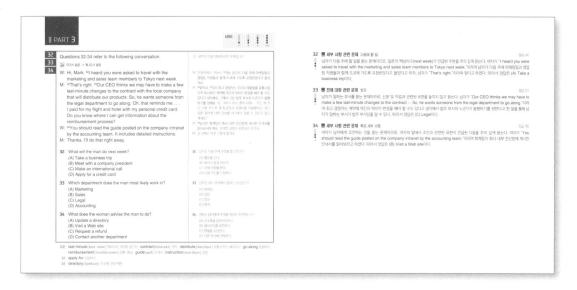

1 지문, 문제, 해석, 정답의 단서

최신 토익 출제 경향이 반영된 지문 및 문제와 함께 수록된 정확한 해석을 보며 지문 및 문제의 내용을 완벽하게 이해할 수 있습니다. 또한, 각 문제별로 표시된 정답의 단서를 확인하여, 모든 문제에 대한 정답의 근거를 정확하게 파악하는 연습을 할 수 있습니다.

2 문제 유형별 상세한 해설 및 문제 풀이 방법

질문 유형별로 가장 효율적인 해결 방법이 적용된 문제 풀이 방법을 제시하였습니다. 대화/지문에서 주의 깊게 들어야 할 부분이나 파악해야 할 사항을 확인하는 단계부터 대화/지문을 들으며 정답을 선택하는 문제 풀이 과정을 읽는 것만으로도 자연스럽게 Part 3·4의 문제 풀이 전략을 익힐 수 있습니다.

3 바꾸어 표현하기

대화/지문의 내용이 질문이나 정답 보기에서 바꾸어 표현된 경우, [대화/지문의 표현 → 정답 보기의 표현] 혹은 [질문의 표현 → 대화/지문의 표현]으로 정리하여 한눈에 확인할 수 있도록 하였습니다. 이를 통해 Part 3·4 풀이 전략을 익히고 나아가 고득점 달성이 가능하도록 하였습니다.

토익 소개 및 시험장 Tips

토익이란 무엇인가?

TOEIC은 Test Of English for International Communication의 약자로 영어가 모국어가 아닌 사람들을 대상으로 언어 본래의 기능인 '커뮤니케이션' 능력에 중점을 두고 일상생활 또는 국제 업무 등에 필요한 실용영어 능력을 평가하는 시험입니다. 토익은 일상생활 및 비즈니스 현장에서 필요로 하는 내용을 평가하기 위해 개발되었고 다음과 같은 실용적인 주제들을 주로 다룹니다.

- ▌ 협력 개발: 연구, 제품 개발
- ▌ 재무 회계: 대출, 투자, 세금, 회계, 은행 업무
- ▌ 일반 업무: 계약, 협상, 마케팅, 판매
- ▌ 기술 영역: 전기, 공업 기술, 컴퓨터, 실험실
- ▌ 사무 영역: 회의, 서류 업무
- ▌ 물품 구입: 쇼핑, 물건 주문, 대금 지불

- ▌ 식사: 레스토랑, 회식, 만찬
- ▌ 문화: 극장, 스포츠, 피크닉
- ▌ 건강: 의료 보험, 병원 진료, 치과
- ▌ 제조: 생산 조립 라인, 공장 경영
- ▌ 직원: 채용, 은퇴, 급여, 진급, 고용 기회
- ▌ 주택: 부동산, 이사, 기업 부지

토익의 파트별 구성

구성		내용	문항 수	시간	배점
Listening Test	Part 1	사진 묘사	6문항 (1번~6번)	45분	495점
	Part 2	질의 응답	25문항 (7번~31번)		
	Part 3	짧은 대화	39문항, 13지문 (32번~70번)		
	Part 4	짧은 담화	30문항, 10지문 (71번~100번)		
Reading Test	Part 5	단문 빈칸 채우기 (문법/어휘)	30문항 (101번~130번)	75분	495점
	Part 6	장문 빈칸 채우기 (문법/어휘/문장 고르기)	16문항, 4지문 (131번~146번)		
	Part 7	지문 읽고 문제 풀기(독해) - 단일 지문 (Single Passage) - 이중 지문 (Double Passages) - 삼중 지문 (Triple Passages)	54문항, 15지문 (147번~200번) - 29문항, 10지문 (147번~175번) - 10문항, 2지문 (176번~185번) - 15문항, 3지문 (186번~200번)		
Total		7 Parts	200문항	120분	990점

토익 접수 방법 및 성적 확인

1. 접수 방법
- 접수 기간을 TOEIC위원회 인터넷 사이트(www.toeic.co.kr) 혹은 공식 애플리케이션에서 확인하고 접수합니다.
- 접수 시 jpg형식의 사진 파일이 필요하므로 미리 준비합니다.

2. 성적 확인
- 시험일로부터 약 10일 이후 TOEIC위원회 인터넷 사이트(www.toeic.co.kr) 혹은 공식 애플리케이션에서 확인합니다. (성적 발표 기간은 회차마다 상이함)
- 시험 접수 시, 우편 수령과 온라인 출력 중 성적 수령 방법을 선택할 수 있습니다.
  * 온라인 출력은 성적 발표 즉시 발급 가능하나, 우편 수령은 약 7일가량의 발송 기간이 소요될 수 있습니다.

시험 당일 준비물

| 신분증 | 연필&지우개 | 시계 | 수험번호를 적어둔 메모 | 오답노트&단어암기장 |

* 시험 당일 신분증이 없으면 시험에 응시할 수 없으므로, 반드시 ETS에서 요구하는 신분증(주민등록증, 운전면허증, 공무원증 등)을 지참해야 합니다.
  ETS에서 인정하는 신분증 종류는 TOEIC위원회 인터넷 사이트(www.toeic.co.kr)에서 확인 가능합니다.

시험 진행 순서

정기시험/추가시험(오전)	추가시험(오후)	진행내용	유의사항
AM 9:30 - 9:45	PM 2:30 - 2:45	답안지 작성 오리엔테이션	10분 전에 고사장에 도착하여, 이름과 수험번호로 고사실을 확인합니다.
AM 9:45 - 9:50	PM 2:45 - 2:50	쉬는 시간	준비해간 오답노트나 단어암기장으로 최종 정리를 합니다. 시험 중간에는 쉬는 시간이 없으므로 화장실에 꼭 다녀오도록 합니다.
AM 9:50 - 10:10	PM 2:50 - 3:10	신분 확인 및 문제지 배부	
AM 10:10 - 10:55	PM 3:10 - 3:55	Listening Test	Part 1과 Part 2는 문제를 풀면서 정답을 바로 답안지에 마킹합니다. Part 3와 Part 4는 문제의 정답 보기 옆에 살짝 표시해두고, Listening Test가 끝난 후 한꺼번에 마킹합니다.
AM 10:55 - 12:10	PM 3:55 - 5:10	Reading Test	각 문제를 풀 때 바로 정답을 마킹합니다.

* 추가시험은 토요일 오전 또는 오후에 시행되므로 이 사항도 꼼꼼히 확인합니다.
* 당일 진행 순서에 대한 더 자세한 내용은 해커스토익(Hackers.co.kr) 사이트에서 확인할 수 있습니다.

▌Part 1 사진 묘사 (6문제)

사진을 가장 잘 묘사한 문장을 4개의 보기 중에서 고르는 유형

문제 형태

문제지	음성
1. 	Number 1. Look at the picture marked number 1 in your test book. (A) He is writing on a sheet of paper. (B) He is reaching for a glass. (C) He is seated near a window. (D) He is opening up a laptop computer.

해설 남자가 창문 근처에 앉아 있는 모습을 seated near a window(창문 근처에 앉아 있다)로 묘사한 (C)가 정답이다.

문제 풀이 전략

1. 보기를 듣기 전에 사진을 묘사할 수 있는 표현을 미리 연상합니다.

보기를 듣기 전에 사진을 보면서 사용 가능한 주어와 등장 인물의 동작이나 사물을 나타내는 동사 및 명사를 미리 연상합니다. 표현을 미리 연상하는 과정에서 사진의 내용을 정확하게 확인하게 되며, 연상했던 표현이 보기에서 사용될 경우 훨씬 명확하게 들을 수 있어 정답 선택이 수월해집니다.

2. 사진을 완벽하게 묘사한 것이 아니라 가장 적절하게 묘사한 보기를 선택합니다.

Part 1은 사진을 완벽하게 묘사한 보기가 아니라 가장 적절하게 묘사한 보기를 선택해야 합니다. 이를 위해 Part 1의 문제를 풀 때 O, ×를 표시하면서 보기를 들으면 오답 보기를 확실히 제거할 수 있어 정확히 정답을 선택할 수 있습니다. 특별히 Part 1에서 자주 출제되는 오답 유형을 알아두면 ×를 표시하면서 훨씬 수월하게 정답을 선택할 수 있습니다.

Part 1 빈출 오답 유형

- 사진 속 사람의 동작을 잘못 묘사한 오답
- 사진에 없는 사람이나 사물을 언급한 오답
- 사진 속 사물의 상태나 위치를 잘못 묘사한 오답
- 사물의 상태를 사람의 동작으로 잘못 묘사한 오답
- 사진에서는 알 수 없는 사실을 진술한 오답
- 혼동하기 쉬운 어휘를 이용한 오답

* 실제 시험을 볼 때, Part 1 디렉션이 나오는 동안 Part 5 문제를 최대한 많이 풀면 전체 시험 시간 조절에 도움이 됩니다. 하지만 "Now, Part 1 will begin"이라는 음성이 들리면 바로 Part 1으로 돌아가서 문제를 풀도록 합니다.

▌Part 2 질의 응답 (25문제)

영어로 된 질문을 듣고 가장 적절한 응답을 3개의 보기 중에서 고르는 유형

문제 형태

문제지	음성
7. Mark your answer on your answer sheet.	Number 7. When is the presentation going to be held? (A) I'm going to discuss sales levels. (B) Sometime on Tuesday. (C) He handled the preparations.

해설 의문사 When을 이용하여 발표가 진행될 시기를 묻고 있는 문제이므로 Sometime on Tuesday라는 시점을 언급한 (B)가 정답이다.

문제 풀이 전략

1. 질문의 첫 단어는 절대 놓치지 않도록 합니다.

Part 2의 문제 유형은 질문의 첫 단어로 결정되므로 절대 첫 단어를 놓치지 않아야 합니다. Part 2에서 평균 11문제 정도 출제되는 의문사 의문문은 첫 단어인 의문사만 들으면 대부분 정답을 선택할 수 있습니다. 그리고 다른 유형의 문제도 첫 단어를 통하여 유형, 시제, 주어 등 문제 풀이와 관련된 기본적인 정보를 파악할 수 있습니다.

2. 오답 유형을 숙지하여 오답 제거 방법을 100% 활용하도록 합니다.

Part 2에서는 오답의 유형이 어느 정도 일정한 패턴으로 사용되고 있습니다. 따라서 오답 유형을 숙지해두어 문제를 풀 때마다 오답 제거 방법을 최대한 활용하도록 합니다. 이를 위해 Part 2의 문제를 풀 때 O, ×를 표시하면서 보기를 들으면 오답 보기를 확실히 제거할 수 있어 정확히 정답을 선택할 수 있습니다.

Part 2 빈출 오답 유형

· 질문에 등장한 단어를 반복하거나, 발음이 유사한 어휘를 사용한 오답

· 동의어, 관련 어휘, 다의어를 사용한 오답

· 주체나 시제를 혼동한 오답

· 정보를 묻는 의문사 의문문에 Yes/No로 응답한 오답

* 실제 시험을 볼 때, Part 2 디렉션이 나오는 동안 Part 5 문제를 최대한 많이 풀면 전체 시험 시간 조절에 도움이 됩니다. 하지만 "Now, let us begin with question number 7"이라는 음성이 들리면 바로 Part 2로 돌아가서 문제를 풀도록 합니다.

Part 3 짧은 대화 (39문제)

· 2~3명이 주고받는 짧은 대화를 듣고 관련 질문에 대한 정답을 고르는 유형
· 구성: 총 13개의 대화에 39문제 출제 (한 대화 당 3문제, 일부 대화는 3문제와 함께 시각 자료가 출제)

문제 형태

문제지	음성
32. What are the speakers mainly discussing? (A) Finding a venue (B) Scheduling a renovation (C) Choosing a menu (D) Organizing a conference 33. What does the woman offer to do? (A) Visit a nearby event hall (B) Revise a travel itinerary (C) Proceed with a booking (D) Contact a facility manager 34. What does the woman mean when she says, "we're all set"? (A) Some furniture will be arranged. (B) Some memos will be circulated. (C) An update will be installed. (D) An area will be large enough.	Questions 32 through 34 refer to the following conversation. W: Joseph, I'm worried it'll be too chilly for the outdoor luncheon we've planned for Wednesday. M: I agree. We'd better book an event hall instead. W: How about Wolford Hall? I'm looking at its Web site now, and it appears to be available. M: Oh, that'd be ideal. That place is near our office, so staff won't have to travel far. W: I can book the hall now, if you want. We need it from 11 A.M. to 2 P.M., right? M: Yeah. Just make sure it can accommodate 50 people. W: It says it'll hold up to 70, so we're all set. M: Perfect. I'll send staff an e-mail with the updated details. Number 32. What are the speakers mainly discussing? Number 33. What does the woman offer to do? Number 34. What does the woman mean when she says, "we're all set"?

해설　32. 대화의 주제를 묻는 문제이다. 여자가 it'll be too chilly for the outdoor luncheon이라며 야외 오찬을 하기에는 날씨가 너무 쌀쌀할 것 같다고 하자, 남자가 We'd better book an event hall instead라며 대신 행사장을 예약하는 것이 낫겠다고 한 뒤, 행사를 위한 장소를 찾는 것에 관한 내용으로 대화가 이어지고 있다. 따라서 정답은 (A)이다.

　　33. 여자가 해주겠다고 제안하는 것을 묻는 문제이다. 여자가 I can book the hall now라며 지금 자신이 그 행사장을 예약할 수 있다고 하였다. 따라서 정답은 (C)이다.

　　34. 여자가 하는 말의 의도를 묻는 문제이다. 남자가 Just make sure it[hall] can accommodate 50 people이라며 행사장이 50명의 사람들을 수용할 수 있는지만 확인하라고 하자, 여자가 it'll hold up to 70, so we're all set이라며 그것은 70명까지 수용할 것이니 우리는 준비가 다 되었다고 한 말을 통해 행사장의 공간이 충분히 클 것임을 알 수 있다. 따라서 정답은 (D)이다.

문제 풀이 전략

1. 대화를 듣기 전에 반드시 질문과 보기를 먼저 읽어야 합니다.

① Part 3의 디렉션을 들려줄 때 32번부터 34번까지의 질문과 보기를 읽으면, 이후 계속해서 대화를 듣기 전에 질문과 보기를 미리 읽을 수 있습니다.

② 질문을 읽을 때에는 질문 유형을 파악한 후, 해당 유형에 따라 어느 부분을 들을지와 어떤 내용을 들을지 듣기 전략을 세웁니다. 시각 자료가 출제된 대화의 경우, 시각 자료를 함께 확인하면서 시각 자료의 종류와 그 내용을 파악합니다.

③ 보기를 읽을 때에는 각 보기를 다르게 구별해주는 어휘를 선택적으로 읽어야 합니다. 특별히 보기가 문장일 경우, 주어가 모두 다르면 주어를, 주어가 모두 같으면 동사 또는 목적어 등의 중요 어휘를 키워드로 결정합니다.

2. 대화를 들으면서 동시에 정답을 선택합니다.

① 질문과 보기를 읽으며 세운 듣기 전략을 토대로, 대화를 들으면서 동시에 각 문제의 정답을 선택합니다.

② 3인 대화의 경우, 대화가 시작하기 전에 "Questions ~ refer to the following conversation with three speakers."라는 음성이 재생되므로 각 대화별 디렉션에도 집중해야 합니다.

③ 대화가 끝난 후 관련된 3개의 질문을 읽어줄 때 다음 대화와 관련된 3개의 질문과 보기를 재빨리 읽으면서 듣기 전략을 다시 세워야 합니다.

④ 만약 대화가 다 끝났는데도 정답을 선택하지 못했다면 가장 정답인 것 같은 보기를 선택하고, 곧바로 다음 대화에 해당하는 질문과 보기를 읽기 시작하는 것이 오답률을 줄이는 현명한 방법입니다.

3. 대화의 초반은 반드시 들어야 합니다.

① 대화에서 초반에 언급된 내용 중 80% 이상이 문제로 출제되므로 대화의 초반은 반드시 들어야 합니다.

② 특별히 대화의 주제를 묻는 문제, 대화자의 직업, 대화의 장소를 묻는 문제에 대한 정답의 단서는 대부분 대화의 초반에 언급됩니다.

③ 초반을 듣지 못하고 놓칠 경우 대화 후반에서 언급된 특정 표현을 사용한 보기를 정답으로 선택하는 오류를 범할 수 있으므로 각별히 주의해야 합니다.

Part 4 짧은 담화 (30문제)

· 짧은 담화를 듣고 관련 질문에 대한 정답을 고르는 유형
· 구성: 총 10개의 지문에 30문제 출제 (한 지문 당 3문제, 일부 지문은 3문제와 함께 시각 자료가 출제)

문제 형태

문제지	음성
	Questions 95 through 97 refer to the following announcement and list.

Department	Manager
Accounting	Janet Lee
Sales	Sarah Bedford
Human Resources	David Weber
Marketing	Michael Brenner

95. What is the purpose of the announcement?

(A) To explain a new project
(B) To describe a job opening
(C) To discuss a recent hire
(D) To verify a policy change

96. Look at the graphic. Which department will Shannon Clark manage?

(A) Accounting
(B) Sales
(C) Human Resources
(D) Marketing

97. What will probably happen on September 1?

(A) A job interview
(B) A product launch
(C) A staff gathering
(D) An employee evaluation

음성:

May I have your attention, please? I just received an e-mail from David Weber in human resources regarding a new manager. Shannon Clark will begin working here next month. Ms. Clark has over a decade of experience working for multinational corporations, so she brings a wealth of knowledge to our company. She will be replacing Michael Brenner, who is retiring this month. One of the other department managers . . . um, Janet Lee . . . has arranged a get-together on September 1 to introduce Ms. Clark. Food and beverages will be provided. Please give her a warm welcome.

Number 95.
What is the purpose of the announcement?

Number 96.
Look at the graphic. Which department will Shannon Clark manage?

Number 97.
What will probably happen on September 1?

해설 95. 공지의 목적을 묻는 문제이다. I just received an e-mail ~ regarding a new manager. Shannon Clark will begin working here next month라며 새로운 관리자에 관련된 이메일을 방금 받았으며, Shannon Clark가 다음 달에 이곳에서 근무를 시작할 것이라고 하였다. 따라서 정답은 (C)이다.

96. Shannon Clark가 관리할 부서를 묻는 문제이다. She[Shannon Clark] will be replacing Michael Brenner, who is retiring this month라며 Shannon Clark은 이달에 은퇴하는 Michael Brenner를 대신할 것이라고 하였으므로, Michael Brenner가 관리자로 일하던 마케팅 부서를 관리하게 될 것임을 표에서 알 수 있다. 따라서 정답은 (D)이다.

97. 9월 1일에 일어날 일을 묻는 문제이다. Janet Lee ~ has arranged a get-together on September 1라며 Janet Lee가 9월 1일에 열릴 모임을 마련했다고 하였다. 따라서 정답은 (C)이다.

문제 풀이 전략

1. 지문을 듣기 전에 반드시 질문과 보기를 먼저 읽어야 합니다.

① Part 4의 디렉션을 들려줄 때 71번부터 73번까지의 질문과 보기를 읽으면, 이후 계속해서 지문을 듣기 전에 질문과 보기를 미리 읽을 수 있습니다.

② 질문을 읽을 때에는 질문 유형을 파악한 후, 해당 유형에 따라 어느 부분을 들을지와 어떤 내용을 들을지 듣기 전략을 세웁니다. 시각 자료가 출제된 담화의 경우, 시각 자료를 함께 확인하면서 시각 자료의 종류와 그 내용을 파악합니다.

③ 보기를 읽을 때에는 각 보기를 다르게 구별해주는 어휘를 선택적으로 읽어야 합니다. 특별히 보기가 문장일 경우, 주어가 모두 다르면 주어를, 주어가 모두 같으면 동사 또는 목적어 등의 중요 어휘를 키워드로 결정합니다.

2. 지문을 들으면서 동시에 정답을 선택합니다.

① 질문과 보기를 읽으며 세운 듣기 전략을 토대로, 지문을 들으면서 동시에 각 문제의 정답을 곧바로 선택합니다.

② 지문의 음성이 끝날 때에는 세 문제의 정답 선택도 완료되어 있어야 합니다.

③ 지문의 음성이 끝난 후 관련된 3개의 질문을 읽어줄 때 다음 지문과 관련된 3개의 질문과 보기를 재빨리 읽으면서 듣기 전략을 다시 세워야 합니다.

④ 만약 지문이 다 끝났는데도 정답을 선택하지 못했다면 가장 정답인 것 같은 보기를 선택하고, 곧바로 다음 지문에 해당하는 질문과 보기를 읽기 시작하는 것이 오답률을 줄이는 현명한 방법입니다.

3. 지문의 초반은 반드시 들어야 합니다.

① 지문에서 초반에 언급된 내용 중 80% 이상이 문제로 출제되므로 지문의 초반을 반드시 들어야 합니다.

② 특별히 지문의 주제/목적 문제나 화자/청자 및 담화 장소 문제처럼 전체 지문 관련 문제에 대한 정답의 단서는 대부분 지문의 초반에 언급됩니다.

③ 초반을 듣지 못하고 놓칠 경우 더 이상 관련된 내용이 언급되지 않아 정답 선택이 어려워질 수 있으므로 주의해야 합니다.

수준별 맞춤 학습 플랜

TEST 01을 마친 후 자신의 환산 점수에 맞는 학습 플랜을 선택하고 매일매일 박스에 체크하며 공부합니다. 각 TEST를 마친 후, 다양한 자료를 활용하여 각 테스트를 꼼꼼하게 리뷰합니다.

* 각 테스트를 마친 후, 해당 테스트의 점수를 교재 앞쪽에 있는 [토익 Listening 목표 달성기]에 기록하여 자신의 점수 변화를 확인할 수 있습니다.

400점 이상
2주 완성 학습 플랜

· 2주 동안 매일 테스트 1회분을 교재 뒤의 Answer Sheet(p.229)를 활용하여 실전처럼 풀어본 후 꼼꼼하게 리뷰합니다.
· 리뷰 시, 틀렸던 문제를 다시 듣고 풀어본 후, 교재 뒤의 **스크립트**를 활용하여 들리지 않았던 부분까지 완벽히 이해합니다.
· 해커스토익(Hackers.co.kr)에서 무료로 제공되는 **지문 및 문제 해석**으로 틀린 지문과 문제의 의미를 확실하게 이해합니다.
· 해커스인강(HackersIngang.com)에서 무료로 제공되는 **단어암기장 및 단어암기 MP3**로 각 TEST의 핵심 어휘 중 모르는 어휘만 체크하여 암기합니다.

	Day 1	Day 2	Day 3	Day 4	Day 5
Week 1	☐ Test 01 풀기 및 리뷰	☐ Test 02 풀기 및 리뷰	☐ Test 03 풀기 및 리뷰	☐ Test 04 풀기 및 리뷰	☐ Test 05 풀기 및 리뷰
Week 2	☐ Test 06 풀기 및 리뷰	☐ Test 07 풀기 및 리뷰	☐ Test 08 풀기 및 리뷰	☐ Test 09 풀기 및 리뷰	☐ Test 10 풀기 및 리뷰

※ 《해커스 토익 실전 1000제 2 Listening 해설집》(별매)으로 리뷰하기
  · 자신이 틀렸던 문제와 난이도 최상 문제를 다시 한번 풀어보고 완벽하게 이해합니다.
  · 틀린 문제는 정답 및 오답 해설을 보며 오답이 왜 오답인지 그 이유까지 확실하게 파악합니다.

300~395점
3주 완성 학습 플랜

· 3주 동안 첫째 날, 둘째 날에 테스트 1회분씩을 풀어본 후 꼼꼼하게 리뷰하고, 셋째 날에는 2회분에 대한 심화 학습을 합니다.
· 리뷰 시, 틀렸던 문제를 다시 듣고 풀어본 후, 교재 뒤의 **스크립트**를 활용하여 들리지 않았던 부분까지 완벽히 이해합니다.
· 심화 학습 시, 리뷰했던 내용을 복습하고 대화/지문의 핵심 어휘를 정리하고 암기합니다.
· 해커스토익(Hackers.co.kr)에서 무료로 제공되는 **지문 및 문제 해석**으로 틀린 지문과 문제의 의미를 확실하게 이해합니다.
· 해커스인강(HackersIngang.com)에서 무료로 제공되는 **단어암기장 및 단어암기 MP3**로 각 TEST의 핵심 어휘를 암기합니다.

	Day 1	Day 2	Day 3	Day 4	Day 5
Week 1	☐ Test 01 풀기 및 리뷰	☐ Test 02 풀기 및 리뷰	☐ Test 01&02 심화 학습	☐ Test 03 풀기 및 리뷰	☐ Test 04 풀기 및 리뷰
Week 2	☐ Test 03&04 심화 학습	☐ Test 05 풀기 및 리뷰	☐ Test 06 풀기 및 리뷰	☐ Test 05&06 심화 학습	☐ Test 07 풀기 및 리뷰
Week 3	☐ Test 08 풀기 및 리뷰	☐ Test 07&08 심화 학습	☐ Test 09 풀기 및 리뷰	☐ Test 10 풀기 및 리뷰	☐ Test 09&10 심화 학습

※ 《해커스 토익 실전 1000제 2 Listening 해설집》(별매)으로 리뷰하기
  · 자신이 틀렸던 문제와 난이도 중 이상의 문제를 다시 한번 풀어보고 완벽하게 이해합니다.
  · 틀린 문제는 정답 및 오답 해설을 보며 오답이 왜 오답인지 그 이유까지 확실하게 파악합니다.
  · 모든 문제마다 표시된 문제 유형을 보며 자신이 자주 틀리는 문제 유형이 무엇인지 파악하고 보완합니다.
  · 대화/지문에 자주색으로 표시된 정답의 단서를 보고 정답을 선택해보며 문제 풀이 노하우를 파악합니다.

295점 이하
4주 완성 학습 플랜

· 4주 동안 이틀에 걸쳐 테스트 1회분을 풀고 꼼꼼하게 리뷰합니다.
· 리뷰 시, 모든 문제를 다시 듣고 풀어본 후, 교재 뒤쪽의 **스크립트**를 활용하여 들리지 않았던 부분까지 완벽하게 이해합니다.
· 해커스토익(Hackers.co.kr)에서 무료로 제공되는 **지문 및 문제 해석**으로 모든 지문과 문제의 의미를 완벽하게 이해합니다.
· 해커스인강(HackersIngang.com)에서 무료로 제공되는 **단어암기장 및 단어암기 MP3**로 각 TEST의 핵심 어휘를 암기합니다.

	Day 1	Day 2	Day 3	Day 4	Day 5
Week 1	☐ Test 01 풀기	☐ Test 01 리뷰	☐ Test 02 풀기	☐ Test 02 리뷰	☐ Test 03 풀기
Week 2	☐ Test 03 리뷰	☐ Test 04 풀기	☐ Test 04 리뷰	☐ Test 05 풀기	☐ Test 05 리뷰
Week 3	☐ Test 06 풀기	☐ Test 06 리뷰	☐ Test 07 풀기	☐ Test 07 리뷰	☐ Test 08 풀기
Week 4	☐ Test 08 리뷰	☐ Test 09 풀기	☐ Test 09 리뷰	☐ Test 10 풀기	☐ Test 10 리뷰

※ ≪해커스 토익 실전 1000제 2 Listening 해설집≫(별매)**으로 리뷰하기**
  · 자신이 틀렸던 문제와 난이도 중 이상의 문제를 다시 한번 풀어보고 완벽하게 이해합니다.
  · 틀린 문제는 정답 및 오답 해설을 보며 오답이 왜 오답인지 그 이유까지 확실하게 파악합니다.
  · 모든 문제마다 표시된 문제 유형을 보며 자신이 자주 틀리는 문제 유형이 무엇인지 파악하고 보완합니다.
  · 대화/지문에 자주색으로 표시된 정답의 단서를 보고 정답을 선택해보며 문제 풀이 노하우를 파악합니다.
  · Part 3·4의 중요한 바꾸어 표현하기를 정리하고 암기합니다.

해커스와 함께라면 여러분의 목표를 더 빠르게 달성할 수 있습니다!
자신의 점수에 맞춰 아래 해커스 교재로 함께 학습하시면 더욱 빠르게 여러분이 목표한 바를 달성할 수 있습니다.

400점 이상	300~395점	295점 이하
≪해커스 토익 Listening≫	≪해커스 토익 750+ LC≫	≪해커스 토익 스타트 Listening≫

▌TEST 01

잠깐! 테스트 전 확인사항

1. 휴대 전화의 전원을 끄셨나요? □ 예
2. Answer Sheet, 연필, 지우개를 준비하셨나요? □ 예
3. MP3를 들을 준비가 되셨나요? □ 예

모든 준비가 완료되었으면 목표 점수를 떠올린 후 테스트를 시작합니다.
TEST 01을 통해 본인의 실력을 평가해 본 후, 본인에게 맞는 학습 플랜(p.20~21)으로 본 교재를 효율적으로 학습해 보세요.

🎧 TEST 01.mp3

실전용·복습용 문제풀이 MP3 무료 다운로드 및 스트리밍 바로듣기 (HackersIngang.com)
* 실제 시험장의 소음까지 재현해 낸 고사장 소음/매미 버전 MP3, 영국식·호주식 발음 집중 MP3, 고속 버전 MP3까지 구매하면 실전에 더욱 완벽히 대비할 수 있습니다.

무료MP3 바로듣기

LISTENING TEST

In this section, you must demonstrate your ability to understand spoken English. This section is divided into four parts and will take approximately 45 minutes to complete. Do not mark the answers in your test book. Use the answer sheet that is provided separately.

PART 1

Directions: For each question, you will listen to four short statements about a picture in your test book. These statements will not be printed and will only be spoken one time. Select the statement that best describes what is happening in the picture and mark the corresponding letter (A), (B), (C), or (D) on the answer sheet.

Sample Answer
Ⓐ ● Ⓒ Ⓓ

The statement that best describes the picture is (B), "The man is sitting at the desk." So, you should mark letter (B) on the answer sheet.

1.

2.

GO ON TO THE NEXT PAGE

3.

4.

5.

6.

GO ON TO THE NEXT PAGE ➤

PART 2

Directions: For each question, you will listen to a statement or question followed by three possible responses spoken in English. They will not be printed and will only be spoken one time. Select the best response and mark the corresponding letter (A), (B), or (C) on your answer sheet.

7. Mark your answer on your answer sheet.

8. Mark your answer on your answer sheet.

9. Mark your answer on your answer sheet.

10. Mark your answer on your answer sheet.

11. Mark your answer on your answer sheet.

12. Mark your answer on your answer sheet.

13. Mark your answer on your answer sheet.

14. Mark your answer on your answer sheet.

15. Mark your answer on your answer sheet.

16. Mark your answer on your answer sheet.

17. Mark your answer on your answer sheet.

18. Mark your answer on your answer sheet.

19. Mark your answer on your answer sheet.

20. Mark your answer on your answer sheet.

21. Mark your answer on your answer sheet.

22. Mark your answer on your answer sheet.

23. Mark your answer on your answer sheet.

24. Mark your answer on your answer sheet.

25. Mark your answer on your answer sheet.

26. Mark your answer on your answer sheet.

27. Mark your answer on your answer sheet.

28. Mark your answer on your answer sheet.

29. Mark your answer on your answer sheet.

30. Mark your answer on your answer sheet.

31. Mark your answer on your answer sheet.

Directions: In this part, you will listen to several conversations between two or more speakers. These conversations will not be printed and will only be spoken one time. For each conversation, you will be asked to answer three questions. Select the best response and mark the corresponding letter (A), (B), (C), or (D) on your answer sheet.

32. What does the woman want to do?

(A) Rent accommodations
(B) Store some furniture
(C) Purchase some household goods
(D) Use a moving service

33. What does the man suggest?

(A) Hiring a professional construction crew
(B) Making an advance payment
(C) Buying some new containers
(D) Considering a longer rental period

34. What will the man most likely do next?

(A) Prepare a contract
(B) Show some options
(C) Cancel a rental commitment
(D) Provide a service address

35. What does the woman ask the man to do?

(A) Pick up some guests
(B) Order a meal
(C) Send some invitations
(D) Select a venue

36. Why does the woman say, "my brother lives in the suburbs"?

(A) To propose an alternative
(B) To request assistance
(C) To reject a suggestion
(D) To show appreciation

37. What does the man say about BK Steakhouse?

(A) It has an outdoor seating area.
(B) It will introduce an online booking system.
(C) It serves affordable menu items.
(D) It offers complimentary valet parking.

38. Where most likely is the conversation taking place?

(A) At a university
(B) At a concert hall
(C) At a theater
(D) At a gallery

39. What does the woman want permission to do?

(A) Obtain a brochure
(B) Take photographs
(C) Attend an event
(D) Tour a facility

40. What does Arthur suggest the woman do?

(A) Purchase a pass
(B) Call a representative
(C) Send a notification
(D) Complete a form

41. Why did the man visit Amsterdam?

(A) To close a deal
(B) To visit a tourist attraction
(C) To attend a conference
(D) To meet some relatives

42. What did the man especially like in the old city center?

(A) A traditional market
(B) A national museum
(C) An art exhibition
(D) A dining establishment

43. What type of information does the woman request?

(A) A flight number
(B) An e-mail address
(C) A business name
(D) A hotel recommendation

GO ON TO THE NEXT PAGE

44. What industry do the speakers most likely work in?

(A) Accounting
(B) Fashion
(C) Marketing
(D) Education

45. Why does the woman say, "she has a month left on her current contract"?

(A) To suggest a new employee is needed soon
(B) To encourage the man to make a decision
(C) To recommend a change to an interview process
(D) To point out a candidate's lack of qualifications

46. What does the man request the woman do?

(A) Review some documents
(B) Arrange some interviews
(C) Make a job offer
(D) Update a schedule

---

47. Who most likely are the speakers?

(A) Investors
(B) Engineers
(C) Writers
(D) Officials

48. What problem does the woman mention?

(A) A bridge is shut down.
(B) A deadline has passed.
(C) A device has malfunctioned.
(D) A copy is missing.

49. What does Raymond say he will do?

(A) Join another team
(B) Replace a laptop
(C) Request a transfer
(D) Visit another floor

---

50. What is the conversation mainly about?

(A) An annual task
(B) An experimental machine
(C) A new employee
(D) A seasonal promotion

51. Why is the man worried?

(A) He did not sign a document.
(B) He was overcharged for a meal.
(C) He cannot register for a class.
(D) He has a scheduling conflict.

52. What will the man probably do next?

(A) Talk to a customer
(B) Make a phone call
(C) Attend a meeting
(D) Cancel a plan

---

53. Why did the woman ask the man to visit her office?

(A) To offer a solution to a problem
(B) To suggest an organizational change
(C) To talk about a sales method
(D) To discuss a performance issue

54. What made Abigail take leave from work?

(A) She is taking an academic course.
(B) She is recovering from an illness.
(C) She is taking care of her children.
(D) She is relocating to a new home.

55. What does the woman offer to do?

(A) Reassign a task
(B) Provide a worker
(C) Change a deadline
(D) Return a report

---

56. Who most likely is the man?

(A) A front desk clerk
(B) A travel agent
(C) A conference organizer
(D) A software developer

57. Why is the hotel closing the fitness center?

(A) To replace some fitness equipment
(B) To improve guest safety
(C) To perform renovations
(D) To hold a special event

58. What has the hotel done for its guests?

(A) Secured access to another facility
(B) Allowed visitors to check in early
(C) Arranged transportation to an event
(D) Canceled a booking for a room

59. Why is the woman calling?

(A) To report a client complaint
(B) To ask about a technical issue
(C) To find out a meeting location
(D) To confirm a presentation topic

60. How can the woman submit a request?

(A) By visiting a department
(B) By logging into a Web site
(C) By following a link
(D) By sending an e-mail

61. What is mentioned about Ms. Harper?

(A) She will review some slide shows.
(B) She rescheduled an appointment.
(C) She was recently promoted.
(D) She is on a business trip.

Portside Public Library Floor Directory	
1st Floor	Lobby
2nd Floor	Novels
3rd Floor	Non-Fictions
4th Floor	Newspapers and Magazines
5th Floor	Computers and Printers

62. What was the man recently notified about?

(A) An account closure
(B) An expired card
(C) An unread message
(D) An unpaid fine

63. Why does the woman suggest visiting the Web site regularly?

(A) To download a form
(B) To make a payment
(C) To reserve a publication
(D) To prevent future problems

64. Look at the graphic. Which floor will the man most likely go to next?

(A) 2nd floor
(B) 3rd floor
(C) 4th floor
(D) 5th floor

GO ON TO THE NEXT PAGE

TEST

01

02 | 03 | 04 | 05 | 06 | 07 | 08 | 09 | 10

해커스 토익 실전 1000제 2 Listening

Westwood Appliance Special Coupons		
	Valid until: Oct 30
10% off any item over $100	15% off any item over $150
20% off any item over $200	25% off any item over $250

65. What task has the woman been assigned?

(A) Reviewing customer opinions
(B) Giving a presentation
(C) Developing a strategy
(D) Making a report

66. According to the woman, what happened last week?

(A) A competitor started offering free shipping.
(B) A rival company released a new model.
(C) A delivery was sent to the wrong address.
(D) An order was canceled by a customer.

67. Look at the graphic. Which discount rate will no longer be available?

(A) 10% off
(B) 15% off
(C) 20% off
(D) 25% off

Building A	Plaza Shopping Center	Central Hospital
Jackson Ave.		
Greendale Subway Station	Building B	Building C
Elm Ave.		
Building D	Monroe Theater	Public Library

9th St.

68. What are the speakers mainly discussing?

(A) A corporate policy
(B) A workshop schedule
(C) A company expansion
(D) A recruitment strategy

69. What is the man impressed with?

(A) A set of instructions
(B) An office space
(C) An employee benefit
(D) A workshop schedule

70. Look at the graphic. Which building does the man refer to?

(A) Building A
(B) Building B
(C) Building C
(D) Building D

Directions: In this part, you will listen to several short talks by a single speaker. These talks will not be printed and will only be spoken one time. For each talk, you will be asked to answer three questions. Select the best response and mark the corresponding letter (A), (B), (C), or (D) on your answer sheet.

71. What is the main purpose of the talk?

(A) To go over a membership procedure
(B) To introduce a facility
(C) To discuss penalties for disregarding rules
(D) To provide guidelines for employees

72. According to the speaker, what is in the rare collections room?

(A) Old photographs
(B) Handwritten drafts of novels
(C) Historic census data
(D) Correspondence from authors

73. What does the speaker ask the listeners to do?

(A) Ensure that they do not litter
(B) Return books to the shelves
(C) Refrain from making loud noises
(D) Notify staff if items are damaged

74. What is mentioned about the Seattle Modern Art Institute?

(A) It recently opened a new branch.
(B) It expanded an existing facility.
(C) It partnered with another gallery.
(D) It announced a special exhibition.

75. What is special about a celebration?

(A) It will not charge an admission fee.
(B) It will be attended by a local celebrity.
(C) It is sponsored by a city council.
(D) It is exclusively for children.

76. What can guests do in the evening?

(A) Join a private museum tour
(B) Participate in contests
(C) Watch a film
(D) Listen to some music

77. Who most likely is the listener?

(A) A business consultant
(B) A travel agent
(C) A photographer
(D) A recruiting manager

78. Why is the speaker traveling to Portland?

(A) To attend an educational session
(B) To meet with some clients
(C) To shoot a new film
(D) To inspect a branch office

79. Why does the speaker say, "Our return flight is on June 30"?

(A) To fix a due date
(B) To show his preference
(C) To cancel an appointment
(D) To indicate his availability

80. Which department does the speaker most likely work in?

(A) Sales
(B) Personnel
(C) Production
(D) Finance

81. What does the speaker say about Ms. Walker?

(A) She made some changes to a project.
(B) She transferred from a different location.
(C) She was the manager of a branch office.
(D) She was hired by the company last year.

82. What will most likely happen on Friday?

(A) A presentation will be given.
(B) A process will be approved.
(C) A team will be formed.
(D) A deadline will be extended.

GO ON TO THE NEXT PAGE

TEST

01

02 | 03 | 04 | 05 | 06 | 07 | 08 | 09 | 10 | 해커스 토익 실전 1000제 2 Listening

83. What is mentioned about the Bronze Gym Turbo?

(A) It comes preassembled.
(B) It only ships to certain countries.
(C) It requires a large amount of space.
(D) It can be used for multiple purposes.

84. According to the speaker, what happened last month?

(A) A new product was released.
(B) A shipping fee was reduced.
(C) A loyalty program was introduced.
(D) A seasonal sale was launched.

85. What can people do on the Bronze Gym Web site?

(A) Access an online account
(B) View user feedback
(C) Track workout progress
(D) Read an instruction manual

---

86. According to the speaker, what did people like about the new advertisement?

(A) It featured famous athletes.
(B) It included humorous elements.
(C) It presented a positive viewpoint.
(D) It focused on a popular sport.

87. Why does the speaker say, "we averaged about 50,000 per day last week"?

(A) To indicate a concern
(B) To support an assertion
(C) To encourage improvement
(D) To express frustration

88. What does the speaker want to do?

(A) Delay a vehicle release
(B) Hold a promotional event
(C) Produce more commercials
(D) Use another search engine

---

89. What is the speech mainly about?

(A) A corporate policy
(B) A market trend
(C) A company objective
(D) A budget increase

90. According to the speaker, what will happen in February?

(A) A factory will be constructed.
(B) Operations will be halted.
(C) An office will be renovated.
(D) Branches will be opened.

91. How can the listeners find information about open positions?

(A) By reading a pamphlet
(B) By attending a meeting
(C) By calling a department head
(D) By checking out a bulletin board

---

92. What problem does the speaker mention?

(A) A submission was late.
(B) A topic is inappropriate.
(C) An article is too lengthy.
(D) A publication was canceled.

93. What does the speaker imply when he says, "Our editor intends to review the article before the end of the week"?

(A) A revision needs to be approved.
(B) A schedule will be confirmed shortly.
(C) A colleague doesn't have to change a plan.
(D) A task must be completed soon.

94. What does the speaker ask the listener to do?

(A) Return a call
(B) Attend an interview
(C) Visit a business
(D) Meet a representative

Delta Shipping New Employee Orientation - June 15	
Session	**Topic**
8:00 A.M. – 10:00 A.M.	Corporate Structure
10:00 A.M. – 12:00 P.M.	Company Policies
LUNCH	
1:00 P.M. – 3:00 P.M.	Pay and Benefits
3:00 P.M. – 5:00 P.M.	Safety and Security

95. What did the speaker do yesterday?

(A) Received a shipment
(B) Arranged a tour
(C) Uploaded a timetable
(D) Printed a map

96. Look at the graphic. Which topic will not be discussed today?

(A) Corporate Structure
(B) Company Policies
(C) Pay and Benefits
(D) Safety and Security

97. Why should the listeners speak to the receptionist?

(A) To request an item
(B) To register for an event
(C) To receive a job assignment
(D) To fill out a form

Washington Dulles: January 1 Departures		
Destination	**Departure Time**	**Flight #**
Detroit	11:12 A.M.	4010
St. Louis	11:20 A.M.	5192
Cleveland	11:25 A.M.	1330
Philadelphia	11:32 A.M.	1250

98. What is mentioned about the storm?

(A) It has lasted longer than a week.
(B) It is causing traffic accidents.
(C) It has resulted in road closures.
(D) It is among the worst in 10 years.

99. Look at the graphic. Which flight was canceled?

(A) Flight 4010
(B) Flight 5192
(C) Flight 1330
(D) Flight 1250

100. According to the speaker, what will happen tomorrow?

(A) An announcement will be made.
(B) A facility will be reopened.
(C) A winter storm will end.
(D) A travel ban will be lifted.

정답 p.164 / 점수 환산표 p.167 / 스크립트 p.168 / 무료 해석 바로 보기(정답 및 정답 음성 포함)

▮ 정답 음성(QR)이나 정답(p.164)을 이용해 채점하시기 바랍니다. 정답 음성에서 Boy는 (B)를, David는 (D)를 나타냅니다.
▮ 점수 환산표(p.167)를 이용하여 본인의 점수를 확인하고, 그에 따른 학습 플랜을 p.20~21에서 선택한 후 실천해 보세요.
▮ 다음 페이지에 있는 Self 체크 리스트를 통해 자신의 문제 풀이 방식과 태도를 점검해 보세요.

Self 체크 리스트

TEST 01은 무사히 잘 마치셨죠?
이제 다음의 Self 체크 리스트를 통해 자신의 테스트 진행 내용을 점검해 볼까요?

1. 나는 테스트가 진행되는 동안 한 번도 중도에 멈추지 않았다.

　□ 예　　　　　　　　□ 아니오

　아니오에 답한 경우, 이유는 무엇인가요?

2. 나는 답안지 표기까지 성실하게 모두 마무리하였다.

　□ 예　　　　　　　　□ 아니오

　아니오에 답한 경우, 이유는 무엇인가요?

3. 나는 Part 2의 25문항을 푸는 동안 완전히 테스트에 집중하였다.

　□ 예　　　　　　　　□ 아니오

　아니오에 답한 경우, 이유는 무엇인가요?

4. 나는 Part 3를 풀 때 음성이 들리기 전에 해당 질문과 보기를 모두 먼저 읽었다.

　□ 예　　　　　　　　□ 아니오

　아니오에 답한 경우, 이유는 무엇인가요?

5. 나는 Part 4를 풀 때 음성이 들리기 전에 해당 질문과 보기를 모두 먼저 읽었다.

　□ 예　　　　　　　　□ 아니오

　아니오에 답한 경우, 이유는 무엇인가요?

6. 개선해야 할 점 또는 나를 위한 충고를 적어보세요.

* 교재의 첫 장으로 돌아가서 자신이 적은 목표 점수를 확인하면서 목표에 대한 의지를 다지기 바랍니다. 개선해야 할 점은 반드시 다음 테스트에 실천해야 합니다. 그것이 가장 중요하며, 그래야만 발전할 수 있습니다.

TEST 02

PART 1
PART 2
PART 3
PART 4
Self 체크 리스트

잠깐! 테스트 전 확인사항
1. 휴대 전화의 전원을 끄셨나요? □ 예
2. Answer Sheet, 연필, 지우개를 준비하셨나요? □ 예
3. MP3를 들을 준비가 되셨나요? □ 예

모든 준비가 완료되었으면 목표 점수를 떠올린 후 테스트를 시작합니다.

🎧 TEST 02.mp3
실전용·복습용 문제풀이 MP3 무료 다운로드 및 스트리밍 바로듣기 (HackersIngang.com)
* 실제 시험장의 소음까지 재현해 낸 고사장 소음/매미 버전 MP3, 영국식·호주식 발음 집중 MP3, 고속 버전 MP3까지
  구매하면 실전에 더욱 완벽히 대비할 수 있습니다.

무료MP3 바로듣기

LISTENING TEST

In this section, you must demonstrate your ability to understand spoken English. This section is divided into four parts and will take approximately 45 minutes to complete. Do not mark the answers in your test book. Use the answer sheet that is provided separately.

PART 1

Directions: For each question, you will listen to four short statements about a picture in your test book. These statements will not be printed and will only be spoken one time. Select the statement that best describes what is happening in the picture and mark the corresponding letter (A), (B), (C), or (D) on the answer sheet.

Sample Answer

The statement that best describes the picture is (B), "The man is sitting at the desk." So, you should mark letter (B) on the answer sheet.

1.

2.

GO ON TO THE NEXT PAGE ➤

3.

4.

5.

6.

GO ON TO THE NEXT PAGE ➤

PART 2

Directions: For each question, you will listen to a statement or question followed by three possible responses spoken in English. They will not be printed and will only be spoken one time. Select the best response and mark the corresponding letter (A), (B), or (C) on your answer sheet.

7. Mark your answer on your answer sheet.

8. Mark your answer on your answer sheet.

9. Mark your answer on your answer sheet.

10. Mark your answer on your answer sheet.

11. Mark your answer on your answer sheet.

12. Mark your answer on your answer sheet.

13. Mark your answer on your answer sheet.

14. Mark your answer on your answer sheet.

15. Mark your answer on your answer sheet.

16. Mark your answer on your answer sheet.

17. Mark your answer on your answer sheet.

18. Mark your answer on your answer sheet.

19. Mark your answer on your answer sheet.

20. Mark your answer on your answer sheet.

21. Mark your answer on your answer sheet.

22. Mark your answer on your answer sheet.

23. Mark your answer on your answer sheet.

24. Mark your answer on your answer sheet.

25. Mark your answer on your answer sheet.

26. Mark your answer on your answer sheet.

27. Mark your answer on your answer sheet.

28. Mark your answer on your answer sheet.

29. Mark your answer on your answer sheet.

30. Mark your answer on your answer sheet.

31. Mark your answer on your answer sheet.

Directions: In this part, you will listen to several conversations between two or more speakers. These conversations will not be printed and will only be spoken one time. For each conversation, you will be asked to answer three questions. Select the best response and mark the corresponding letter (A), (B), (C), or (D) on your answer sheet.

32. Who is the woman?

(A) A newspaper editor
(B) A television reporter
(C) A health-care worker
(D) A store owner

33. What information was incorrectly printed?

(A) The location of a branch
(B) The date of an opening
(C) The name of a company
(D) The price of a product

34. What does the man offer to do?

(A) Reprint an advertisement
(B) Proofread a newspaper article
(C) Inform a coworker of a mistake
(D) Transfer the woman's call

35. What type of event is taking place today?

(A) A cooking course
(B) A food exposition
(C) A company gathering
(D) A restaurant opening

36. What was the man responsible for?

(A) Listing new items on a menu
(B) Showing guests to their seats
(C) Preparing ingredients for a dish
(D) Tracking event attendance

37. What will the man probably do next?

(A) Bring dishes to a kitchen
(B) Serve some special meals
(C) Talk to a chef
(D) Change the time of an event

38. What is the conversation mainly about?

(A) A company policy
(B) A training workshop
(C) A corporate fund-raiser
(D) An employee club

39. What does the woman mean when she says, "I'm not very experienced"?

(A) She does not want to compete.
(B) She will inquire about an event.
(C) She cannot complete an assignment.
(D) She is eager to receive instruction.

40. What does the man say he will do this afternoon?

(A) Pay an application fee
(B) Send a document
(C) Provide some equipment
(D) E-mail a group organizer

41. What is the problem?

(A) Insufficient funding was provided.
(B) A document was misplaced.
(C) A project was canceled.
(D) Incorrect information was submitted.

42. Where does the woman have to go?

(A) To a product launch
(B) To a departmental meeting
(C) To a business lunch
(D) To an employee orientation

43. What does the man plan to do on Wednesday?

(A) Organize an office space
(B) Contact some employees
(C) Release a company document
(D) Correct some charts

GO ON TO THE NEXT PAGE

44. What is the woman concerned about?

(A) A product did poorly in a trial.
(B) Some complaints were made.
(C) An engineer intends to resign.
(D) Some measurements are inaccurate.

45. What did the man recently do?

(A) Contacted a customer
(B) Carried out some tests
(C) Asked for a cost estimate
(D) Drafted a device manual

46. What does the man ask about?

(A) An informational session
(B) An evaluation summary
(C) An assignment deadline
(D) A shift schedule

---

47. Where most likely does the conversation take place?

(A) At a public office
(B) At a shopping mall
(C) At a convenience store
(D) At a welfare center

48. What does the woman instruct Robert to do?

(A) Provide some chocolate recipes
(B) Retain a copy of a receipt
(C) Offer additional marketing support
(D) Perform tasks at the same time

49. Who most likely is John Pence?

(A) An event planner
(B) A journalist
(C) A government official
(D) A store cashier

---

50. Why does the man visit the business?

(A) To request a discount
(B) To confirm a payment
(C) To speak with an instructor
(D) To inquire about an offering

51. Why was the evening class canceled?

(A) A trainer was unavailable.
(B) A room had been booked.
(C) Student registration was low.
(D) A facility's hours were reduced.

52. What does the woman offer to do?

(A) Review a business pamphlet
(B) Deal with a transaction
(C) Suggest an alternative course
(D) Get a handout

---

53. Who most likely is the man?

(A) An equipment salesperson
(B) A repair technician
(C) A building inspector
(D) A construction worker

54. What problem does the man mention?

(A) Some instructions have been misplaced.
(B) Some parts have not been delivered.
(C) A component is malfunctioning.
(D) A machine was never installed.

55. Why will Janice call the building manager?

(A) To request a replacement part
(B) To report on some work
(C) To obtain access to an office
(D) To arrange an appointment

---

56. Where most likely are the speakers?

(A) At a train station
(B) At a bus stop
(C) At a taxi stand
(D) At an airport

57. Why is the woman unable to board?

(A) She left a meeting late.
(B) She could not find a taxi.
(C) She has forgotten her ticket.
(D) She was caught in traffic.

58. What does the man offer to do?

(A) Direct the woman to a gate
(B) Provide a seat upgrade
(C) Make another booking
(D) Store some extra luggage

59. Who most likely is the woman?

(A) A keynote speaker
(B) An event organizer
(C) A corporate spokesperson
(D) A financial advisor

60. What will the woman do in April?

(A) Give a speech
(B) Travel to another country
(C) Conduct training
(D) Attend a seminar

61. Why does the man say, "It'll be held on April 4"?

(A) To imply that another speaker is available
(B) To suggest that the woman postpone a visit
(C) To indicate that the woman will miss an event
(D) To announce a planned schedule change

Austin Airport Terminal B		
Departure Time	**Destination**	**Gate**
7:55 P.M.	Atlanta	B2
8:10 P.M.	Memphis	B7
8:25 P.M.	Savannah	B37
8:40 P.M.	Denver	B69

62. Why is the man calling?

(A) To file a complaint
(B) To order a taxi
(C) To request a class upgrade
(D) To report a plan change

63. Look at the graphic. Where will the speakers most likely meet?

(A) Gate B2
(B) Gate B7
(C) Gate B37
(D) Gate B69

64. What does the man suggest?

(A) Sitting together during a flight
(B) Having dinner at a hotel
(C) Taking public transportation
(D) Discussing a sales strategy

GO ON TO THE NEXT PAGE

Show Name	Channel
Wake-Up Pittsburgh	3
Morning Buzz	5
Pennsylvania Today	7
Mornings with Jerry	10

65. Who most likely are the speakers?

(A) Television program hosts
(B) Event planners
(C) Food critics
(D) Dining establishment personnel

66. According to the woman, what happened last weekend?

(A) A popular local show was delayed.
(B) A business was at full capacity.
(C) A supervisor made an announcement.
(D) A worker held a surprise celebration.

67. Look at the graphic. Which channel will Harold Newman appear on?

(A) Channel 3
(B) Channel 5
(C) Channel 7
(D) Channel 10

The Boston Fine Arts Museum Map

	Northern Wing Paintings	
Western Wing Photography	Lobby	Eastern Wing Sculptures
	Southern Wing Ceramics	

68. What is the conversation mainly about?

(A) A security problem
(B) A workplace training program
(C) A beginning of a first duty
(D) A purchase of an artwork

69. Look at the graphic. Where will the man be stationed?

(A) In the Western Wing
(B) In the Northern Wing
(C) In the Eastern Wing
(D) In the Southern Wing

70. What will the woman probably do next?

(A) Contact a supervisor
(B) Go to an office
(C) Provide some paperwork
(D) Retrieve a uniform

Directions: In this part, you will listen to several short talks by a single speaker. These talks will not be printed and will only be spoken one time. For each talk, you will be asked to answer three questions. Select the best response and mark the corresponding letter (A), (B), (C), or (D) on your answer sheet.

71. What is the purpose of the message?

(A) To explain a premium increase
(B) To provide insurance information
(C) To apologize for a miscalculation
(D) To describe a loyalty program

72. What detail does the speaker need?

(A) A coverage start date
(B) A driving test score
(C) A transaction amount
(D) A vehicle type

73. What does the speaker ask the listener to do?

(A) Review a quote online
(B) Arrange an appointment
(C) Return a phone call
(D) Renew a contract

74. Where most likely is the talk taking place?

(A) At a medical convention
(B) At a press conference
(C) At a shareholder's meeting
(D) At a fund-raising event

75. According to the speaker, what will happen in nine months?

(A) A charity goal will be achieved.
(B) A facility will be completed.
(C) A new medication will be released.
(D) An operations manager will be promoted.

76. What will be made available in the future?

(A) A preview of an upcoming product line
(B) Details about a recently constructed facility
(C) An overview of the company's research projects
(D) Information about employment opportunities

77. According to the speaker, what do some workers plan to do?

(A) Take part in a festival
(B) Undergo some special training
(C) Enter a cooking competition
(D) Modify a restaurant menu

78. When will the store return to its regular hours?

(A) On June 8
(B) On June 9
(C) On June 10
(D) On June 11

79. How can the listeners request a reservation?

(A) By texting a restaurant
(B) By leaving a voice message
(C) By visiting a company Web site
(D) By sending an e-mail

80. Who most likely is the speaker?

(A) A hardware developer
(B) A computer technician
(C) An electrical engineer
(D) A laptop manufacturer

81. Why does the speaker say, "Just be aware that the newest model costs $500"?

(A) To point out an increase in prices
(B) To emphasize the importance of a warranty
(C) To provide information about a sale
(D) To recommend replacing a device

82. What can the listener get for free?

(A) A file transfer
(B) A laptop case
(C) A computer repair
(D) A software program

GO ON TO THE NEXT PAGE

83. What is the purpose of the talk?

(A) To explain an enrollment procedure
(B) To provide details about a program
(C) To encourage the listeners to volunteer
(D) To introduce a guest speaker

84. What does the speaker say about some project managers?

(A) They will lead presentations.
(B) They will be selecting teams.
(C) They will conduct evaluations.
(D) They will be assessing proposals.

85. What will be provided to the listeners?

(A) A free meal
(B) Copies of a survey form
(C) Contact details for speakers
(D) An information packet

---

86. What will most likely happen at the end of May?

(A) A firm will open a new office.
(B) A business deal will be completed.
(C) An executive will leave a job.
(D) An industry event will be held.

87. What does the speaker imply when he says, "it currently employs about 15,000 staff members"?

(A) A corporate headquarters must be expanded.
(B) A business has experienced tremendous growth.
(C) An organization needs to reduce its workforce.
(D) A company merger will impact many people.

88. What is mentioned about Dale Fenny?

(A) He founded the firm.
(B) He made a public announcement.
(C) He has applied for a new job.
(D) He is in the financial field.

---

89. What does Harford Snow promise to do?

(A) Provide the lowest rates
(B) Inspect properties at no charge
(C) Perform a task within a few hours
(D) Contact customers before arriving

90. According to the speaker, what service is available for an extra fee?

(A) Safety training
(B) Driveway cleaning
(C) Equipment repair
(D) Ice removal

91. What information might the listeners get on the company's Web site?

(A) Appointment availability
(B) Consumer reviews
(C) Discount options
(D) Refund instructions

---

92. What is mentioned about *The Time Was Then*?

(A) It was criticized by some experts.
(B) It features a famous actress.
(C) It was only shown in select theaters.
(D) It has achieved great success.

93. Why does the speaker say, "Gabriela has worked on hundreds of projects"?

(A) To introduce a recipient
(B) To explain a decision
(C) To offer some praise
(D) To confirm a rumor

94. What does the speaker say she will do in August?

(A) Promote a recent film
(B) Start a new project
(C) Collaborate with a mentor
(D) Travel for a premiere

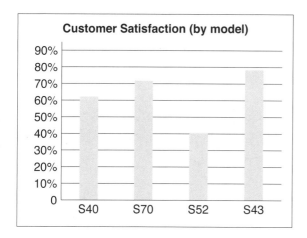

Customer Satisfaction (by model)

Employment Workshop
Saturday, February 21

Online Job Search Resources	9:00-10:30
Importance of Networking	10:30-12:00
Lunch	
Résumés & Cover Letters	1:00-2:30
Preparing for an Interview	2:30-4:00

95. Who most likely are the listeners?

(A) Research assistants
(B) Marketing specialists
(C) Sales associates
(D) Product designers

96. Look at the graphic. Which model was released in May?

(A) S40
(B) S70
(C) S52
(D) S43

97. What does the speaker want to do?

(A) Release a revised model
(B) Lower a device's price
(C) Update an advertising campaign
(D) Conduct a questionnaire

98. What does the speaker plan to do in April?

(A) Start a new job
(B) Take some tests
(C) Volunteer at a center
(D) Register for classes

99. What problem does the speaker mention?

(A) She failed an exam.
(B) She forgot a prior commitment.
(C) She missed a workshop.
(D) She did not meet a deadline.

100. Look at the graphic. Which session will the speaker probably miss?

(A) Online Job Search Resources
(B) Importance of Networking
(C) Résumés & Cover Letters
(D) Preparing for an Interview

정답 p.164 / 점수 환산표 p.167 / 스크립트 p.174 / 무료 해석 바로 보기(정답 및 정답 음성 포함)

▌정답 음성(QR)이나 정답(p.164)을 이용해 채점하시기 바랍니다. 정답 음성에서 Boy는 (B)를, David는 (D)를 나타냅니다.
▌다음 페이지에 있는 Self 체크 리스트를 통해 자신의 문제 풀이 방식과 태도를 점검해 보세요.

Self 체크 리스트

TEST 02는 무사히 잘 마치셨죠?
이제 다음의 Self 체크 리스트를 통해 자신의 테스트 진행 내용을 점검해 볼까요?

1. 나는 테스트가 진행되는 동안 한 번도 중도에 멈추지 않았다.

   ☐ 예　　　　　　　☐ 아니오

   아니오에 답한 경우, 이유는 무엇인가요?

2. 나는 답안지 표기까지 성실하게 모두 마무리하였다.

   ☐ 예　　　　　　　☐ 아니오

   아니오에 답한 경우, 이유는 무엇인가요?

3. 나는 Part 2의 25문항을 푸는 동안 완전히 테스트에 집중하였다.

   ☐ 예　　　　　　　☐ 아니오

   아니오에 답한 경우, 이유는 무엇인가요?

4. 나는 Part 3를 풀 때 음성이 들리기 전에 해당 질문과 보기를 모두 먼저 읽었다.

   ☐ 예　　　　　　　☐ 아니오

   아니오에 답한 경우, 이유는 무엇인가요?

5. 나는 Part 4를 풀 때 음성이 들리기 전에 해당 질문과 보기를 모두 먼저 읽었다.

   ☐ 예　　　　　　　☐ 아니오

   아니오에 답한 경우, 이유는 무엇인가요?

6. 개선해야 할 점 또는 나를 위한 충고를 적어보세요.

* 교재의 첫 장으로 돌아가서 자신이 적은 목표 점수를 확인하면서 목표에 대한 의지를 다지기 바랍니다. 개선해야 할 점은 반드시 다음 테스트에 실천해야 합니다. 그것이 가장 중요하며, 그래야만 발전할 수 있습니다.

▐ TEST 03

PART 1
PART 2
PART 3
PART 4
Self 체크 리스트

잠깐! 테스트 전 확인사항

1. 휴대 전화의 전원을 끄셨나요? □ 예
2. Answer Sheet, 연필, 지우개를 준비하셨나요? □ 예
3. MP3를 들을 준비가 되셨나요? □ 예

모든 준비가 완료되었으면 목표 점수를 떠올린 후 테스트를 시작합니다.

🎧 TEST 03.mp3

실전용·복습용 문제풀이 MP3 무료 다운로드 및 스트리밍 바로듣기 (HackersIngang.com)
* 실제 시험장의 소음까지 재현해 낸 고사장 소음/매미 버전 MP3, 영국식·호주식 발음 집중 MP3, 고속 버전 MP3까지
  구매하면 실전에 더욱 완벽히 대비할 수 있습니다.

무료MP3 바로듣기

LISTENING TEST

In this section, you must demonstrate your ability to understand spoken English. This section is divided into four parts and will take approximately 45 minutes to complete. Do not mark the answers in your test book. Use the answer sheet that is provided separately.

PART 1

Directions: For each question, you will listen to four short statements about a picture in your test book. These statements will not be printed and will only be spoken one time. Select the statement that best describes what is happening in the picture and mark the corresponding letter (A), (B), (C), or (D) on the answer sheet.

Sample Answer

The statement that best describes the picture is (B), "The man is sitting at the desk." So, you should mark letter (B) on the answer sheet.

1.

2.

GO ON TO THE NEXT PAGE ➡

3.

4.

5.

6.

GO ON TO THE NEXT PAGE

PART 2

Directions: For each question, you will listen to a statement or question followed by three possible responses spoken in English. They will not be printed and will only be spoken one time. Select the best response and mark the corresponding letter (A), (B), or (C) on your answer sheet.

7. Mark your answer on your answer sheet.

8. Mark your answer on your answer sheet.

9. Mark your answer on your answer sheet.

10. Mark your answer on your answer sheet.

11. Mark your answer on your answer sheet.

12. Mark your answer on your answer sheet.

13. Mark your answer on your answer sheet.

14. Mark your answer on your answer sheet.

15. Mark your answer on your answer sheet.

16. Mark your answer on your answer sheet.

17. Mark your answer on your answer sheet.

18. Mark your answer on your answer sheet.

19. Mark your answer on your answer sheet.

20. Mark your answer on your answer sheet.

21. Mark your answer on your answer sheet.

22. Mark your answer on your answer sheet.

23. Mark your answer on your answer sheet.

24. Mark your answer on your answer sheet.

25. Mark your answer on your answer sheet.

26. Mark your answer on your answer sheet.

27. Mark your answer on your answer sheet.

28. Mark your answer on your answer sheet.

29. Mark your answer on your answer sheet.

30. Mark your answer on your answer sheet.

31. Mark your answer on your answer sheet.

PART 3

Directions: In this part, you will listen to several conversations between two or more speakers. These conversations will not be printed and will only be spoken one time. For each conversation, you will be asked to answer three questions. Select the best response and mark the corresponding letter (A), (B), (C), or (D) on your answer sheet.

32. What will the man do next week?
    (A) Take a business trip
    (B) Meet with a company president
    (C) Make an international call
    (D) Apply for a credit card

33. Which department does the man most likely work in?
    (A) Marketing
    (B) Sales
    (C) Legal
    (D) Accounting

34. What does the woman advise the man to do?
    (A) Update a directory
    (B) Visit a Web site
    (C) Request a refund
    (D) Contact another department

35. What did Mitch recently do?
    (A) Led a meeting
    (B) Watched a presentation
    (C) Ordered some merchandise
    (D) Returned from a vacation

36. What is the woman's problem?
    (A) She was denied a request.
    (B) She cannot locate a product.
    (C) She received improper instructions.
    (D) She is not familiar with a brand.

37. What does Ben offer to do?
    (A) Talk to a customer
    (B) Update a database
    (C) Check a storage area
    (D) Test an electronic device

38. Where is the conversation most likely taking place?
    (A) In a theater
    (B) In a department store
    (C) In a hotel
    (D) In a government office

39. What does the woman ask for?
    (A) A description of an item
    (B) The name of an owner
    (C) The date of a visit
    (D) A confirmation of a payment

40. What will the man most likely do next?
    (A) Make a payment
    (B) Show an identification card
    (C) Pose for a photograph
    (D) Fill out an application form

41. What will begin at 4 P.M.?
    (A) A social gathering
    (B) A private consultation
    (C) A training session
    (D) A cooking class

42. Why did the women arrive early?
    (A) To sample some dishes
    (B) To volunteer their services
    (C) To make revisions to a plan
    (D) To rehearse some music

43. What does the man ask the women to do?
    (A) Clean up a space
    (B) Stop by a market
    (C) Cut up some produce
    (D) Move some tables

GO ON TO THE NEXT PAGE

44. Where most likely are the speakers?

(A) At a theater
(B) At a restaurant
(C) At a shopping complex
(D) At a stadium

45. What is mentioned about the man's coworker?

(A) He invited some friends over.
(B) He is able to attend an event.
(C) He is a season ticket holder.
(D) He worked an extra shift.

46. Why does the man say, "I've got a hot dog and soda"?

(A) To calculate an amount
(B) To point out a mistake
(C) To indicate a preference
(D) To turn down an offer

47. What type of event does the woman want flowers for?

(A) A retirement celebration
(B) An award presentation
(C) A graduation ceremony
(D) A company outing

48. Why does the man apologize?

(A) A delivery service is not available.
(B) A store has increased its prices.
(C) A product is not in stock.
(D) An order has not been prepared.

49. What does the man recommend?

(A) Browsing an online catalog
(B) Contacting a different branch
(C) Ordering another product
(D) Sending a gift card

50. Where most likely are the speakers?

(A) In a convention center
(B) In a corporate office
(C) In a hotel
(D) In a mall

51. Why does the man say, "Bently Furniture specializes in commercial furniture"?

(A) To accept an offer
(B) To indicate a problem
(C) To suggest an alternative
(D) To explain a decision

52. Why will the woman make a phone call?

(A) To inquire about product availability
(B) To request a confirmation number
(C) To provide some feedback
(D) To confirm a delivery time

53. What does the man ask the woman about?

(A) A departure time
(B) A first-class ticket
(C) A luggage policy
(D) A gate location

54. What does the man say he will do?

(A) Wait for a shuttle bus
(B) Make some business calls
(C) Charge to a corporate credit card
(D) Accept a free upgrade

55. What does the woman recommend?

(A) Looking at a digital board
(B) Using a station facility
(C) Paying for wireless Internet
(D) Following other passengers

56. What is the report about?

(A) Consumer complaints
(B) Production costs
(C) Clothing lines
(D) Potential markets

57. Who is Fred Diamond?

(A) An investor
(B) A client
(C) A designer
(D) An intern

58. What will the woman probably do next?

(A) Print a handout
(B) Read an e-mail
(C) Explain a decision
(D) Correct a document

---

59. According to the man, what will the speakers mostly discuss?

(A) An effort to hire additional teachers
(B) A change to voting regulations
(C) A city's community festivals
(D) A politician's professional background

60. What news does the woman announce?

(A) An early retirement
(B) A budget increase
(C) An award nomination
(D) A project delay

61. What is mentioned about city schools?

(A) They have highly trained staff.
(B) They may reduce class sizes.
(C) They will receive more supplies.
(D) They can enroll more students.

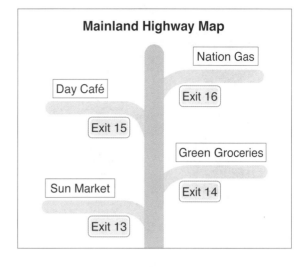

Mainland Highway Map

62. What type of event is taking place today?

(A) A training session
(B) A welcoming party
(C) A birthday celebration
(D) A branch opening

63. Look at the graphic. Which highway exit did the man most likely take?

(A) Exit 13
(B) Exit 14
(C) Exit 15
(D) Exit 16

64. What does the man offer to do?

(A) Drop off a vehicle
(B) Fill up a gas tank
(C) Pick up some beverages
(D) Call some suppliers

GO ON TO THE NEXT PAGE

H88 - $850

C34 - $1,350

F56 - $1,100

X12 - $975

Barton Inc. Volunteer Day!

Office Volunteer Goals

- Easton City: 10
- Lowerville: 15
- New Clemson: 20
- Bloomington: 25

65. According to the man, who is the device for?

(A) A colleague
(B) A relative
(C) A friend
(D) A client

66. What feature does the man want to prioritize?

(A) Portability
(B) Battery life
(C) Affordability
(D) Display size

67. Look at the graphic. Which laptop does the woman recommend?

(A) H88
(B) C34
(C) F56
(D) X12

68. Who most likely are the speakers?

(A) School teachers
(B) Public relations personnel
(C) IT specialists
(D) Media representatives

69. Look at the graphic. Which office was most recently established?

(A) Easton City
(B) Lowerville
(C) New Clemson
(D) Bloomington

70. What do the speakers plan to do?

(A) Encourage some workers to make donations
(B) Participate in an upcoming event
(C) Announce goals to their colleagues
(D) Coordinate activities with an organizer

PART 4

Directions: In this part, you will listen to several short talks by a single speaker. These talks will not be printed and will only be spoken one time. For each talk, you will be asked to answer three questions. Select the best response and mark the corresponding letter (A), (B), (C), or (D) on your answer sheet.

71. Where is the announcement most likely being made?

(A) In a supermarket
(B) In a restaurant
(C) In an electronics store
(D) In an office building

72. What are the listeners instructed to present to an attendant?

(A) A voucher slip
(B) A parking pass
(C) A proof of purchase
(D) An identification card

73. What is mentioned about the parking spaces near the elevators?

(A) They meet government standards.
(B) They are for small vehicles.
(C) They are reserved for employees.
(D) They require a permit to use.

74. Why is the speaker calling?

(A) To request some bank information
(B) To alert a customer about a new policy
(C) To offer a financial product
(D) To confirm an account opening

75. What will the listener be eligible for?

(A) Investing in some high-interest funds
(B) Receiving discounts from partners
(C) Transferring money overseas for free
(D) Ordering a special business card

76. What does the speaker mean when he says, "You've been pre-approved for this process"?

(A) A security check has been successful.
(B) A customer doesn't have to apply for a service.
(C) A bank will contact the customer soon.
(D) A request has been registered.

77. Who most likely are the listeners?

(A) Festival attendees
(B) Music school students
(C) Studio technicians
(D) Record store staff

78. According to the speaker, what happened in April?

(A) An event was announced.
(B) A concert was postponed.
(C) A band was formed.
(D) An album was released.

79. What does the speaker say about Philip Waterfield?

(A) He plans to record more music.
(B) He rarely gives live performances.
(C) He has appeared on television.
(D) He was given an award.

80. According to the speaker, what does Mr. Vang plan to do on June 14?

(A) Verify an itinerary
(B) Conclude a business trip
(C) Depart on a cruise
(D) Pay a remaining balance

81. What does the speaker mean when he says, "Premier cabins include queen-size beds"?

(A) Inaccurate information was provided.
(B) A handout is outdated.
(C) A reservation needs to be changed.
(D) Larger accommodations were added.

82. What was included in a brochure?

(A) Some photographs
(B) A price list
(C) Some coupons
(D) A phone number

GO ON TO THE NEXT PAGE

83. What problem does the speaker mention?

(A) A venue has been overbooked.
(B) Some schedules were not updated.
(C) Some equipment is not working.
(D) A speaker cannot attend an event.

84. Who is Shawn Murray?

(A) A government official
(B) A convention organizer
(C) A company founder
(D) A television celebrity

85. What does the speaker suggest?

(A) Waiting for another announcement
(B) Going to a ballroom early
(C) Watching a short video clip
(D) Buying some merchandise

---

86. What does the speaker say the listeners can do?

(A) Choose an instructor
(B) Reserve a facility
(C) Rent some skates
(D) Use a coupon

87. According to the speaker, what do some people qualify for?

(A) Training lessons
(B) Free admission
(C) Complimentary gear
(D) Annual passes

88. Why should the listeners dial one?

(A) To hear about different rates
(B) To reserve a storage locker
(C) To learn about a schedule
(D) To replay a message

---

89. What is mentioned about Lucy Mayfield?

(A) She received an award.
(B) She founded an organization.
(C) She is a college professor.
(D) She partnered with other researchers.

90. According to the speaker, what will Ms. Mayfield discuss?

(A) New government regulations
(B) Threats to sea life
(C) Increased pollution levels
(D) Goals of a foundation

91. Why does the speaker say, "She'll be leaving at noon to give a seminar"?

(A) To point out a change
(B) To stress a time constraint
(C) To promote an upcoming event
(D) To express gratitude

---

92. Where are the listeners?

(A) In a living room
(B) In a bedroom
(C) In a kitchen
(D) In a private office

93. According to the speaker, what is famous in the house?

(A) Some artwork
(B) Some furniture
(C) Some book collections
(D) Some room designs

94. What does the speaker suggest?

(A) Walking around a property
(B) Reading a display board
(C) Heading toward an exit
(D) Looking at some papers

City Library	Coerver Hospital	Building A
N. Dearborn St.		
Building B	4th Ave. / Metro Station / 5th Ave.	Lonster Park
N. Monroe St.		
Building C	Stark Theater	Building D

Artist	Title of Work
Mark Rubin	*Wall with Flowers*
Lola Hays	*Daylight and More*
Ken Hamilton	*Tower Heights*
Sandy Meyer	*Reaching for the Sky*

95. Look at the graphic. In which building does the listener have an appointment?

(A) Building A
(B) Building B
(C) Building C
(D) Building D

96. According to the speaker, why should the listener arrive early?

(A) To relax before a procedure
(B) To find a parking spot
(C) To complete some paperwork
(D) To take an X-ray

97. What does the listener have to bring with him?

(A) An identification card
(B) A medical record
(C) An insurance document
(D) A questionnaire form

98. What is the speaker mainly discussing?

(A) A celebrity visit
(B) A fund-raising event
(C) A gallery opening
(D) A special exhibition

99. Look at the graphic. Which piece has yet to be delivered?

(A) *Wall with Flowers*
(B) *Daylight and More*
(C) *Tower Heights*
(D) *Reaching for the Sky*

100. What will probably happen this afternoon?

(A) Some paintings will be sold.
(B) Some tickets will be given away.
(C) A notice will be posted online.
(D) A guest will give a short talk.

정답 p.164 / 점수 환산표 p.167 / 스크립트 p.180 / 무료 해석 바로 보기(정답 및 정답 음성 포함)

▌정답 음성(QR)이나 정답(p.164)을 이용해 채점하시기 바랍니다. 정답 음성에서 Boy는 (B)를, David는 (D)를 나타냅니다.
▌다음 페이지에 있는 Self 체크 리스트를 통해 자신의 문제 풀이 방식과 태도를 점검해 보세요.

Self 체크 리스트

TEST 03는 무사히 잘 마치셨죠?
이제 다음의 Self 체크 리스트를 통해 자신의 테스트 진행 내용을 점검해 볼까요?

1. 나는 테스트가 진행되는 동안 한 번도 중도에 멈추지 않았다.

   ☐ 예   ☐ 아니오

   아니오에 답한 경우, 이유는 무엇인가요?

2. 나는 답안지 표기까지 성실하게 모두 마무리하였다.

   ☐ 예   ☐ 아니오

   아니오에 답한 경우, 이유는 무엇인가요?

3. 나는 Part 2의 25문항을 푸는 동안 완전히 테스트에 집중하였다.

   ☐ 예   ☐ 아니오

   아니오에 답한 경우, 이유는 무엇인가요?

4. 나는 Part 3를 풀 때 음성이 들리기 전에 해당 질문과 보기를 모두 먼저 읽었다.

   ☐ 예   ☐ 아니오

   아니오에 답한 경우, 이유는 무엇인가요?

5. 나는 Part 4를 풀 때 음성이 들리기 전에 해당 질문과 보기를 모두 먼저 읽었다.

   ☐ 예   ☐ 아니오

   아니오에 답한 경우, 이유는 무엇인가요?

6. 개선해야 할 점 또는 나를 위한 충고를 적어보세요.

* 교재의 첫 장으로 돌아가서 자신이 적은 목표 점수를 확인하면서 목표에 대한 의지를 다지기 바랍니다. 개선해야 할 점은 반드시 다음 테스트에 실천해야 합니다. 그것이 가장 중요하며, 그래야만 발전할 수 있습니다.

▌TEST 04

PART 1
PART 2
PART 3
PART 4
Self 체크 리스트

잠깐! 테스트 전 확인사항

1. 휴대 전화의 전원을 끄셨나요? □ 예
2. Answer Sheet, 연필, 지우개를 준비하셨나요? □ 예
3. MP3를 들을 준비가 되셨나요? □ 예

모든 준비가 완료되었으면 목표 점수를 떠올린 후 테스트를 시작합니다.

🎧 TEST 04.mp3

실전용·복습용 문제풀이 MP3 무료 다운로드 및 스트리밍 바로듣기 (HackersIngang.com)

* 실제 시험장의 소음까지 재현해 낸 고사장 소음/매미 버전 MP3, 영국식·호주식 발음 집중 MP3, 고속 버전 MP3까지
  구매하면 실전에 더욱 완벽히 대비할 수 있습니다.

무료MP3 바로듣기

LISTENING TEST

In this section, you must demonstrate your ability to understand spoken English. This section is divided into four parts and will take approximately 45 minutes to complete. Do not mark the answers in your test book. Use the answer sheet that is provided separately.

PART 1

Directions: For each question, you will listen to four short statements about a picture in your test book. These statements will not be printed and will only be spoken one time. Select the statement that best describes what is happening in the picture and mark the corresponding letter (A), (B), (C), or (D) on the answer sheet.

Sample Answer
Ⓐ ● Ⓒ Ⓓ

The statement that best describes the picture is (B), "The man is sitting at the desk." So, you should mark letter (B) on the answer sheet.

1.

2.

GO ON TO THE NEXT PAGE

3.

4.

5.

6.

GO ON TO THE NEXT PAGE

TEST | 01 | 02 | 03 | **04** | 05 | 06 | 07 | 08 | 09 | 10

해커스 토익 실전 1000제 2 Listening

PART 2

Directions: For each question, you will listen to a statement or question followed by three possible responses spoken in English. They will not be printed and will only be spoken one time. Select the best response and mark the corresponding letter (A), (B), or (C) on your answer sheet.

7. Mark your answer on your answer sheet.

8. Mark your answer on your answer sheet.

9. Mark your answer on your answer sheet.

10. Mark your answer on your answer sheet.

11. Mark your answer on your answer sheet.

12. Mark your answer on your answer sheet.

13. Mark your answer on your answer sheet.

14. Mark your answer on your answer sheet.

15. Mark your answer on your answer sheet.

16. Mark your answer on your answer sheet.

17. Mark your answer on your answer sheet.

18. Mark your answer on your answer sheet.

19. Mark your answer on your answer sheet.

20. Mark your answer on your answer sheet.

21. Mark your answer on your answer sheet.

22. Mark your answer on your answer sheet.

23. Mark your answer on your answer sheet.

24. Mark your answer on your answer sheet.

25. Mark your answer on your answer sheet.

26. Mark your answer on your answer sheet.

27. Mark your answer on your answer sheet.

28. Mark your answer on your answer sheet.

29. Mark your answer on your answer sheet.

30. Mark your answer on your answer sheet.

31. Mark your answer on your answer sheet.

PART 3

Directions: In this part, you will listen to several conversations between two or more speakers. These conversations will not be printed and will only be spoken one time. For each conversation, you will be asked to answer three questions. Select the best response and mark the corresponding letter (A), (B), (C), or (D) on your answer sheet.

32. Where do the speakers most likely work?
(A) At a medical facility
(B) At a law firm
(C) At a community center
(D) At an educational institution

33. What does the man ask the woman to do?
(A) Reschedule a summer vacation
(B) Attend training workshops
(C) Work additional hours
(D) Try a different position

34. What does the man say about Jack?
(A) He will take some leave.
(B) He will move to another office.
(C) He will return to university.
(D) He will receive a promotion.

35. Why does the woman say, "I have four children"?
(A) To request an alternative
(B) To reject an offer
(C) To point out a problem
(D) To specify a requirement

36. What is mentioned about the Newman station wagon?
(A) It was released in the past year.
(B) It has many safety features.
(C) It is relatively fuel-efficient.
(D) It is available at a reduced rate.

37. What does the woman want to do?
(A) Speak to a manager
(B) Drive a vehicle briefly
(C) Look at a different model
(D) Read through a car manual

38. What is the conversation mainly about?
(A) Exchanging a product
(B) Extending a warranty
(C) Refunding a fee
(D) Repairing an item

39. What did the man do yesterday?
(A) Visited a retail outlet
(B) Purchased a device
(C) Replaced a component
(D) Contacted a service center

40. What will the man most likely do next?
(A) Select a model
(B) Complete a form
(C) Show a receipt
(D) Make a payment

41. What are the speakers mainly discussing?
(A) A software installation
(B) A training session
(C) A departmental meeting
(D) A product demonstration

42. What did Mr. Stevens request that staff members do?
(A) Download a program
(B) Change a security setting
(C) Provide an account password
(D) Meet with a technician

43. What will the man most likely do next?
(A) Cancel a workshop
(B) Send e-mails to clients
(C) Give instructions to coworkers
(D) Book a meeting room

GO ON TO THE NEXT PAGE

44. What most likely is the man's job?

(A) Corporate executive
(B) Personal driver
(C) Administrative assistant
(D) Security guard

45. What does the woman say a meeting will be about?

(A) A business convention
(B) A charity fund-raiser
(C) A construction project
(D) An advertising campaign

46. What does the man offer to do?

(A) Return at a later time
(B) Wait for the woman
(C) Reschedule an appointment
(D) Review marketing materials

47. Who most likely are the speakers?

(A) Real estate agents
(B) Construction workers
(C) Interior decorators
(D) Building managers

48. What does Anne ask about?

(A) The size of a room
(B) The location of an item
(C) The cost of an order
(D) The budget of a project

49. What will the man probably do next?

(A) Unpack a box
(B) Install a device
(C) Talk to a client
(D) Go to a shop

50. What does the man ask the woman to do?

(A) Find a coworker
(B) Move a vehicle
(C) Repair a device
(D) Help a customer

51. What task does the woman say she will finish later?

(A) Sweeping some aisles
(B) Throwing out some trash
(C) Stocking some products
(D) Changing some price labels

52. What does the man suggest doing?

(A) Filling up a container
(B) Using a credit card again
(C) Talking to a supervisor
(D) Moving to another machine

53. What does the man invite the woman to do?

(A) Go to a new restaurant
(B) Visit an amusement park
(C) Attend an exhibition
(D) Watch a film

54. Why is the man unable to meet the woman before 8 P.M. on Saturday?

(A) He will be eating with coworkers.
(B) He will be working overtime.
(C) He will be returning from a trip.
(D) He will be going to a gallery.

55. What does the woman say she will do today?

(A) Check a schedule
(B) Make a reservation
(C) Purchase some tickets
(D) Meet some friends

56. What did the man do?

    (A) Sliced a freshly made cake
    (B) Requested some dessert
    (C) Confirmed a booking
    (D) Measured some ingredients

57. Why does the woman say, "There's a bag in the pantry"?

    (A) To express confusion
    (B) To explain a mistake
    (C) To offer a solution
    (D) To indicate concern

58. What is mentioned about the man?

    (A) He wants a different task.
    (B) He will purchase some flour.
    (C) He forgot about a reservation.
    (D) He was recently hired.

---

59. What does the woman ask for?

    (A) A brand comparison
    (B) A wood sample
    (C) A price estimate
    (D) A product recommendation

60. What problem does the woman mention?

    (A) She ordered too much of a product.
    (B) She did not bring an item.
    (C) She cannot return before 7 P.M.
    (D) She wrote down the wrong amount.

61. What does the man suggest that the woman do?

    (A) Visit a different branch
    (B) Return to her residence
    (C) Measure a structure
    (D) Pay for her purchase

Step 1: Pre-production materials inspection

▼

Step 2: Random product sampling

▼

Step 3: Performance testing

▼

Step 4: Production report

▼

Step 5: Pre-shipment inspection

62. Why is the woman late?

    (A) A shipment just arrived.
    (B) A factory machine broke down.
    (C) A worker required instructions.
    (D) A client called about an order.

63. Look at the graphic. Which step will be eliminated?

    (A) Step 2
    (B) Step 3
    (C) Step 4
    (D) Step 5

64. What does the woman say will happen next year?

    (A) A storage facility will be constructed.
    (B) A hiring process will be changed.
    (C) An appliance model will be discontinued.
    (D) An employee orientation will be held.

GO ON TO THE NEXT PAGE

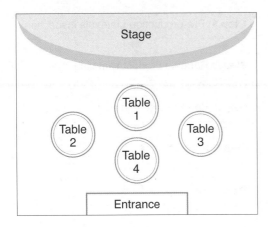

Factory Training Schedule	
Session	**Start time**
Basic safety	8 A.M.
Machine maintenance	9 A.M.
Warehouse regulations	10:30 A.M.
Quality control	11:30 A.M.

65. Who is Mr. Grimes?

   (A) An award recipient
   (B) An event host
   (C) A foundation head
   (D) An association donor

66. Look at the graphic. Where will Mr. Grimes be seated?

   (A) At Table 1
   (B) At Table 2
   (C) At Table 3
   (D) At Table 4

67. What responsibility is given to the man?

   (A) Collecting coats from people
   (B) Stacking some chairs
   (C) Passing on some information
   (D) Arranging transportation for guests

68. Look at the graphic. Which session will be postponed?

   (A) Basic safety
   (B) Machine maintenance
   (C) Warehouse regulations
   (D) Quality control

69. What did the man create?

   (A) A name tag
   (B) A sign-up sheet
   (C) A training booklet
   (D) A program

70. Where will the man most likely go next?

   (A) To a conference room
   (B) To a packaging area
   (C) To a warehouse
   (D) To an office

Directions: In this part, you will listen to several short talks by a single speaker. These talks will not be printed and will only be spoken one time. For each talk, you will be asked to answer three questions. Select the best response and mark the corresponding letter (A), (B), (C), or (D) on your answer sheet.

71. What is the talk mainly about?

(A) The schedule of a train
(B) Some details regarding a boat ride
(C) Some rules for a wildlife park
(D) The amenities of a resort

72. What does the speaker say is located on the lower level?

(A) Some luggage
(B) A seat
(C) A vehicle
(D) Some refreshments

73. What does the speaker suggest doing?

(A) Watching for wildlife
(B) Taking out a ticket
(C) Forming a line
(D) Reviewing an area map

74. Who most likely are the listeners?

(A) Post office workers
(B) Corporate receptionists
(C) Hotel guests
(D) Apartment tenants

75. What problem does the speaker mention?

(A) Outgoing mail can no longer be left at a desk.
(B) Access to a building is going to be restricted.
(C) Some packages have gone missing.
(D) Some staff are not able to carry out a task.

76. According to the speaker, why will slips be left in mail slots?

(A) To request signatures from renters
(B) To inform people about parcels
(C) To provide updates on a project
(D) To collect votes on a proposal

77. Where do the listeners work?

(A) At a construction company
(B) At a law office
(C) At a conference center
(D) At a government agency

78. What is mentioned about Sandra Boyd?

(A) She has been transferred.
(B) She coordinated some repairs.
(C) She is a personal assistant.
(D) She reported some issues.

79. What does the speaker mean when he says, "we have scheduled it for Saturday afternoon"?

(A) The listeners will not participate in an event.
(B) The listeners will work overtime.
(C) The listeners will not be disturbed.
(D) The listeners will be provided with instructions.

80. What was sent out two weeks ago?

(A) A newsletter
(B) A registration form
(C) A contract
(D) A reminder letter

81. What can the listener do online?

(A) Read a user agreement
(B) Update personal information
(C) Submit a payment
(D) Learn about loan options

82. Why would the listener contact the speaker?

(A) To make an inquiry
(B) To close an account
(C) To activate a credit card
(D) To apply for a mortgage

GO ON TO THE NEXT PAGE

83. According to the speaker, what did Jason Ferguson do?

(A) Gave a talk
(B) Joined an association
(C) Founded a publication
(D) Accepted a prize

84. What is the Career Achievement Award given for?

(A) Raising the standard of journalism
(B) Creating successful marketing campaigns
(C) Increasing magazine subscriptions
(D) Developing innovative business practices

85. What will probably happen next?

(A) Some nominees will be named.
(B) Some group photographs will be taken.
(C) A brief video will be shown.
(D) A recipient will come on stage.

86. What prevented the speaker from calling sooner?

(A) A business trip
(B) A medical appointment
(C) Luncheon arrangements
(D) Inspection preparations

87. What does the speaker mean when he says, "The shipment is scheduled to arrive tomorrow"?

(A) An order was placed on time.
(B) A delivery is behind schedule.
(C) A job can begin as planned.
(D) A fee was paid to expedite an order.

88. What will a worker give to the listener?

(A) A revised schedule
(B) A set of blueprints
(C) A box of supplies
(D) A billing statement

89. What is mentioned about the game on August 18?

(A) It will be streamed online.
(B) It will begin later than expected.
(C) It has been moved to a new venue.
(D) It has generated a lot of interest.

90. According to the speaker, what did David Polanski do last week?

(A) Met with another team's coach
(B) Purchased additional uniforms
(C) Organized a team practice
(D) Spoke with a media representative

91. What will probably happen next?

(A) An interview will be conducted.
(B) An advertisement will be played.
(C) A weather forecast will be given.
(D) A game score will be announced.

92. What did Superherbal recently do?

(A) Conducted a survey
(B) Changed an ingredient
(C) Launched a product
(D) Updated a Web site

93. What is mentioned about AdaptoPro?

(A) It was featured on a TV program.
(B) It has received positive feedback.
(C) It is available for online purchase.
(D) It will be sold in a variety of flavors.

94. Why does the speaker say, "This will not happen again for a while"?

(A) To explain a change to a company policy
(B) To suggest that the listeners check a schedule
(C) To indicate that a service will be canceled
(D) To encourage the listeners to buy some items

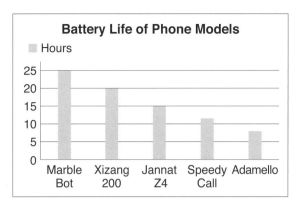

Battery Life of Phone Models

■ Hours

	Condition		
	Good	**Fair**	**Replace**
Headlights		✓	
Brake pads			✓
Timing belt			✓
Exhaust pipe			✓
Tires		✓	

95. What is a new feature of the MarbleBot smartphone?

(A) A fast processor
(B) A fingerprint sensor
(C) A wide screen
(D) An advanced camera

96. Look at the graphic. Which model is the MarbleBot's main competitor?

(A) Xizang 200
(B) Jannat Z4
(C) SpeedyCall
(D) Adamello

97. What was released by GadgetAssessor. com?

(A) A company profile
(B) A product manual
(C) A list of ranked devices
(D) A series of photos

98. According to the speaker, what does the listener plan to do tomorrow?

(A) Test drive a vehicle
(B) Go on a road trip
(C) Secure a rental car
(D) Review a billing statement

99. Look at the graphic. Which component has an issue that needs to be addressed?

(A) Headlights
(B) Brake pads
(C) Timing belt
(D) Exhaust system

100. Why does the speaker want to talk to the listener?

(A) To offer an explanation
(B) To discuss alternative options
(C) To explain promotion conditions
(D) To arrange a pick-up time

정답 p.164 / 점수 환산표 p.167 / 스크립트 p.186 / 무료 해석 바로 보기(정답 및 정답 음성 포함)

▌정답 음성(QR)이나 정답(p.164)을 이용해 채점하시기 바랍니다. 정답 음성에서 Boy는 (B)를, David는 (D)를 나타냅니다.
▌다음 페이지에 있는 Self 체크 리스트를 통해 자신의 문제 풀이 방식과 태도를 점검해 보세요.

TEST 04 PART 4 **77**

Self 체크 리스트

TEST 04는 무사히 잘 마치셨죠?
이제 다음의 **Self** 체크 리스트를 통해 자신의 테스트 진행 내용을 점검해 볼까요?

1. 나는 테스트가 진행되는 동안 한 번도 중도에 멈추지 않았다.

   ☐ 예 ☐ 아니오

   아니오에 답한 경우, 이유는 무엇인가요?

2. 나는 답안지 표기까지 성실하게 모두 마무리하였다.

   ☐ 예 ☐ 아니오

   아니오에 답한 경우, 이유는 무엇인가요?

3. 나는 Part 2의 25문항을 푸는 동안 완전히 테스트에 집중하였다.

   ☐ 예 ☐ 아니오

   아니오에 답한 경우, 이유는 무엇인가요?

4. 나는 Part 3를 풀 때 음성이 들리기 전에 해당 질문과 보기를 모두 먼저 읽었다.

   ☐ 예 ☐ 아니오

   아니오에 답한 경우, 이유는 무엇인가요?

5. 나는 Part 4를 풀 때 음성이 들리기 전에 해당 질문과 보기를 모두 먼저 읽었다.

   ☐ 예 ☐ 아니오

   아니오에 답한 경우, 이유는 무엇인가요?

6. 개선해야 할 점 또는 나를 위한 충고를 적어보세요.

* 교재의 첫 장으로 돌아가서 자신이 적은 목표 점수를 확인하면서 목표에 대한 의지를 다지기 바랍니다. 개선해야 할 점은 반드시 다음 테스트에
실천해야 합니다. 그것이 가장 중요하며, 그래야만 발전할 수 있습니다.

▌TEST 05

PART **1**
PART **2**
PART **3**
PART **4**
Self 체크 리스트

잠깐! 테스트 전 확인사항

1. 휴대 전화의 전원을 끄셨나요? □ 예
2. Answer Sheet, 연필, 지우개를 준비하셨나요? □ 예
3. MP3를 들을 준비가 되셨나요? □ 예

모든 준비가 완료되었으면 목표 점수를 떠올린 후 테스트를 시작합니다.

🎧 TEST 05.mp3

실전용·복습용 문제풀이 MP3 무료 다운로드 및 스트리밍 바로듣기 (HackersIngang.com)
* 실제 시험장의 소음까지 재현해 낸 고사장 소음/매미 버전 MP3, 영국식·호주식 발음 집중 MP3, 고속 버전 MP3까지
  구매하면 실전에 더욱 완벽히 대비할 수 있습니다.

무료MP3 바로듣기

LISTENING TEST

In this section, you must demonstrate your ability to understand spoken English. This section is divided into four parts and will take approximately 45 minutes to complete. Do not mark the answers in your test book. Use the answer sheet that is provided separately.

PART 1

Directions: For each question, you will listen to four short statements about a picture in your test book. These statements will not be printed and will only be spoken one time. Select the statement that best describes what is happening in the picture and mark the corresponding letter (A), (B), (C), or (D) on the answer sheet.

Sample Answer
Ⓐ ● Ⓒ Ⓓ

The statement that best describes the picture is (B), "The man is sitting at the desk." So, you should mark letter (B) on the answer sheet.

1.

2.

GO ON TO THE NEXT PAGE

3.

4.

5.

6.

GO ON TO THE NEXT PAGE

PART 2

Directions: For each question, you will listen to a statement or question followed by three possible responses spoken in English. They will not be printed and will only be spoken one time. Select the best response and mark the corresponding letter (A), (B), or (C) on your answer sheet.

7. Mark your answer on your answer sheet.

8. Mark your answer on your answer sheet.

9. Mark your answer on your answer sheet.

10. Mark your answer on your answer sheet.

11. Mark your answer on your answer sheet.

12. Mark your answer on your answer sheet.

13. Mark your answer on your answer sheet.

14. Mark your answer on your answer sheet.

15. Mark your answer on your answer sheet.

16. Mark your answer on your answer sheet.

17. Mark your answer on your answer sheet.

18. Mark your answer on your answer sheet.

19. Mark your answer on your answer sheet.

20. Mark your answer on your answer sheet.

21. Mark your answer on your answer sheet.

22. Mark your answer on your answer sheet.

23. Mark your answer on your answer sheet.

24. Mark your answer on your answer sheet.

25. Mark your answer on your answer sheet.

26. Mark your answer on your answer sheet.

27. Mark your answer on your answer sheet.

28. Mark your answer on your answer sheet.

29. Mark your answer on your answer sheet.

30. Mark your answer on your answer sheet.

31. Mark your answer on your answer sheet.

PART 3

Directions: In this part, you will listen to several conversations between two or more speakers. These conversations will not be printed and will only be spoken one time. For each conversation, you will be asked to answer three questions. Select the best response and mark the corresponding letter (A), (B), (C), or (D) on your answer sheet.

32. Where most likely is the conversation taking place?

(A) At a resort hotel
(B) At a car repair shop
(C) At an automobile rental agency
(D) At a tour office

33. What does the man inquire about?

(A) The availability of tickets
(B) The location of a facility
(C) Baggage storage space
(D) Expected drop-off times

34. What does the woman ask the man to do?

(A) Provide a form of identification
(B) Pay a percentage of a fee
(C) Describe his lost luggage
(D) Get his vehicle from a parking lot

35. What type of business most likely is Spectrum?

(A) An art supply store
(B) A construction firm
(C) A painting company
(D) A moving service

36. Why is the man calling?

(A) To ask about a product
(B) To inquire about a charge
(C) To request a billing statement
(D) To confirm an order

37. What does the man say he will do next?

(A) Call an interior designer
(B) Send a payment
(C) Look at some paint samples
(D) Take some measurements

38. Why did the woman visit the community center?

(A) To apply for a position
(B) To sign up for a contest
(C) To register for a course
(D) To hand in a finished work

39. Why is the woman worried?

(A) She does not have writing experience.
(B) She cannot be present for a seminar.
(C) She might not have enough time to prepare.
(D) She did not submit the correct document.

40. What does the man imply when he says, "that magazine is sold across the country"?

(A) Her work could be read by many.
(B) An event is popular nationwide.
(C) The magazine has a long history.
(D) A copy of a publication will be easy to find.

41. What did the man recently do?

(A) Traveled to Seattle
(B) Helped to organize a sale
(C) Requested another assignment
(D) Cooperated with a marketing team

42. What problem does the woman mention?

(A) A promotion has to be canceled.
(B) An incorrect branch was included.
(C) A program is not properly loading.
(D) A report was never turned in.

43. What does the man say he will do?

(A) Revise some material
(B) Meet with a supervisor
(C) Update his work schedule
(D) Design a Web site

GO ON TO THE NEXT PAGE

44. Why did the man arrive early?

(A) To assemble store shelves
(B) To repair some consoles
(C) To unpack some merchandise
(D) To send a shipment

45. Why should the speakers finish a task now?

(A) Trucks need to be loaded.
(B) Customers are waiting at an entrance.
(C) A manager has given more assignments.
(D) A sales event has already begun.

46. What does the man suggest?

(A) Clearing out a storage room
(B) Requesting additional assistance
(C) Asking shoppers to return later
(D) Delaying the store opening

---

47. What problem does the woman mention?

(A) A branch is currently understaffed.
(B) A theater requires new equipment.
(C) A film release has been postponed.
(D) A staff member missed a shift.

48. What does the man mean when he says, "This is the busiest time of the year"?

(A) He needs to check a schedule.
(B) He agrees with a recommendation.
(C) He wants to promote a service.
(D) He has completed a task.

49. What will probably happen later today?

(A) Some interviews will be held.
(B) A Web site will be officially launched.
(C) Some employees will undergo training.
(D) A posting will be posted.

---

50. What is the purpose of the call?

(A) To apply for membership
(B) To reserve accommodations
(C) To book some tickets
(D) To ask about transportation costs

51. What is the man concerned about?

(A) Guide availability
(B) Program duration
(C) A starting time
(D) A tour price

52. How can visitors receive a discount?

(A) By paying in advance
(B) By showing up early
(C) By being a cardholder
(D) By getting a family pass

---

53. What did the man do several hours ago?

(A) Met a recording artist
(B) Signed some paperwork
(C) Agreed to a deal
(D) Viewed a rental unit

54. Who is Janet Davidson?

(A) A professional photographer
(B) A building owner
(C) A real estate agent
(D) An office secretary

55. What does the woman ask the man to do?

(A) Make an appointment
(B) Update a schedule
(C) Confirm a layout
(D) Pay a deposit

---

56. What are the speakers mainly discussing?

(A) A change to a safety regulation
(B) Preparations for an activity
(C) An itinerary for a trip
(D) Complications with a vessel

57. What does the woman mention about Splash World?

(A) It extended operational hours.
(B) It is currently closed.
(C) It is located nearby.
(D) It restocked some goods.

58. What does the man ask about?

(A) A group's departure time
(B) A supplier's branch location
(C) A product's model number
(D) A business's contact information

59. What is the conversation mainly about?

(A) Moving plans
(B) Opening hours
(C) Staff hiring
(D) Business strategy

60. What does the woman recommend?

(A) Introducing new items to the menu
(B) Advertising in a neighborhood
(C) Reducing the number of dishes
(D) Paying for some repairs

61. What does Steven say he will do?

(A) Prepare ingredients for a recipe
(B) Examine the results of a survey
(C) Hand out flyers to passers-by
(D) Hold a meeting with employees

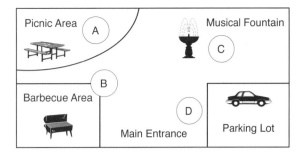

62. Why does the woman apologize?

(A) She did not bring some items.
(B) She cannot attend an event.
(C) She forgot to buy some tickets.
(D) She parked in the wrong area.

63. Look at the graphic. Where most likely will the speakers sit?

(A) Area A
(B) Area B
(C) Area C
(D) Area D

64. What will the woman probably do next?

(A) Park a vehicle
(B) Check a map
(C) Ask for some directions
(D) Purchase some drinks

GO ON TO THE NEXT PAGE

Exton Building Directory	
Floor 1	
101	Markus Swan
102	Tom Olsen
Floor 2	
201	Ahmed Abdul
202	Harvey Pinkerton

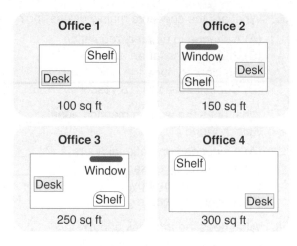

Office 1 — 100 sq ft
Office 2 — 150 sq ft
Office 3 — 250 sq ft
Office 4 — 300 sq ft

65. What did the woman already do?

(A) Canceled an appointment
(B) Went to a different floor
(C) Spoke to another receptionist
(D) Updated some information

66. Why did Mr. Pinkerton move into a new office?

(A) He began a special marketing project.
(B) He required a larger workspace.
(C) He received a promotion.
(D) He joined another department.

67. Look at the graphic. Which office will the woman head to?

(A) 101
(B) 102
(C) 201
(D) 202

68. Who most likely is the woman?

(A) A financial consultant
(B) An engineer
(C) An architect
(D) A Web designer

69. Look at the graphic. Which office will the woman use?

(A) Office 1
(B) Office 2
(C) Office 3
(D) Office 4

70. What will the woman probably do next?

(A) Go on a building tour
(B) Meet with a manager
(C) Participate in an orientation
(D) Introduce herself to coworkers

PART 4

Directions: In this part, you will listen to several short talks by a single speaker. These talks will not be printed and will only be spoken one time. For each talk, you will be asked to answer three questions. Select the best response and mark the corresponding letter (A), (B), (C), or (D) on your answer sheet.

71. Who is Wan Cheol Shin?

(A) A musical performer
(B) A famous actor
(C) A symphony conductor
(D) A guest speaker

72. What will be available at the event?

(A) Free brochures
(B) Refreshments
(C) Music recordings
(D) Signed posters

73. Why would the listeners call the provided telephone number?

(A) To check performance times
(B) To inquire about tickets
(C) To learn about an artist
(D) To purchase a CD

74. What is the announcement mainly about?

(A) A company event
(B) A change of location
(C) A temporary closure
(D) A staff reassignment

75. What will happen next Friday?

(A) The building will be renovated.
(B) Insect problems will be resolved.
(C) Tenant feedback will be collected.
(D) Broken equipment will be repaired.

76. What does the speaker mean when she says, "The rest of you are in luck"?

(A) A new benefit will be offered.
(B) A team assignment was canceled.
(C) Some employees can take a day off.
(D) Some staff members will get a pay raise.

77. Where does the talk most likely take place?

(A) At a job orientation
(B) At a product launch
(C) At a trade fair
(D) At a fashion seminar

78. What were given to the listeners?

(A) Event programs
(B) Performance reports
(C) Personal name tags
(D) Fabric samples

79. What will the participants do in the afternoon?

(A) Look at new apparel
(B) Watch a presentation
(C) Take part in group activities
(D) Review some documents

80. What did a technician do this morning?

(A) Installed some machinery
(B) Inspected a device
(C) Updated some software
(D) Relocated some supplies

81. Why does the speaker say, "a delivery will be made this week"?

(A) To make a correction
(B) To show surprise
(C) To offer assurance
(D) To confirm some speculation

82. What does the speaker suggest doing?

(A) Waiting for a specialist
(B) Speaking with a team manager
(C) Adjusting a work schedule
(D) Using another machine

GO ON TO THE NEXT PAGE

83. Who most likely is the speaker?

(A) A personal assistant
(B) A program manager
(C) A park caretaker
(D) A city administrator

84. According to the speaker, what does the listener want to do?

(A) Volunteer at an outing
(B) Arrange a tour
(C) Make a booking
(D) Join a civic organization

85. Why might the listener visit a Web site?

(A) To pay a deposit
(B) To view some images
(C) To upload a review
(D) To check for updates

---

86. What most likely do the listeners do for work?

(A) Provide technical support
(B) Develop new software programs
(C) Consult companies
(D) Sell products over the phone

87. According to the speaker, why are communication skills important?

(A) They make it easier to find new customers.
(B) They increase the likelihood of being hired.
(C) They allow customers to feel assured.
(D) They motivate other employees.

88. What does the speaker ask the listeners to do?

(A) Provide feedback
(B) Contact some clients
(C) Watch a short video
(D) Participate in exercises

---

89. What is the main topic of the news report?

(A) An upcoming election
(B) A selected award recipient
(C) A medical facility
(D) A construction project

90. What is mentioned about Maude Evans?

(A) She retired a year ago.
(B) She works at a hospital.
(C) She joined the city council.
(D) She owns a local business.

91. According to the speaker, who will attend a gathering?

(A) A health care professional
(B) Performing artists
(C) Government representatives
(D) A foundation president

---

92. What did the speaker do this morning?

(A) Notified people of a postponement
(B) Put in a special food order
(C) Inquired about space at a restaurant
(D) Sampled some dessert options

93. What does the speaker mean when he says, "I'm headed to the airport now"?

(A) He will reach a destination on time.
(B) He has taken a coworker's suggestion.
(C) He is unable to carry out a task.
(D) He has already made a reservation.

94. According to the speaker, why should a reservation be made quickly?

(A) A client has given short notice on a request.
(B) A scheduled event is approaching.
(C) A discount will be canceled soon.
(D) A restaurant will be closing shortly.

Burger Shack Combo Options

The Veggie

Mushroom Burger
Greek Salad

The Western

Barbecue Burger
Onion Rings

The Deluxe

Double Patty Burger
Garden Salad

The Swiss

Cheddar Burger
French Fries

---

95. What was Dawn Rather hired to do?

(A) Improve an ordering system
(B) Conduct some customer surveys
(C) Promote an updated lunch menu
(D) Collaborate with professional cooks

96. Look at the graphic. Which meal combo does the speaker refer to?

(A) The Veggie
(B) The Western
(C) The Deluxe
(D) The Swiss

97. What does the speaker say will happen in July?

(A) A major campaign will be concluded.
(B) A special promotion will be announced.
(C) A new symbol will be revealed.
(D) A fast food restaurant branch will open.

Calgary Music Festival Lineup

Wednesday	Thursday	Friday	Saturday	Sunday
Blue Wing	Time Bandit	Karl Slocum	Smooth Moves	DJ Jacobs

98. Who most likely is Lisa Gomez?

(A) A news reporter
(B) An event organizer
(C) An amateur musician
(D) A band manager

99. Look at the graphic. When will DJ James Money perform?

(A) On Thursday
(B) On Friday
(C) On Saturday
(D) On Sunday

100. According to the speaker, what will half of the money raised by ticket sales be used for?

(A) Supporting a local organization
(B) Promoting young artists
(C) Providing free albums to attendees
(D) Giving scholarships to students

정답 p.165 / 점수 환산표 p.167 / 스크립트 p.192 / 무료 해석 바로 보기(정답 및 정답 음성 포함)

▮ 정답 음성(QR)이나 정답(p.165)을 이용해 채점하시기 바랍니다. 정답 음성에서 Boy는 (B)를, David는 (D)를 나타냅니다.
▮ 다음 페이지에 있는 Self 체크 리스트를 통해 자신의 문제 풀이 방식과 태도를 점검해 보세요.

Self 체크 리스트

TEST 05는 무사히 잘 마치셨죠?
이제 다음의 Self 체크 리스트를 통해 자신의 테스트 진행 내용을 점검해 볼까요?

1. 나는 테스트가 진행되는 동안 한 번도 중도에 멈추지 않았다.

   ☐ 예   ☐ 아니오

   아니오에 답한 경우, 이유는 무엇인가요?

2. 나는 답안지 표기까지 성실하게 모두 마무리하였다.

   ☐ 예   ☐ 아니오

   아니오에 답한 경우, 이유는 무엇인가요?

3. 나는 Part 2의 25문항을 푸는 동안 완전히 테스트에 집중하였다.

   ☐ 예   ☐ 아니오

   아니오에 답한 경우, 이유는 무엇인가요?

4. 나는 Part 3를 풀 때 음성이 들리기 전에 해당 질문과 보기를 모두 먼저 읽었다.

   ☐ 예   ☐ 아니오

   아니오에 답한 경우, 이유는 무엇인가요?

5. 나는 Part 4를 풀 때 음성이 들리기 전에 해당 질문과 보기를 모두 먼저 읽었다.

   ☐ 예   ☐ 아니오

   아니오에 답한 경우, 이유는 무엇인가요?

6. 개선해야 할 점 또는 나를 위한 충고를 적어보세요.

* 교재의 첫 장으로 돌아가서 자신이 적은 목표 점수를 확인하면서 목표에 대한 의지를 다지기 바랍니다. 개선해야 할 점은 반드시 다음 테스트에 실천해야 합니다. 그것이 가장 중요하며, 그래야만 발전할 수 있습니다.

TEST 06

PART 1
PART 2
PART 3
PART 4
Self 체크 리스트

잠깐! 테스트 전 확인사항

1. 휴대 전화의 전원을 끄셨나요? □ 예
2. Answer Sheet, 연필, 지우개를 준비하셨나요? □ 예
3. MP3를 들을 준비가 되셨나요? □ 예

모든 준비가 완료되었으면 목표 점수를 떠올린 후 테스트를 시작합니다.

🎧 TEST 06.mp3

실전용·복습용 문제풀이 MP3 무료 다운로드 및 스트리밍 바로듣기 (HackersIngang.com)

* 실제 시험장의 소음까지 재현해 낸 고사장 소음/매미 버전 MP3, 영국식·호주식 발음 집중 MP3, 고속 버전 MP3까지
  구매하면 실전에 더욱 완벽히 대비할 수 있습니다.

무료MP3 바로듣기

LISTENING TEST

In this section, you must demonstrate your ability to understand spoken English. This section is divided into four parts and will take approximately 45 minutes to complete. Do not mark the answers in your test book. Use the answer sheet that is provided separately.

PART 1

Directions: For each question, you will listen to four short statements about a picture in your test book. These statements will not be printed and will only be spoken one time. Select the statement that best describes what is happening in the picture and mark the corresponding letter (A), (B), (C), or (D) on the answer sheet.

Sample Answer
Ⓐ ● Ⓒ Ⓓ

The statement that best describes the picture is (B), "The man is sitting at the desk." So, you should mark letter (B) on the answer sheet.

1.

2.

GO ON TO THE NEXT PAGE ➡

3.

4.

5.

6.

GO ON TO THE NEXT PAGE

PART 2

Directions: For each question, you will listen to a statement or question followed by three possible responses spoken in English. They will not be printed and will only be spoken one time. Select the best response and mark the corresponding letter (A), (B), or (C) on your answer sheet.

7. Mark your answer on your answer sheet.

8. Mark your answer on your answer sheet.

9. Mark your answer on your answer sheet.

10. Mark your answer on your answer sheet.

11. Mark your answer on your answer sheet.

12. Mark your answer on your answer sheet.

13. Mark your answer on your answer sheet.

14. Mark your answer on your answer sheet.

15. Mark your answer on your answer sheet.

16. Mark your answer on your answer sheet.

17. Mark your answer on your answer sheet.

18. Mark your answer on your answer sheet.

19. Mark your answer on your answer sheet.

20. Mark your answer on your answer sheet.

21. Mark your answer on your answer sheet.

22. Mark your answer on your answer sheet.

23. Mark your answer on your answer sheet.

24. Mark your answer on your answer sheet.

25. Mark your answer on your answer sheet.

26. Mark your answer on your answer sheet.

27. Mark your answer on your answer sheet.

28. Mark your answer on your answer sheet.

29. Mark your answer on your answer sheet.

30. Mark your answer on your answer sheet.

31. Mark your answer on your answer sheet.

PART 3

Directions: In this part, you will listen to several conversations between two or more speakers. These conversations will not be printed and will only be spoken one time. For each conversation, you will be asked to answer three questions. Select the best response and mark the corresponding letter (A), (B), (C), or (D) on your answer sheet.

32. What are the speakers mainly discussing?

(A) A newspaper subscription
(B) A journalist position
(C) A magazine closure
(D) An article correction

33. What does the woman suggest?

(A) Sending a copy of identification
(B) Paying for a service in advance
(C) Trying a different format
(D) Talking to a publisher

34. What will the woman most likely do next?

(A) Update some information
(B) Send an invoice
(C) Change a mailing address
(D) Rewrite some articles

35. What industry do the speakers most likely work in?

(A) Fitness
(B) Transportation
(C) Construction
(D) Interior design

36. What problem does the woman mention?

(A) Customers have made complaints.
(B) A discount will reduce overall profits.
(C) A delivery will arrive too late.
(D) Machines were not installed properly.

37. What will Brandon inquire about?

(A) Opening a facility
(B) Canceling an order
(C) Signing a contract
(D) Delaying a project

38. Where is the conversation most likely taking place?

(A) A tourist office
(B) A transit station
(C) A department store
(D) An outdoor market

39. Why is the museum closed today?

(A) A special holiday was declared.
(B) A safety issue has been raised.
(C) A new exhibition is being set up.
(D) A charity event will be held.

40. What does the man ask the woman to do?

(A) Recommend a restaurant
(B) Organize transportation
(C) Provide directions
(D) Suggest an activity

41. Which department do the speakers most likely work in?

(A) Legal
(B) Customer service
(C) Sales
(D) Human resources

42. Why does the woman say, "We may need more time"?

(A) To stress that a deadline is flexible
(B) To indicate that a process is incomplete
(C) To suggest that a task will be difficult
(D) To propose that a request be approved

43. What will the speakers probably do next?

(A) Speak with an applicant
(B) Post a notice
(C) Cancel a meeting
(D) Consult with a superior

GO ON TO THE NEXT PAGE

44. Why is the woman calling?

(A) To provide an update
(B) To address a concern
(C) To postpone an event
(D) To confirm a schedule

45. What does the woman say about Polly Mitchell?

(A) She has relevant experience.
(B) She is a media representative.
(C) She was recently promoted.
(D) She is a new employee.

46. What does the man ask the woman to do?

(A) Review a proposal
(B) Send a document
(C) Read an e-mail
(D) Write a statement

47. Why is the man unable to perform a task?

(A) He works in another section.
(B) He cannot locate an item.
(C) He has not received training.
(D) He is busy with a customer.

48. What information does the woman require?

(A) A discount amount
(B) A delivery date
(C) A serial number
(D) A product name

49. How can the customer qualify for a discount?

(A) By submitting a payment
(B) By completing a questionnaire
(C) By using a delivery service
(D) By creating an online account

50. What is the purpose of the woman's visit?

(A) To deposit a check
(B) To replace an item
(C) To inquire about a credit card
(D) To open up an account

51. What is a benefit of using the Gavin Premium Credit Card?

(A) Discounted purchases
(B) Reward points
(C) An interest-free period
(D) A complimentary service

52. What does the man suggest the woman do?

(A) Speak to a bank manager
(B) Read through a pamphlet
(C) Increase a credit limit
(D) Apply for a debit card

53. What are the speakers mainly discussing?

(A) A live concert
(B) An awards ceremony
(C) A gallery opening
(D) A charitable auction

54. What is mentioned about Ms. Holmes?

(A) She is arranging the catering.
(B) She organized an event.
(C) She has taught painting.
(D) She will give a talk.

55. What does the woman say she will do?

(A) Contact an artist
(B) Confirm some information
(C) Update a Web site
(D) Set up some equipment

56. What type of product was released last month?

(A) A clothing item
(B) A home appliance
(C) A cooking utensil
(D) A soft drink

57. What does Brad think needs to be changed?

(A) A marketing strategy
(B) An advertising agency
(C) The price of a product
(D) The design of a logo

58. What does the woman suggest?

(A) Hiring a management consultant
(B) Collecting additional opinions
(C) Creating a social media page
(D) Holding a promotional event

---

59. What did the man do this morning?

(A) Contacted an establishment
(B) Mailed out some invitations
(C) Booked some accommodations
(D) Sampled food options

60. What does the woman mean when she says, "you'd better keep looking"?

(A) An item has gone missing.
(B) A larger venue is required.
(C) A service is not suitable.
(D) An executive is not pleased.

61. Who most likely is Richard Seymore?

(A) An advisor
(B) A veterinarian
(C) An investor
(D) An engineer

Model	Detachable Keyboard	Stylus	Charging Pad
Wind SG	✓		✓
Blaze		✓	✓
Millennium	✓	✓	
Super Turbo	✓		✓

62. Why does the woman need a tablet computer?

(A) To communicate with clients
(B) To make online purchases
(C) To stay in touch with a friend
(D) To participate in a course

63. Look at the graphic. Which model will the woman most likely buy?

(A) Wind SG
(B) Blaze
(C) Millennium
(D) Super Turbo

64. According to the man, what is the woman unable to receive?

(A) A refund
(B) A discount
(C) A warranty
(D) A gift

GO ON TO THE NEXT PAGE

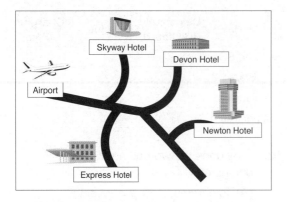

Hilltop Bistro	
Coffee	£1.50
Tomato Soup	£4.00
Roast Beef	£12.00
Salad	£3.50
TOTAL	**£21.00**

65. What problem does the woman mention?

(A) A flight has been missed.
(B) A vehicle has been damaged.
(C) A departure has been delayed.
(D) A reservation has been lost.

66. Look at the graphic. Which hotel does the man recommend?

(A) Skyway Hotel
(B) Devon Hotel
(C) Express Hotel
(D) Newton Hotel

67. What will the woman probably do next?

(A) Purchase a ticket
(B) Rent a car
(C) Call a hotel
(D) Take a shuttle

68. Who most likely is the woman?

(A) A chef
(B) A waitress
(C) A nutritionist
(D) A cashier

69. What did the man especially like?

(A) The view of the river
(B) The outdoor seating area
(C) The music performance
(D) The affordable prices

70. Look at the graphic. Which amount will be removed from the bill?

(A) £1.50
(B) £4.00
(C) £12.00
(D) £3.50

PART 4

Directions: In this part, you will listen to several short talks by a single speaker. These talks will not be printed and will only be spoken one time. For each talk, you will be asked to answer three questions. Select the best response and mark the corresponding letter (A), (B), (C), or (D) on your answer sheet.

71. Who most likely is the speaker?

(A) A recruiting manager
(B) A sales representative
(C) A business consultant
(D) A company president

72. What does the speaker attribute the company's success to?

(A) Rapid expansion
(B) New employees
(C) Quality service
(D) Reliable products

73. What will most likely happen next?

(A) A performance will be held.
(B) A promotion will be announced.
(C) A demonstration will be given.
(D) A speech will be made.

74. What does the speaker say about Ventra Tower?

(A) It is located on the outskirts of a city.
(B) It includes a multistory parking area.
(C) It is near a public transportation facility.
(D) It contains a variety of residential units.

75. Why does the speaker recommend a five-year lease?

(A) To save on rental expenses
(B) To receive additional services
(C) To reduce a security deposit amount
(D) To gain access to a private space

76. Why does the speaker say, "We are already accepting applications"?

(A) To describe a submission process
(B) To give a reason for a change
(C) To draw attention to a deadline
(D) To encourage prompt action

77. What type of business is being advertised?

(A) A shipping company
(B) An airline
(C) A hotel
(D) A travel agency

78. What is being offered to celebrate an opening?

(A) A rewards program
(B) A free service
(C) A special sale
(D) A local product

79. What can the listeners do with a company's mobile application?

(A) Make changes to reservations
(B) Chat in real-time with a representative
(C) Compare prices with other companies
(D) Acquire some up-to-date information

80. Why is the speaker calling?

(A) To explain a delay
(B) To confirm a decision
(C) To request a service
(D) To propose a change

81. Why does the speaker say, "The EZ Clean on Elma Street sold for $190,000"?

(A) To answer an inquiry
(B) To recommend a business
(C) To justify a suggestion
(D) To specify a location

82. What does the speaker mention about the listener's business?

(A) It will find a buyer soon.
(B) It should temporarily shut down.
(C) It should reinvest some profits.
(D) It will be listed for sale.

GO ON TO THE NEXT PAGE

83. What is the talk mainly about?

(A) A disciplinary measure
(B) A training program
(C) A recruitment goal
(D) A safety concern

84. According to the speaker, what will the listeners be responsible for?

(A) Completing an evaluation
(B) Approving a plan
(C) Developing a course
(D) Forming a team

85. What does the speaker ask the listeners to do next Monday?

(A) Select a candidate
(B) Give a presentation
(C) Attend a session
(D) Submit a document

---

86. What is the audition for?

(A) An orchestra
(B) A choir
(C) A movie
(D) A play

87. What will most likely be done by noon?

(A) Equipment will be repaired.
(B) A decision will be made.
(C) A contest will be held.
(D) Information will be shared.

88. What does the speaker ask the listeners to do?

(A) Review photographs
(B) Try on different outfits
(C) Meet with a director
(D) Go to another floor

---

89. What type of product is being introduced?

(A) A universal remote
(B) A kitchen appliance
(C) A computer program
(D) A gaming device

90. According to the speaker, what did Focus Incorporated do last month?

(A) Participated in a conference
(B) Reduced a product price
(C) Released a software update
(D) Partnered with a company

91. What does the speaker imply when she says, "There's no risk involved"?

(A) A full refund is available.
(B) A contract is not enforceable.
(C) An extended warranty is offered.
(D) A device is not dangerous.

---

92. What is mentioned about Green Shields?

(A) It purchased another company.
(B) It announced a new service.
(C) It expanded into other countries.
(D) It changed a customer policy.

93. Why does the listener qualify for a discount?

(A) He often posts online reviews.
(B) He recently bought his first insurance policy.
(C) He booked an overseas vacation package.
(D) He frequently buys a product.

94. What does the speaker suggest?

(A) Reading printed information
(B) Viewing digital contents
(C) Signing in to an account
(D) Visiting a nearby business

Product A	Product B
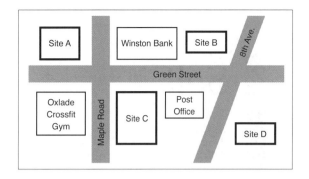	
$10.00	$15.00
Product C	**Product D**
CANADA	
$20.00	$25.00

95. Who most likely is the speaker?

(A) A travel guide
(B) A museum employee
(C) A store owner
(D) A salesperson

96. Look at the graphic. How much does the product recommended by the speaker cost?

(A) $10.00
(B) $15.00
(C) $20.00
(D) $25.00

97. What will the listeners most likely do at 1 P.M.?

(A) Board a bus
(B) Eat a meal
(C) Make a payment
(D) Visit a park

98. Where most likely is the announcement taking place?

(A) In a fitness center
(B) In a shopping complex
(C) In a parking lot
(D) In a financial institution

99. According to the speaker, what must the listeners do to receive a parking pass?

(A) Complete a survey
(B) Sign an agreement
(C) E-mail an employee
(D) Present a card

100. Look at the graphic. Where can the listeners park for free on May 15?

(A) Site A
(B) Site B
(C) Site C
(D) Site D

▌정답 음성(QR)이나 정답(p.165)을 이용해 채점하시기 바랍니다. 정답 음성에서 Boy는 (B)를, David는 (D)를 나타냅니다.
▌다음 페이지에 있는 Self 체크 리스트를 통해 자신의 문제 풀이 방식과 태도를 점검해 보세요.

TEST | 01 | 02 | 03 | 04 | 05 | 06 | 07 | 08 | 09 | 10 | 해커스 토익 실전 1000제 2 Listening

Self 체크 리스트

TEST 06는 무사히 잘 마치셨죠?
이제 다음의 Self 체크 리스트를 통해 자신의 테스트 진행 내용을 점검해 볼까요?

1. 나는 테스트가 진행되는 동안 한 번도 중도에 멈추지 않았다.

   ☐ 예   ☐ 아니오

   아니오에 답한 경우, 이유는 무엇인가요?

2. 나는 답안지 표기까지 성실하게 모두 마무리하였다.

   ☐ 예   ☐ 아니오

   아니오에 답한 경우, 이유는 무엇인가요?

3. 나는 Part 2의 25문항을 푸는 동안 완전히 테스트에 집중하였다.

   ☐ 예   ☐ 아니오

   아니오에 답한 경우, 이유는 무엇인가요?

4. 나는 Part 3를 풀 때 음성이 들리기 전에 해당 질문과 보기를 모두 먼저 읽었다.

   ☐ 예   ☐ 아니오

   아니오에 답한 경우, 이유는 무엇인가요?

5. 나는 Part 4를 풀 때 음성이 들리기 전에 해당 질문과 보기를 모두 먼저 읽었다.

   ☐ 예   ☐ 아니오

   아니오에 답한 경우, 이유는 무엇인가요?

6. 개선해야 할 점 또는 나를 위한 충고를 적어보세요.

* 교재의 첫 장으로 돌아가서 자신이 적은 목표 점수를 확인하면서 목표에 대한 의지를 다지기 바랍니다. 개선해야 할 점은 반드시 다음 테스트에
실천해야 합니다. 그것이 가장 중요하며, 그래야만 발전할 수 있습니다.

TEST 07

PART 1
PART 2
PART 3
PART 4
Self 체크 리스트

잠깐! 테스트 전 확인사항
1. 휴대 전화의 전원을 끄셨나요? □ 예
2. Answer Sheet, 연필, 지우개를 준비하셨나요? □ 예
3. MP3를 들을 준비가 되셨나요? □ 예

모든 준비가 완료되었으면 목표 점수를 떠올린 후 테스트를 시작합니다.

🎧 TEST 07.mp3
실전용·복습용 문제풀이 MP3 무료 다운로드 및 스트리밍 바로듣기 (HackersIngang.com)
* 실제 시험장의 소음까지 재현해 낸 고사장 소음/매미 버전 MP3, 영국식·호주식 발음 집중 MP3, 고속 버전 MP3까지
구매하면 실전에 더욱 완벽히 대비할 수 있습니다.

무료MP3 바로듣기

LISTENING TEST

In this section, you must demonstrate your ability to understand spoken English. This section is divided into four parts and will take approximately 45 minutes to complete. Do not mark the answers in your test book. Use the answer sheet that is provided separately.

PART 1

Directions: For each question, you will listen to four short statements about a picture in your test book. These statements will not be printed and will only be spoken one time. Select the statement that best describes what is happening in the picture and mark the corresponding letter (A), (B), (C), or (D) on the answer sheet.

Sample Answer

The statement that best describes the picture is (B), "The man is sitting at the desk." So, you should mark letter (B) on the answer sheet.

1.

2.

GO ON TO THE NEXT PAGE

3.

4.

5.

6.

GO ON TO THE NEXT PAGE

PART 2

Directions: For each question, you will listen to a statement or question followed by three possible responses spoken in English. They will not be printed and will only be spoken one time. Select the best response and mark the corresponding letter (A), (B), or (C) on your answer sheet.

7. Mark your answer on your answer sheet.

8. Mark your answer on your answer sheet.

9. Mark your answer on your answer sheet.

10. Mark your answer on your answer sheet.

11. Mark your answer on your answer sheet.

12. Mark your answer on your answer sheet.

13. Mark your answer on your answer sheet.

14. Mark your answer on your answer sheet.

15. Mark your answer on your answer sheet.

16. Mark your answer on your answer sheet.

17. Mark your answer on your answer sheet.

18. Mark your answer on your answer sheet.

19. Mark your answer on your answer sheet.

20. Mark your answer on your answer sheet.

21. Mark your answer on your answer sheet.

22. Mark your answer on your answer sheet.

23. Mark your answer on your answer sheet.

24. Mark your answer on your answer sheet.

25. Mark your answer on your answer sheet.

26. Mark your answer on your answer sheet.

27. Mark your answer on your answer sheet.

28. Mark your answer on your answer sheet.

29. Mark your answer on your answer sheet.

30. Mark your answer on your answer sheet.

31. Mark your answer on your answer sheet.

Directions: In this part, you will listen to several conversations between two or more speakers. These conversations will not be printed and will only be spoken one time. For each conversation, you will be asked to answer three questions. Select the best response and mark the corresponding letter (A), (B), (C), or (D) on your answer sheet.

32. According to the woman, what needs to be changed?

(A) An online database
(B) The details in a brochure
(C) A personnel policy
(D) The date of an event

33. What has Sun Nam been tasked with?

(A) Arranging a consultation
(B) Editing a report
(C) Leading a team
(D) Contacting an executive

34. What does the woman say she will do later today?

(A) Revise the format of a flyer
(B) Bring files to an administrator
(C) Leave for a trade fair
(D) Speak to a colleague

35. What did the man buy on Monday?

(A) Dishware
(B) Beverages
(C) Furniture
(D) Appliances

36. What problem does the man mention?

(A) A warranty has expired.
(B) Some merchandise is too small.
(C) An item is damaged.
(D) A product was not shipped.

37. What is the man told to do?

(A) Return to a service desk
(B) Find a similar item
(C) Ask a supervisor for help
(D) Contact another branch

38. What does the woman ask about?

(A) When some dishes will be prepared
(B) Why some menu items are unavailable
(C) Where a group should be seated
(D) What an entrée is served with

39. Why does the woman say, "One of them just left"?

(A) To explain why a manager is upset
(B) To emphasize a problem's seriousness
(C) To criticize a coworker's decision
(D) To check if a restaurant will close

40. What does the woman suggest?

(A) Reducing a charge
(B) Bringing in more staff
(C) Canceling some orders
(D) Offering guests a free meal

41. What is the conversation mainly about?

(A) A partnership with an organization
(B) A way to raise money
(C) An event for volunteers
(D) A method for boosting morale

42. According to the man, what technique does the organization use?

(A) Advertising on television
(B) Giving away gifts
(C) Charging membership fees
(D) Organizing special events

43. What does the man offer to do?

(A) Develop a plan
(B) Announce a decision
(C) Assemble a team
(D) Contact a company

GO ON TO THE NEXT PAGE

44. What concern does the woman mention?

(A) She might need to leave early.
(B) She cannot afford to buy passes.
(C) She could not reach her relatives.
(D) She may have to miss an event.

45. What does the man recommend?

(A) Gathering more information
(B) Taking time to make a choice
(C) Coming with family members
(D) Getting some vouchers

46. What does the man say he did last year?

(A) Volunteered his services
(B) Harvested produce
(C) Operated a booth
(D) Met up with acquaintances

---

47. What does the woman ask permission to do?

(A) Take a personal day
(B) Attend a dental conference
(C) Extend a vacation
(D) Cancel an engagement

48. What will happen on Thursday?

(A) New employees will be trained.
(B) A workshop will be conducted.
(C) A clinic will close for the holidays.
(D) Course materials will be made.

49. What does the man suggest?

(A) Asking a supervisor for time off
(B) Verifying an address
(C) Rescheduling an appointment
(D) Taking notes at a seminar

---

50. What did the man do last month?

(A) Reviewed a document
(B) Signed a contract
(C) Contacted a publishing agent
(D) Drafted a manuscript

51. Why is the woman excited?

(A) She is going to give a public reading.
(B) She recently met a famous author.
(C) She was nominated for an award.
(D) She has been selected for publication.

52. What does the man say about The Oxford Club?

(A) It is closed this Tuesday afternoon.
(B) It is often busy during the week.
(C) It is situated near his workplace.
(D) It is one of his favorite cafés.

---

53. Where most likely do the speakers work?

(A) At a warehouse
(B) At a department store
(C) At a supermarket
(D) At a travel agency

54. Why is Gary unable to help on Saturday?

(A) He is going on a family vacation.
(B) He will take a class on baking.
(C) He is attending an annual workshop.
(D) He has a medical appointment.

55. What will the woman most likely do next?

(A) Cancel an order
(B) Talk to coworkers
(C) Write a check
(D) Purchase supplies

---

56. Why is the man calling?

(A) To apply for Internet banking
(B) To request a new credit card
(C) To open a bank account
(D) To report a transaction error

57. What must the man do?

(A) Update his account information
(B) Explain a company policy
(C) Enter an extension number
(D) Complete a form online

58. What does the man want to change?

(A) A billing address
(B) A spending restriction
(C) His credit card provider
(D) His contact information

59. What industry does the woman most likely work in?

(A) Advertising
(B) Recruitment
(C) Software development
(D) Smartphone manufacturing

60. What does the man imply when he says, "she just moved into a house close to your office"?

(A) Ms. Phillips got a new temporary job recently.
(B) Ms. Phillips will be able to commute to work.
(C) Ms. Phillips can make it on time.
(D) Ms. Phillips has been relocated to a branch nearby.

61. What does the woman ask for?

(A) A summary of qualifications
(B) A completed application form
(C) A professional certificate
(D) A list of suitable candidates

Wilson Language Academy Spanish Tutors	
Tutor Name	**Available Days**
Diego Lopez	Mondays and Thursdays
Sarah Rodriguez	Wednesdays
Jose Garcia	Fridays
Jennifer Alcon	Saturdays and Sundays

62. Why is the man going to Madrid?

(A) To take a facility tour
(B) To attend a business conference
(C) To negotiate a merger
(D) To meet with a client

63. Look at the graphic. Who will the man most likely study Spanish with?

(A) Diego Lopez
(B) Sarah Rodriguez
(C) Jose Garcia
(D) Jennifer Alcon

64. What does the woman ask the man to do?

(A) Provide contact information
(B) Pay a lesson fee
(C) Contact an instructor
(D) Confirm registration

GO ON TO THE NEXT PAGE

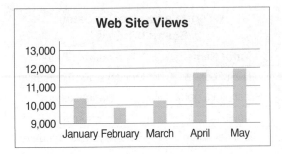

Web Site Views

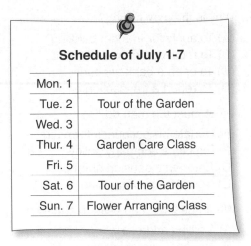

Schedule of July 1-7

Mon. 1	
Tue. 2	Tour of the Garden
Wed. 3	
Thur. 4	Garden Care Class
Fri. 5	
Sat. 6	Tour of the Garden
Sun. 7	Flower Arranging Class

65. What did the man recently do?

(A) Became a company spokesperson
(B) Created a mobile phone application
(C) Presented a promotional idea
(D) Assigned a task

66. What problem is mentioned?

(A) An advertisement is too long.
(B) Some instructions lack clarity.
(C) A launch event cannot be postponed.
(D) A message is overly complicated.

67. Look at the graphic. When was a previous campaign released?

(A) In February
(B) In March
(C) In April
(D) In May

68. Who is Myra Lawrence?

(A) A university instructor
(B) A professional gardener
(C) A Web site designer
(D) A facility manager

69. Look at the graphic. When will the man probably visit the botanical garden?

(A) On July 2
(B) On July 4
(C) On July 6
(D) On July 7

70. What is the man instructed to do?

(A) Purchase materials in advance
(B) Change an appointment time
(C) Select an online link
(D) E-mail a registration form

PART 4

Directions: In this part, you will listen to several short talks by a single speaker. These talks will not be printed and will only be spoken one time. For each talk, you will be asked to answer three questions. Select the best response and mark the corresponding letter (A), (B), (C), or (D) on your answer sheet.

71. What facility does the teahouse include?

(A) A parking lot
(B) A stage for performances
(C) A private library
(D) An area for sleeping

72. What is mentioned about the teahouse?

(A) It overlooks the entire city.
(B) It hosted many notable events.
(C) It has innovative architectural features.
(D) It was owned by the royal family.

73. According to the speaker, what is the teahouse now used as?

(A) A venue for government ceremonies
(B) A destination for visiting tourists
(C) A location for live shows
(D) A facility for storing historic artifacts

74. What kind of business is being advertised?

(A) A gardening company
(B) A flower shop
(C) A banquet hall
(D) An interior design firm

75. According to the speaker, why should the listeners visit Green Solutions?

(A) To browse through merchandise
(B) To make a booking
(C) To place a customized order
(D) To get an initial estimate

76. How can the listeners receive a price reduction?

(A) By printing out a coupon
(B) By placing a phone call
(C) By mentioning a commercial
(D) By making a minimum purchase

77. What did the speaker do last weekend?

(A) Bought a painting
(B) Attended an art fair
(C) Met with an artist
(D) Opened an art gallery

78. What does the speaker imply when he says, "it's in a busy location"?

(A) Some visitors will be late.
(B) A business will be expanded.
(C) A fee will be increased.
(D) Artwork will receive a lot of attention.

79. What does the speaker offer to do?

(A) Print out some invitations
(B) Advertise an event
(C) Create an invoice
(D) Contact museum curators

80. What does the speaker mention about the commuter train system?

(A) It failed a government inspection.
(B) It had to be completely shut down.
(C) It is disliked by some individuals.
(D) It recently underwent repairs.

81. What did Mary Stenos do on Wednesday?

(A) Met with media representatives
(B) Stopped by a construction site
(C) Announced new regulations
(D) Launched an online forum

82. According to the speaker, why should the listeners visit the Web site?

(A) To download some brochures
(B) To check the status of a project
(C) To submit questions about a plan
(D) To view a schedule for a conference

GO ON TO THE NEXT PAGE

83. What is being advertised?

(A) A staffing company
(B) A talent agency
(C) A legal firm
(D) A consulting service

84. What service does Ace Solutions provide?

(A) Camera installation
(B) Certification courses
(C) Background checks
(D) On-site training

85. What does the speaker recommend that the listeners do?

(A) Provide feedback on a service
(B) Sign up for a newsletter
(C) Renew a membership
(D) Take advantage of an offer

86. Where most likely are the listeners?

(A) At a writing seminar
(B) At a literary reading
(C) At an awards ceremony
(D) At a fiction convention

87. What is the speaker's newest work about?

(A) Her favorite author
(B) The history of South Africa
(C) Her personal experiences
(D) The psychology of children

88. Why does the speaker say, "Copies have been placed in the back of the room"?

(A) To make a correction
(B) To ask for assistance
(C) To encourage purchases
(D) To initiate an exercise

89. Where are the listeners?

(A) At a shareholder meeting
(B) At a convention
(C) At an orientation
(D) At a manufacturing plant tour

90. What do some companies contract Lifan to do?

(A) Conduct quality control testing
(B) Promote their products
(C) Ship goods internationally
(D) Manufacture components

91. What most likely will happen next?

(A) A customer survey will be discussed.
(B) A speaker will take the stage.
(C) New products will be revealed.
(D) Additional handouts will be distributed.

92. Why is an agent unable to be reached?

(A) She is taking a leave.
(B) She is at a film festival.
(C) She has turned her mobile phone off.
(D) She has to meet with a client.

93. What does the speaker mean when she says, "Most of your parts have been in action movies"?

(A) A director has voiced some concerns.
(B) A screenplay can still be revised.
(C) A role matches a performer's experience.
(D) A proposal might seem unfitting.

94. What will the speaker provide to the listener?

(A) An audition schedule
(B) A draft of a script
(C) Some legal documents
(D) Some contact information

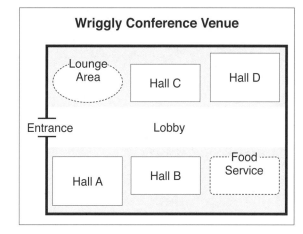

Wriggly Conference Venue

- Lounge Area
- Hall C
- Hall D
- Entrance
- Lobby
- Hall A
- Hall B
- Food Service

Presidential Palace - Manila
CUSTOMER RECEIPT

Guest: Beverly Gilder   Room: 1713

Charge	Amount
Room Rate	$138.99
Mini-Bar	$8.98
Dry Cleaning	$15.79
Spa Services	$46.00
Tax	$20.97
Total Paid	**$230.73**

95. Who most likely is the speaker addressing?

(A) Students
(B) Jobseekers
(C) College administrators
(D) Business representatives

96. What is mentioned about Global Education?

(A) It has had difficulty finding employees recently.
(B) It has offices around the world.
(C) It has reserved the largest booth.
(D) It has not participated in the event before.

97. Look at the graphic. Where will engineering staff be located?

(A) In Hall A
(B) In Hall B
(C) In Hall C
(D) In Hall D

98. What did the speaker fail to do?

(A) Book a room in advance
(B) Review some details
(C) Request a copy of a statement
(D) Report an error to a supervisor

99. Look at the graphic. How much will the speaker probably be refunded?

(A) $138.99
(B) $8.98
(C) $15.79
(D) $46.00

100. What will the speaker most likely do on Friday?

(A) Submit a document
(B) Leave for a trip
(C) Contact a hotel
(D) Respond to an e-mail

Self 체크 리스트

TEST 07은 무사히 잘 마치셨죠?
이제 다음의 Self 체크 리스트를 통해 자신의 테스트 진행 내용을 점검해 볼까요?

1. 나는 테스트가 진행되는 동안 한 번도 중도에 멈추지 않았다.

   ☐ 예   ☐ 아니오

   아니오에 답한 경우, 이유는 무엇인가요?

2. 나는 답안지 표기까지 성실하게 모두 마무리하였다.

   ☐ 예   ☐ 아니오

   아니오에 답한 경우, 이유는 무엇인가요?

3. 나는 Part 2의 25문항을 푸는 동안 완전히 테스트에 집중하였다.

   ☐ 예   ☐ 아니오

   아니오에 답한 경우, 이유는 무엇인가요?

4. 나는 Part 3를 풀 때 음성이 들리기 전에 해당 질문과 보기를 모두 먼저 읽었다.

   ☐ 예   ☐ 아니오

   아니오에 답한 경우, 이유는 무엇인가요?

5. 나는 Part 4를 풀 때 음성이 들리기 전에 해당 질문과 보기를 모두 먼저 읽었다.

   ☐ 예   ☐ 아니오

   아니오에 답한 경우, 이유는 무엇인가요?

6. 개선해야 할 점 또는 나를 위한 충고를 적어보세요.

* 교재의 첫 장으로 돌아가서 자신이 적은 목표 점수를 확인하면서 목표에 대한 의지를 다지기 바랍니다. 개선해야 할 점은 반드시 다음 테스트에
  실천해야 합니다. 그것이 가장 중요하며, 그래야만 발전할 수 있습니다.

▌TEST 08

PART 1
PART 2
PART 3
PART 4
Self 체크 리스트

잠깐! 테스트 전 확인사항

1. 휴대 전화의 전원을 끄셨나요? ☐ 예
2. Answer Sheet, 연필, 지우개를 준비하셨나요? ☐ 예
3. MP3를 들을 준비가 되셨나요? ☐ 예

모든 준비가 완료되었으면 목표 점수를 떠올린 후 테스트를 시작합니다.

🎧 TEST 08.mp3

실전용·복습용 문제풀이 MP3 무료 다운로드 및 스트리밍 바로듣기 (HackersIngang.com)

* 실제 시험장의 소음까지 재현해 낸 고사장 소음/매미 버전 MP3, 영국식·호주식 발음 집중 MP3, 고속 버전 MP3까지
  구매하면 실전에 더욱 완벽히 대비할 수 있습니다.

무료MP3 바로듣기

LISTENING TEST

In this section, you must demonstrate your ability to understand spoken English. This section is divided into four parts and will take approximately 45 minutes to complete. Do not mark the answers in your test book. Use the answer sheet that is provided separately.

PART 1

Directions: For each question, you will listen to four short statements about a picture in your test book. These statements will not be printed and will only be spoken one time. Select the statement that best describes what is happening in the picture and mark the corresponding letter (A), (B), (C), or (D) on the answer sheet.

Sample Answer

The statement that best describes the picture is (B), "The man is sitting at the desk." So, you should mark letter (B) on the answer sheet.

1.

2.

GO ON TO THE NEXT PAGE

3.

4.

5.

6.

GO ON TO THE NEXT PAGE

PART 2

Directions: For each question, you will listen to a statement or question followed by three possible responses spoken in English. They will not be printed and will only be spoken one time. Select the best response and mark the corresponding letter (A), (B), or (C) on your answer sheet.

7. Mark your answer on your answer sheet.

8. Mark your answer on your answer sheet.

9. Mark your answer on your answer sheet.

10. Mark your answer on your answer sheet.

11. Mark your answer on your answer sheet.

12. Mark your answer on your answer sheet.

13. Mark your answer on your answer sheet.

14. Mark your answer on your answer sheet.

15. Mark your answer on your answer sheet.

16. Mark your answer on your answer sheet.

17. Mark your answer on your answer sheet.

18. Mark your answer on your answer sheet.

19. Mark your answer on your answer sheet.

20. Mark your answer on your answer sheet.

21. Mark your answer on your answer sheet.

22. Mark your answer on your answer sheet.

23. Mark your answer on your answer sheet.

24. Mark your answer on your answer sheet.

25. Mark your answer on your answer sheet.

26. Mark your answer on your answer sheet.

27. Mark your answer on your answer sheet.

28. Mark your answer on your answer sheet.

29. Mark your answer on your answer sheet.

30. Mark your answer on your answer sheet.

31. Mark your answer on your answer sheet.

PART 3

Directions: In this part, you will listen to several conversations between two or more speakers. These conversations will not be printed and will only be spoken one time. For each conversation, you will be asked to answer three questions. Select the best response and mark the corresponding letter (A), (B), (C), or (D) on your answer sheet.

32. Where most likely are the speakers?
(A) At a car dealership
(B) At a gas station
(C) At an auto mechanic shop
(D) At a rental agency

33. What does the man ask the woman about?
(A) Whether a vehicle was damaged
(B) Why an agreement was not signed
(C) How much fuel she used
(D) What features a car has

34. Why is the woman being charged extra?
(A) She did not arrive on time.
(B) She requested a cleaning service.
(C) She did not refill the gas tank.
(D) She agreed to an upgrade.

35. What does the man say about the book fair?
(A) It was held at a local library.
(B) It was featured in a major magazine.
(C) It provided reading materials to kids.
(D) It had a lower turnout than anticipated.

36. Why does the man say, "I suggested running an online marketing campaign a few months ago"?
(A) To provide a reason for a decision
(B) To express agreement with an opinion
(C) To show concern about a plan
(D) To indicate a preference for an option

37. What was Ms. Gabbert unable to do?
(A) Use more funds for an event
(B) Meet with a financial consultant
(C) Participate in a company event
(D) Review a project budget

38. What did the woman do last Thursday?
(A) Submitted an article
(B) Created a social media profile
(C) Interviewed a local chef
(D) Hosted an opening event

39. According to the man, what did Lima Kitchen recently do?
(A) Developed an online page
(B) Started business operations
(C) Offered discount coupons
(D) Remodeled a dining area

40. What will the woman most likely do next?
(A) Edit a story
(B) Visit a restaurant
(C) Meet with a colleague
(D) Make an online post

41. What are the speakers mainly discussing?
(A) The benefits of employee training
(B) The effects of increased competition
(C) The details of new regulations
(D) The possibility of expansion

42. Why is Allen concerned?
(A) He has received multiple complaints.
(B) He does not want to lose customers.
(C) He is unable to afford some equipment.
(D) He could not find a moving company.

43. What does the woman recommend?
(A) Ordering mechanical equipment
(B) Stopping by a vacant facility
(C) Buying a nearby property
(D) Constructing more branches

GO ON TO THE NEXT PAGE

44. Where do the speakers most likely work?

(A) At a supermarket
(B) At an advertising firm
(C) At a movie production company
(D) At a bakery

45. Why is the woman concerned?

(A) A sale is not drawing customers.
(B) A commercial lacks some information.
(C) A video is longer than anticipated.
(D) A store interior is not fully prepared.

46. What does the man mean when he says, "You specifically asked for that content to be included"?

(A) He cannot meet a deadline.
(B) He will not perform a task.
(C) He is confused by a request.
(D) He was misinformed about a project.

---

47. Who most likely is the man?

(A) A fashion designer
(B) A customer service representative
(C) A Web site developer
(D) A post office worker

48. According to the man, what did the woman fail to do?

(A) Provide payment confirmation
(B) Input correct information
(C) Print a receipt
(D) Log in to a Web page

49. According to the man, what should the woman do with a code?

(A) Submit it online
(B) E-mail it to an employee
(C) Present it to a manager
(D) Write it on a billing statement

---

50. What does the woman say about her work?

(A) It can be stressful at times.
(B) It is challenging for new employees.
(C) It requires regular business trips.
(D) It involves repetitive movements.

51. What type of business does the woman work in?

(A) A clothing distributor
(B) A footwear factory
(C) A medical facility
(D) A retail store

52. What does the man suggest the woman do?

(A) Seek out a physical therapist
(B) Consider alternative professions
(C) Discuss a situation with a supervisor
(D) Request some additional safety equipment

---

53. What issue does the man mention?

(A) A Web site is experiencing a glitch.
(B) A scheduling conflict has occurred.
(C) A job opening has received little interest.
(D) An application was submitted after a due date.

54. What does the woman offer to do?

(A) Contact employees of another company
(B) Redesign a social media site
(C) Arrange an appointment with a recruiter
(D) Review programmer applications

55. What does the woman ask the man to do?

(A) Edit a recruitment posting
(B) Lead an upcoming meeting
(C) Post some information online
(D) Give her an update this afternoon

---

56. Where most likely is the conversation taking place?

(A) At a hardware store
(B) At an auto repair shop
(C) At a snow removal company
(D) At a medical center

57. What does Shawn say he will do?

(A) Borrow some equipment
(B) Take a bus home
(C) Make a purchase
(D) Pay back some money

58. What will the woman most likely do next?

(A) Transport items to another location
(B) Post a message online
(C) Change the hours of operation
(D) Check the weather forecast

59. Who most likely is the man?

(A) A marketing manager
(B) A television host
(C) A company president
(D) A luggage designer

60. What is unique about the ES32 suitcase?

(A) Its fabric options
(B) Its portability
(C) Its accessories
(D) Its durability

61. What will probably happen in October?

(A) A product will be updated.
(B) A bag line will be introduced.
(C) A discount will be discontinued.
(D) A suitcase will be recalled.

Newark Film Festival Schedule – Friday, July 18	
Film Name	**Time**
Hazard	12:30 – 2:00 P.M.
Low Horizon	2:30 – 4:00 P.M.
City Stories	4:30 – 6:00 P.M.
Chords	6:30 – 8:00 P.M.

62. What is the woman's problem?

(A) She misplaced an item.
(B) She cannot make a payment.
(C) She cannot locate a venue.
(D) She arrived late for an event.

63. Look at the graphic. What time will the movie the woman will watch begin?

(A) At 12:30 P.M.
(B) At 2:30 P.M.
(C) At 4:30 P.M.
(D) At 6:30 P.M.

64. What does the woman ask about?

(A) A theater location
(B) A parking regulation
(C) A ticket cost
(D) A screening time

TEST | 01 | 02 | 03 | 04 | 05 | 06 | 07 | 08 | 09 | 10

해커스 토익 실전 1000제 2 Listening

GO ON TO THE NEXT PAGE

```
Engel's Department Store

Purchase Date: July 17

Item                        Price
Wriggly deluxe sneakers... $24.99
JPX T-shirt (Sale Item)...... $35.32
Kent dress shirt................. $25.14
Teton shorts..................... $22.25

        Sales Tax: 8%
        Total: $116.32

Payment Method: Credit Card
```

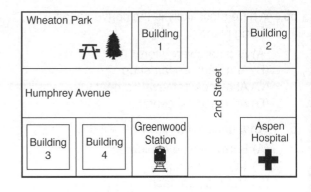

65. What is the conversation mainly about?

(A) An incorrect charge
(B) A return policy
(C) A damaged garment
(D) An employee discount

66. What does the man offer to do?

(A) Exchange some clothing
(B) Provide a voucher
(C) Mark down an item
(D) Print out a new receipt

67. Look at the graphic. What brand does the woman want to return?

(A) Wriggly
(B) JPX
(C) Kent
(D) Teton

68. Look at the graphic. Where will the speakers most likely meet?

(A) Building 1
(B) Building 2
(C) Building 3
(D) Building 4

69. Why is the man unable to go to a lunch appointment?

(A) He has to sign some papers.
(B) He needs more time for a task.
(C) He will assist a client.
(D) He is working from home.

70. What is the man excited about?

(A) He will be promoted.
(B) He will receive a bonus.
(C) He will take a vacation.
(D) He will be transferred.

Directions: In this part, you will listen to several short talks by a single speaker. These talks will not be printed and will only be spoken one time. For each talk, you will be asked to answer three questions. Select the best response and mark the corresponding letter (A), (B), (C), or (D) on your answer sheet.

71. Where is the talk most likely taking place?

(A) In corporate office
(B) In a shopping mall
(C) In a repair shop
(D) In a convention center

72. According to the speaker, what is a feature of the Clear Flow XS?

(A) It has speed settings.
(B) It is self-cleaning.
(C) It has multiple racks.
(D) It is energy efficient.

73. What will the speaker probably do next?

(A) Answer people's questions
(B) Pass out some pamphlets
(C) Show how a dishwasher works
(D) Discuss some payment options

74. What does the speaker say he received?

(A) A copy of a talk
(B) Some photographs
(C) Some charts
(D) An event program

75. What does the speaker recommend?

(A) Discussing an investment strategy
(B) Including some graphics
(C) Checking the accuracy of some data
(D) Increasing the length of a speech

76. What does the speaker mean when he says, "June 15 works best for us"?

(A) A venue space will be available.
(B) A proposed date has been accepted.
(C) A presentation must be rescheduled.
(D) A meeting can continue as planned.

77. What is being advertised?

(A) Landscaping services
(B) Financial products
(C) Luxury homes
(D) Lakefront land

78. What added benefit is available to buyers?

(A) Free property inspections
(B) Ready access to utilities
(C) Special mortgage rates
(D) Professional consultations

79. According to the speaker, why would the listeners contact the office?

(A) To set up a customer account
(B) To gain entry to a building
(C) To arrange a tour of a location
(D) To inquire about some rates

80. Where are the listeners?

(A) At a senior facility
(B) At a public school
(C) At a community center
(D) At a medical clinic

81. What is mentioned about the listeners?

(A) They will work on weekdays only.
(B) They will plan various events.
(C) They have received certification.
(D) They have watched a video.

82. What does the speaker offer to do?

(A) Modify a program
(B) Distribute copies of a handbook
(C) Lead a brainstorming session
(D) Respond to questions

GO ON TO THE NEXT PAGE

83. Who most likely are the listeners?

(A) Audio engineers
(B) Opera singers
(C) Security guards
(D) Instrument players

84. What does the speaker ask the listeners to bring with them?

(A) An instrument case
(B) Some copies of notes
(C) A seating plan
(D) Some invitation cards

85. Why does the speaker say, "This season's gala show will be attended by our main donors"?

(A) To justify the cost of an upcoming performance
(B) To point out some changes to a guest list
(C) To emphasize the importance of an event
(D) To suggest a need for additional funding

86. What did the speaker do this morning?

(A) Posted an advertisement for a job opening
(B) Met with the owner of prominent resort
(C) Read a message from an executive
(D) Assigned staff members to new roles

87. What is mentioned about the mentorship program?

(A) It has been used at a headquarters office.
(B) It will require extensive staff training.
(C) It has been successful at other companies.
(D) It will ensure there are many candidates for promotion.

88. What does the speaker ask the listeners to do?

(A) Conduct performance evaluations
(B) Review a list of candidates for promotion
(C) Develop a manual for management trainees
(D) Recommend participants for a program

89. According to the speaker, what did Marsha Summers do?

(A) Appeared on television programs
(B) Arranged a business trip
(C) Wrote an article for a magazine
(D) Conducted some scientific research

90. What will the speaker ask Ms. Summers about?

(A) A media organization
(B) A fundraising event
(C) An environmental group
(D) A business venture

91. What does the speaker recommend the listeners do?

(A) Make a donation
(B) Purchase a publication
(C) Download a schedule
(D) Post a question

92. What is the talk mainly about?

(A) A historical landmark
(B) A restoration project
(C) A tour itinerary
(D) A fundraising campaign

93. What does the speaker mean when she says, "the building was badly damaged in a recent storm"?

(A) An assessment needs to be made.
(B) A destination will not be visited.
(C) A repair effort has been stopped.
(D) A fundraiser will be launched soon.

94. What will the listeners probably do next?

(A) Participate in an auction
(B) Take out their passes
(C) Learn about a structure
(D) Head to a vehicle

Bus No.	Destination	Departure Time
4491	Antoine Bridge	09:20
4619	Tigerville	10:40
5518	Suzuki Stadium	12:00
6675	Hawthorne Park	14:30

95. Why is Highway 45 closed?

(A) A bridge is being inspected.
(B) An accident has occurred.
(C) A structure is being repaired.
(D) A parade has begun.

96. Look at the graphic. Which bus does the speaker refer to?

(A) Bus 4491
(B) Bus 4619
(C) Bus 5518
(D) Bus 6675

97. What does the speaker remind the listeners about?

(A) An upcoming event
(B) An additional fee
(C) A changed policy
(D) A new facility

 East Street Parking Garage Fees

1 hr. – $3
2 hrs. – $6
3 hrs. – $8
4 hrs. – $10

(4 hrs. max)

98. What task was the listener given?

(A) Looking up an exercise class
(B) Organizing a company event
(C) Coaching a soccer team
(D) Promoting a sports competition

99. According to the speaker, what is located near a workplace?

(A) A park
(B) An arena
(C) A community center
(D) A workout facility

100. Look at the graphic. What amount will the listeners most likely be charged for parking?

(A) $3
(B) $6
(C) $8
(D) $10

정답 p.165 / 점수 환산표 p.167 / 스크립트 p.210 / 무료 해석 바로 보기(정답 및 정답 음성 포함)

▌정답 음성(QR)이나 정답(p.165)을 이용해 채점하시기 바랍니다. 정답 음성에서 Boy는 (B)를, David는 (D)를 나타냅니다.
▌다음 페이지에 있는 Self 체크 리스트를 통해 자신의 문제 풀이 방식과 태도를 점검해 보세요.

Self 체크 리스트

TEST 08은 무사히 잘 마치셨죠?
이제 다음의 Self 체크 리스트를 통해 자신의 테스트 진행 내용을 점검해 볼까요?

1. 나는 테스트가 진행되는 동안 한 번도 중도에 멈추지 않았다.

☐ 예   ☐ 아니오

아니오에 답한 경우, 이유는 무엇인가요?

2. 나는 답안지 표기까지 성실하게 모두 마무리하였다.

☐ 예   ☐ 아니오

아니오에 답한 경우, 이유는 무엇인가요?

3. 나는 Part 2의 25문항을 푸는 동안 완전히 테스트에 집중하였다.

☐ 예   ☐ 아니오

아니오에 답한 경우, 이유는 무엇인가요?

4. 나는 Part 3를 풀 때 음성이 들리기 전에 해당 질문과 보기를 모두 먼저 읽었다.

☐ 예   ☐ 아니오

아니오에 답한 경우, 이유는 무엇인가요?

5. 나는 Part 4를 풀 때 음성이 들리기 전에 해당 질문과 보기를 모두 먼저 읽었다.

☐ 예   ☐ 아니오

아니오에 답한 경우, 이유는 무엇인가요?

6. 개선해야 할 점 또는 나를 위한 충고를 적어보세요.

* 교재의 첫 장으로 돌아가서 자신이 적은 목표 점수를 확인하면서 목표에 대한 의지를 다지기 바랍니다. 개선해야 할 점은 반드시 다음 테스트에
실천해야 합니다. 그것이 가장 중요하며, 그래야만 발전할 수 있습니다.

TEST 09

PART 1
PART 2
PART 3
PART 4
Self 체크 리스트

잠깐! 테스트 전 확인사항

1. 휴대 전화의 전원을 끄셨나요? □ 예
2. Answer Sheet, 연필, 지우개를 준비하셨나요? □ 예
3. MP3를 들을 준비가 되셨나요? □ 예

모든 준비가 완료되었으면 목표 점수를 떠올린 후 테스트를 시작합니다.

🎧 TEST 09.mp3

실전용·복습용 문제풀이 MP3 무료 다운로드 및 스트리밍 바로듣기 (HackersIngang.com)
* 실제 시험장의 소음까지 재현해 낸 고사장 소음/매미 버전 MP3, 영국식·호주식 발음 집중 MP3, 고속 버전 MP3까지
  구매하면 실전에 더욱 완벽히 대비할 수 있습니다.

무료MP3 바로듣기

LISTENING TEST

In this section, you must demonstrate your ability to understand spoken English. This section is divided into four parts and will take approximately 45 minutes to complete. Do not mark the answers in your test book. Use the answer sheet that is provided separately.

PART 1

Directions: For each question, you will listen to four short statements about a picture in your test book. These statements will not be printed and will only be spoken one time. Select the statement that best describes what is happening in the picture and mark the corresponding letter (A), (B), (C), or (D) on the answer sheet.

Sample Answer
Ⓐ ● Ⓒ Ⓓ

The statement that best describes the picture is (B), "The man is sitting at the desk." So, you should mark letter (B) on the answer sheet.

1.

2.

GO ON TO THE NEXT PAGE

3.

4.

5.

6.

GO ON TO THE NEXT PAGE

PART 2

Directions: For each question, you will listen to a statement or question followed by three possible responses spoken in English. They will not be printed and will only be spoken one time. Select the best response and mark the corresponding letter (A), (B), or (C) on your answer sheet.

7. Mark your answer on your answer sheet.

8. Mark your answer on your answer sheet.

9. Mark your answer on your answer sheet.

10. Mark your answer on your answer sheet.

11. Mark your answer on your answer sheet.

12. Mark your answer on your answer sheet.

13. Mark your answer on your answer sheet.

14. Mark your answer on your answer sheet.

15. Mark your answer on your answer sheet.

16. Mark your answer on your answer sheet.

17. Mark your answer on your answer sheet.

18. Mark your answer on your answer sheet.

19. Mark your answer on your answer sheet.

20. Mark your answer on your answer sheet.

21. Mark your answer on your answer sheet.

22. Mark your answer on your answer sheet.

23. Mark your answer on your answer sheet.

24. Mark your answer on your answer sheet.

25. Mark your answer on your answer sheet.

26. Mark your answer on your answer sheet.

27. Mark your answer on your answer sheet.

28. Mark your answer on your answer sheet.

29. Mark your answer on your answer sheet.

30. Mark your answer on your answer sheet.

31. Mark your answer on your answer sheet.

PART 3

Directions: In this part, you will listen to several conversations between two or more speakers. These conversations will not be printed and will only be spoken one time. For each conversation, you will be asked to answer three questions. Select the best response and mark the corresponding letter (A), (B), (C), or (D) on your answer sheet.

32. Why is the man calling?
(A) To discuss carpet samples
(B) To change a schedule
(C) To inquire about a company
(D) To report a shipment delay

33. What request does the woman make?
(A) That a specific product be used
(B) That staff call before arriving
(C) That work be done on a different day
(D) That she be given more color options

34. What does the man offer to do?
(A) Show up early
(B) Expedite a delivery
(C) Refund a payment
(D) Provide a discount

35. What does the man ask the woman to give a talk about?
(A) Returns on recent investments
(B) International manufacturing
(C) A company expansion
(D) A new consumer trend

36. Why is the woman unable to prepare a presentation?
(A) She is going to meet investors.
(B) She is working on an analysis.
(C) She has to go on a business trip.
(D) She has to run errands.

37. What does the man suggest?
(A) Postponing a task
(B) Consulting with a team leader
(C) Requesting a coworker's help
(D) Updating a schedule

38. Why is the man calling?
(A) To order some lunch
(B) To confirm an appointment
(C) To change a booking
(D) To ask for directions

39. What does the man imply when he says, "It's supposed to rain on Thursday"?
(A) He cannot reschedule his lunch.
(B) He needs another option to consider.
(C) He knows other restaurants to visit.
(D) He would like to make a new proposal.

40. What does the woman suggest?
(A) Arriving at a later time
(B) Going to a different branch
(C) Speaking to a manager
(D) Reserving a private room

41. Why does the man need the report by tomorrow?
(A) He has to take it to a workshop.
(B) He has to submit it for publication.
(C) He wants to show it to an executive.
(D) He wants to proofread a section.

42. What information is the woman waiting for?
(A) Survey results
(B) Numerical data
(C) Financial estimates
(D) Product descriptions

43. What does the man want the woman to do?
(A) Deliver an item to an employee
(B) Share some data with a client
(C) Print copies of a contract
(D) Get help from a coworker

GO ON TO THE NEXT PAGE

44. What industry do the speakers most likely work in?

(A) Event planning
(B) Hospitality
(C) Shipping
(D) Publishing

45. What problem does the woman mention?

(A) A venue has not been confirmed.
(B) Some clients did not receive a package.
(C) A pamphlet is missing some information.
(D) Some materials cannot be found.

46. Why does the man say, "We'll attend another expo in Miami next month"?

(A) To explain a decision
(B) To indicate a problem
(C) To get a plan approved
(D) To suggest a location

47. Who most likely are the speakers?

(A) Stage engineers
(B) Performers
(C) Sound directors
(D) Security personnel

48. What problem does Fred mention?

(A) A device has malfunctioned.
(B) An event has been delayed.
(C) A tool has been misplaced.
(D) A room is inaccessible.

49. What does the woman offer to do?

(A) Move some furniture
(B) Check a storage area
(C) Install some equipment
(D) Move an arrival time forward

50. What is the woman's problem?

(A) She ordered the wrong item.
(B) She cannot redeem a voucher.
(C) Her computer stopped working.
(D) Her laptop case is broken.

51. According to the man, what requires an additional charge?

(A) Extending a warranty
(B) Repairing a computer
(C) Upgrading a device
(D) Shipping a product

52. What does the man ask for?

(A) A home address
(B) A product name
(C) A warranty number
(D) A purchase receipt

53. Where most likely are the speakers?

(A) At a clothing retailer
(B) At a tailor shop
(C) At a dry cleaner
(D) At a design studio

54. What information does Hailey provide?

(A) A cost estimate
(B) A delivery date
(C) A business address
(D) An order number

55. What will the man probably do next Tuesday?

(A) Take a measurement
(B) Call an establishment
(C) Meet with a client
(D) Cancel an appointment

56. Why does the man want to hire the woman's company?

(A) He was impressed by an advertisement.
(B) He enjoyed its food in the past.
(C) It offers a diverse menu.
(D) It was highly recommended.

57. What will most likely happen tomorrow?

(A) Some prices will be adjusted.
(B) Some entrées will be sampled.
(C) A business meeting will take place.
(D) A function date will be announced.

58. What does the woman suggest the man do?

(A) Call her company's supervisor
(B) Browse some information online
(C) Make a reservation in advance
(D) Send out invitations to guests

59. What is the business planning to do?

(A) Hire more employees
(B) Open another department
(C) Introduce a new policy
(D) Make arrangements for a conference

60. What is the woman looking forward to?

(A) Receiving another promotion
(B) Sharing duties with colleagues
(C) Spending less on uniforms
(D) Saving time before work

61. What is the woman worried about?

(A) Some complaints from customers
(B) The comfort of the new clothing
(C) A meeting with the restaurant manager
(D) The cost of new materials

62. Who most likely is the man?

(A) A research assistant
(B) A graphic designer
(C) A business partner
(D) A human resources employee

63. Look at the graphic. Where will the company logo be placed?

(A) Spot A
(B) Spot B
(C) Spot C
(D) Spot D

64. What will the woman probably do next?

(A) Revise the company logo
(B) Order some business cards
(C) Send a list of contact information
(D) Share some feedback

GO ON TO THE NEXT PAGE

Box Comes With:

Parts A: 3-foot poles
Parts B: 7-foot poles
Parts C: 2-inch pegs
Parts D: 5-inch pegs

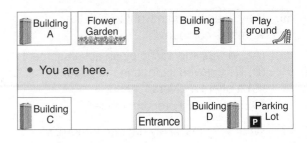

● You are here.

65. Why is the woman calling?

(A) To purchase a product
(B) To confirm a delivery
(C) To make a complaint
(D) To request a refund

66. Look at the graphic. What was not included in the box?

(A) Parts A
(B) Parts B
(C) Parts C
(D) Parts D

67. What will the woman probably do later today?

(A) Visit a retail establishment
(B) Shop for a similar product online
(C) Receive a store gift certificate
(D) Return a recently purchased item

68. Who most likely is the man?

(A) A security guard
(B) A property manager
(C) A construction worker
(D) A delivery person

69. Look at the graphic. Which building is the man going to?

(A) Building A
(B) Building B
(C) Building C
(D) Building D

70. What does the woman say about the complex?

(A) It will be inspected in January.
(B) It has many vacant units.
(C) It has several new tenants.
(D) It will be expanded next year.

PART 4

Directions: In this part, you will listen to several short talks by a single speaker. These talks will not be printed and will only be spoken one time. For each talk, you will be asked to answer three questions. Select the best response and mark the corresponding letter (A), (B), (C), or (D) on your answer sheet.

71. What is available at the information counter?

   (A) Event calendars
   (B) Entrance passes
   (C) Venue maps
   (D) Sign-up sheets

72. What does the speaker recommend the listeners do?

   (A) Become museum members
   (B) Go to a special display
   (C) Take pictures of artifacts
   (D) Meet in the lobby

73. According to the speaker, what do people qualify for?

   (A) A gift bag
   (B) A private tour
   (C) A price reduction
   (D) A parking permit

74. What does the speaker ask the listeners to do?

   (A) Provide feedback on a plan
   (B) Send an e-mail to clients
   (C) Check the deadline for a project
   (D) Prepare items for transport

75. What does the speaker imply when he says, "there are 500 staff members now"?

   (A) A new office is more spacious.
   (B) A workforce will be expanded.
   (C) A policy will be implemented.
   (D) A hiring plan is effective.

76. What is mentioned about the Westport area?

   (A) It attracts visitors from other cities.
   (B) It contains lots of free parking spaces.
   (C) It includes great dining establishments.
   (D) It features public recreation facilities.

77. What field does the speaker work in?

   (A) Interior decoration
   (B) Construction management
   (C) Event planning
   (D) Landscaping design

78. What does the speaker recommend?

   (A) Hiring another specialist
   (B) Touring a park for inspiration
   (C) Redecorating an indoor space
   (D) Installing a fountain

79. What does the speaker ask Mr. Carranza to do?

   (A) Return a phone call
   (B) Decide on a meeting place
   (C) Look over a planned budget
   (D) Start working on a project

80. Why is the speaker surprised?

   (A) The weather did not affect attendance.
   (B) The guest speaker canceled at the last minute.
   (C) The association was recently formed.
   (D) Many new members came to the meeting.

81. What does the speaker mean when he says, "I'm sure most of you already knew that"?

   (A) A study has been published.
   (B) An organization plans to expand.
   (C) A guest is well known.
   (D) A project was previously announced.

82. What is the focus of the initiative?

   (A) Increasing exercise among youth
   (B) Promoting better student diets
   (C) Updating educational standards
   (D) Improving heart attack recovery

GO ON TO THE NEXT PAGE

해커스토익 실전 1000제 2 Listening

83. Why is the announcement being given?

(A) To explain a new system
(B) To introduce an inspector
(C) To provide some reminders
(D) To review safety regulations

84. What items will the listeners most likely pick up?

(A) New tools
(B) Order forms
(C) Shift schedules
(D) Safety goggles

85. What are the listeners asked to do before leaving?

(A) Make some repairs
(B) Clean their workspaces
(C) Get approval from a supervisor
(D) Set up some equipment

86. Which department do the listeners most likely work in?

(A) Sales
(B) Research
(C) Marketing
(D) Finance

87. Why does the speaker say, "this means our company get-together will be canceled"?

(A) To introduce an alternative location
(B) To suggest that workers will be busy
(C) To indicate that a forecast has changed
(D) To emphasize the importance of team-building activity

88. According to the speaker, what will the listeners do?

(A) Visit a retail outlet
(B) Distribute samples
(C) Contact customers
(D) Produce a document

89. What kind of business is being advertised?

(A) A used clothing outlet
(B) A furniture store
(C) A moving company
(D) A computer repair shop

90. According to the advertisement, what is provided to customers?

(A) Brand-new merchandise
(B) Customizable services
(C) Reasonably priced products
(D) Partial rebates

91. According to the speaker, how can customers receive membership?

(A) By completing a purchase
(B) By paying an annual fee
(C) By filling out an application form
(D) By submitting an item for auction

92. What is the topic of the talk?

(A) A new promotional project
(B) International travel destinations
(C) Accommodation options
(D) A corporate retreat

93. What does the speaker say will happen in the spring?

(A) An agency will hire staff.
(B) A company will downsize.
(C) A policy will be enacted.
(D) A campaign will begin.

94. What are the listeners instructed to do?

(A) Finalize some tourism handouts
(B) Draft a preliminary budget
(C) Create a list of potential partners
(D) Contact prospective customers

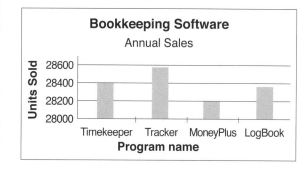

Bookkeeping Software
Annual Sales

Item	Quantity
Office Mark	Order #18240
Item	**Quantity**
Edge Cubical Partition	30
Coleman Desk	10
Brentwood File Cabinet	5
Aero Chair	15

95. Who most likely are the listeners?

(A) Computer programmers
(B) Accountants
(C) Small business owners
(D) Board members

96. Look at the graphic. Which program will be replaced in February?

(A) Timekeeper
(B) Tracker
(C) MoneyPlus
(D) LogBook

97. According to the speaker, what should the listeners do?

(A) Suggest new features
(B) Install an application
(C) Break up into groups
(D) Speak with a representative

98. What did the speaker recently learn about?

(A) The condition of some furniture
(B) An opening of an office
(C) The costs of some upgrades
(D) An increase in staff size

99. Look at the graphic. Which quantity is no longer accurate?

(A) 5
(B) 10
(C) 15
(D) 30

100. What information will the speaker provide?

(A) Payment details
(B) A discount code
(C) A delivery address
(D) Contact number

정답 p.166 / 점수 환산표 p.167 / 스크립트 p.216 / 무료 해석 바로 보기(정답 및 정답 음성 포함)

▮ 정답 음성(QR)이나 정답(p.166)을 이용해 채점하시기 바랍니다. 정답 음성에서 Boy는 (B)를, David는 (D)를 나타냅니다.
▮ 다음 페이지에 있는 Self 체크 리스트를 통해 자신의 문제 풀이 방식과 태도를 점검해 보세요.

Self 체크 리스트

TEST 09는 무사히 잘 마치셨죠?
이제 다음의 Self 체크 리스트를 통해 자신의 테스트 진행 내용을 점검해 볼까요?

1. 나는 테스트가 진행되는 동안 한 번도 중도에 멈추지 않았다.

   ☐ 예   ☐ 아니오

   아니오에 답한 경우, 이유는 무엇인가요?

2. 나는 답안지 표기까지 성실하게 모두 마무리하였다.

   ☐ 예   ☐ 아니오

   아니오에 답한 경우, 이유는 무엇인가요?

3. 나는 Part 2의 25문항을 푸는 동안 완전히 테스트에 집중하였다.

   ☐ 예   ☐ 아니오

   아니오에 답한 경우, 이유는 무엇인가요?

4. 나는 Part 3를 풀 때 음성이 들리기 전에 해당 질문과 보기를 모두 먼저 읽었다.

   ☐ 예   ☐ 아니오

   아니오에 답한 경우, 이유는 무엇인가요?

5. 나는 Part 4를 풀 때 음성이 들리기 전에 해당 질문과 보기를 모두 먼저 읽었다.

   ☐ 예   ☐ 아니오

   아니오에 답한 경우, 이유는 무엇인가요?

6. 개선해야 할 점 또는 나를 위한 충고를 적어보세요.

* 교재의 첫 장으로 돌아가서 자신이 적은 목표 점수를 확인하면서 목표에 대한 의지를 다지기 바랍니다. 개선해야 할 점은 반드시 다음 테스트에 실천해야 합니다. 그것이 가장 중요하며, 그래야만 발전할 수 있습니다.

▍TEST 10

PART **1**
PART **2**
PART **3**
PART **4**
Self 체크 리스트

잠깐! 테스트 전 확인사항
1. 휴대 전화의 전원을 끄셨나요? □ 예
2. Answer Sheet, 연필, 지우개를 준비하셨나요? □ 예
3. MP3를 들을 준비가 되셨나요? □ 예

모든 준비가 완료되었으면 목표 점수를 떠올린 후 테스트를 시작합니다.

무료MP3 바로듣기

TEST 10.mp3
실전용·복습용 문제풀이 MP3 무료 다운로드 및 스트리밍 바로듣기 (HackersIngang.com)
* 실제 시험장의 소음까지 재현해 낸 고사장 소음/매미 버전 MP3, 영국식·호주식 발음 집중 MP3, 고속 버전 MP3까지
구매하면 실전에 더욱 완벽히 대비할 수 있습니다.

LISTENING TEST

In this section, you must demonstrate your ability to understand spoken English. This section is divided into four parts and will take approximately 45 minutes to complete. Do not mark the answers in your test book. Use the answer sheet that is provided separately.

PART 1

Directions: For each question, you will listen to four short statements about a picture in your test book. These statements will not be printed and will only be spoken one time. Select the statement that best describes what is happening in the picture and mark the corresponding letter (A), (B), (C), or (D) on the answer sheet.

Sample Answer

The statement that best describes the picture is (B), "The man is sitting at the desk." So, you should mark letter (B) on the answer sheet.

1.

2.

GO ON TO THE NEXT PAGE →

3.

4.

5.

6.

GO ON TO THE NEXT PAGE

PART 2

Directions: For each question, you will listen to a statement or question followed by three possible responses spoken in English. They will not be printed and will only be spoken one time. Select the best response and mark the corresponding letter (A), (B), or (C) on your answer sheet.

7. Mark your answer on your answer sheet.

8. Mark your answer on your answer sheet.

9. Mark your answer on your answer sheet.

10. Mark your answer on your answer sheet.

11. Mark your answer on your answer sheet.

12. Mark your answer on your answer sheet.

13. Mark your answer on your answer sheet.

14. Mark your answer on your answer sheet.

15. Mark your answer on your answer sheet.

16. Mark your answer on your answer sheet.

17. Mark your answer on your answer sheet.

18. Mark your answer on your answer sheet.

19. Mark your answer on your answer sheet.

20. Mark your answer on your answer sheet.

21. Mark your answer on your answer sheet.

22. Mark your answer on your answer sheet.

23. Mark your answer on your answer sheet.

24. Mark your answer on your answer sheet.

25. Mark your answer on your answer sheet.

26. Mark your answer on your answer sheet.

27. Mark your answer on your answer sheet.

28. Mark your answer on your answer sheet.

29. Mark your answer on your answer sheet.

30. Mark your answer on your answer sheet.

31. Mark your answer on your answer sheet.

PART 3

Directions: In this part, you will listen to several conversations between two or more speakers. These conversations will not be printed and will only be spoken one time. For each conversation, you will be asked to answer three questions. Select the best response and mark the corresponding letter (A), (B), (C), or (D) on your answer sheet.

32. Why was the man's trip disappointing?

(A) He could not attend a business seminar.
(B) He was unable to explore a city.
(C) He had to return home early.
(D) He was not able to secure a deal.

33. What is mentioned about Cape Town?

(A) It features a new public monument.
(B) It charges an admission fee for parks.
(C) It has several outdoor recreational spaces.
(D) It offers tourists free walking tours.

34. What did the man do in Cape Town?

(A) Attended a lecture
(B) Photographed a monument
(C) Visited a park
(D) Watched a performance

35. What is being launched?

(A) A trade magazine
(B) A company Web site
(C) A clothing collection
(D) An electronic device

36. What is mentioned about the event?

(A) It has attracted many online writers.
(B) It was organized by several teams.
(C) It has impressed the company president.
(D) It was promoted in a local newspaper.

37. According to the man, what does Emily Scott plan to do?

(A) Publish an article
(B) Try out a product
(C) Attend a future launch
(D) Review a Web site

38. What is the conversation mainly about?

(A) Conducting a survey
(B) Addressing a complaint
(C) Analyzing a trend
(D) Developing a product

39. What problem does the woman mention?

(A) Employees lack expertise.
(B) Demand has declined.
(C) Workers are expressing frustration.
(D) Information seems inaccurate.

40. What will Sam most likely do next?

(A) Meet with a designer
(B) Train a recent hire
(C) Write a job advertisement
(D) Review an application

41. Why does the woman visit the shop?

(A) To upgrade her insurance
(B) To have a tool repaired
(C) To rent some equipment
(D) To enroll in some classes

42. What does the woman mean when she says, "I can practice with them after I complete the lessons"?

(A) She accepts a requirement.
(B) She will extend a contract.
(C) She is willing to pay extra.
(D) She wants a rule to be changed.

43. What will the man probably do next?

(A) Explain a lesson schedule
(B) Process a fee payment
(C) Provide some insurance forms
(D) Examine an identification card

GO ON TO THE NEXT PAGE

44. What caused the woman to be late?

(A) An extended meeting
(B) Road congestion
(C) Inclement weather
(D) An automobile accident

45. Why does the woman drive to work?

(A) She carpools with other coworkers.
(B) She commutes from a different town.
(C) She does not like walking in cold weather.
(D) She does not like riding public transportation.

46. What does the man say he will do for the woman?

(A) Give her a map
(B) Drive her to the office
(C) Send her a link
(D) Meet her at a station

---

47. Why is the woman calling?

(A) To check an event date
(B) To cancel a reservation
(C) To request a ticket refund
(D) To inquire about a discount

48. What does the man suggest the woman do?

(A) Attend an exhibit
(B) Download a coupon
(C) Contact another employee
(D) Submit some online forms

49. Why does the woman say, "I picked up a brochure yesterday"?

(A) To explain a decision
(B) To reject a suggestion
(C) To confirm a plan
(D) To point out an error

---

50. What problem does the woman mention?

(A) Some goods are placed in the wrong aisle.
(B) A customer created a mess in the store.
(C) A client is complaining about a charge.
(D) A warehouse is missing some supplies.

51. What does Gustavo offer to do?

(A) Provide a colleague with training materials
(B) Check on a delivery's arrival time
(C) Clean out a storage area
(D) Show a coworker an item's location

52. What will the men most likely do after lunch?

(A) Speak to an executive
(B) Repair a broken mop
(C) Place some products on shelves
(D) Order some new cereals

---

53. What type of event is taking place?

(A) A convention
(B) An investors meeting
(C) A corporate outing
(D) A marketing class

54. According to the woman, what were attendees impressed with?

(A) A foreign product
(B) An online service
(C) A finance talk
(D) An investment opportunity

55. According to the man, what will be uploaded to a Web site?

(A) Video recordings
(B) Event photos
(C) Lecture transcripts
(D) Attendee feedback

---

56. Who is Felicity Gifford?

(A) A workshop teacher
(B) A class participant
(C) A university professor
(D) A library employee

57. Why will the woman rearrange some furniture?

(A) An event will have many attendees.
(B) A venue has been changed.
(C) An activity has been planned by the instructor.
(D) A classroom will be cleaned.

58. What does the man recommend?

(A) Removing unnecessary seating
(B) Keeping a door open
(C) Handing out library brochures
(D) Having an employee at the door

---

59. What are the speakers mainly discussing?

(A) Membership levels
(B) Contract negotiations
(C) A poster for an association
(D) A brochure for a festival

60. Where does the man most likely work?

(A) At a graphic design firm
(B) At a community center
(C) At a law office
(D) At a print shop

61. What does the man agree to do?

(A) Volunteer his services
(B) Join an association
(C) Coordinate with a business
(D) Read over a document

EZ Home Cleaning Packages			
Basic	Standard	Superior	Ultimate
$50	$60	$70	$80

62. How did the woman learn about a cleaning service?

(A) By using a search engine
(B) By checking social media
(C) By reading a flyer
(D) By talking to a relative

63. Look at the graphic. Which package will the woman probably choose?

(A) Basic
(B) Standard
(C) Superior
(D) Ultimate

64. When will workers most likely visit the woman's home?

(A) On Saturday
(B) On Sunday
(C) On Monday
(D) On Tuesday

GO ON TO THE NEXT PAGE

65. Look at the graphic. Which film did the speakers' company make?

(A) *South of London*
(B) *The Escapee*
(C) *Wanderers*
(D) *Running Out of Time*

66. What did the speakers' company do this year?

(A) Raised its advertising budget
(B) Produced numerous commercials
(C) Screened films before a test audience
(D) Delayed the release of a movie

67. According to the woman, what will happen later today?

(A) A new film will be announced.
(B) A meeting will be convened.
(C) A survey will be publicized online.
(D) A celebration will take place.

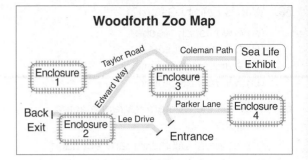

Woodforth Zoo Map

68. What does the woman inquire about?

(A) The reason for a transfer
(B) The time of an arrival
(C) The origin of some animals
(D) The location of a zoo

69. What does the man request the woman do?

(A) Check a facility's condition
(B) Transport a food container
(C) Clean a building exterior
(D) Train an animal for a show

70. Look at the graphic. Where will the new animals live?

(A) In Enclosure 1
(B) In Enclosure 2
(C) In Enclosure 3
(D) In Enclosure 4

PART 4

Directions: In this part, you will listen to several short talks by a single speaker. These talks will not be printed and will only be spoken one time. For each talk, you will be asked to answer three questions. Select the best response and mark the corresponding letter (A), (B), (C), or (D) on your answer sheet.

71. Where most likely are the listeners?

(A) At a bookstore
(B) At a university
(C) At a museum
(D) At a library

72. What does the speaker say will take place?

(A) Library cards will be distributed.
(B) Books will be sold to visitors.
(C) Attendees will compete in a contest.
(D) Prices will be reduced.

73. Why does the speaker thank Camdale Enterprises?

(A) For funding an event
(B) For creating a scholarship
(C) For promoting a fair
(D) For sending novels

74. What does the speaker say about the municipal government?

(A) It provided funds for an event.
(B) It launched a promotional campaign.
(C) It regulated the use of fireworks.
(D) It invited industry leaders to a gathering.

75. What does the speaker imply when he says, "thousands of people are expected to travel to Harrisburg over the weekend"?

(A) A show has grown in size.
(B) A festival has economic benefits.
(C) Tourists will have limited hotel options.
(D) Organizers need to change arrangements.

76. What will the listeners probably hear next?

(A) An interview
(B) A commercial
(C) A talk show
(D) A traffic report

77. Why are camera flashes prohibited?

(A) They upset the performers.
(B) They distract the guide.
(C) They frighten the wildlife.
(D) They bother other guests.

78. What does the speaker tell the listeners to do?

(A) Leave their bags at the entrance
(B) Meet at the snack bar
(C) Take some beverages along
(D) Remain on the shuttle

79. According to the speaker, what can the listeners do after seeing the African wildlife compound?

(A) Get something to eat
(B) Browse through some souvenirs
(C) Look at some displays
(D) Watch a demonstration

80. What will open on April 14?

(A) A department store
(B) A performance arts theater
(C) A dining facility
(D) A child care center

81. According to the speaker, what is located on the fifth floor?

(A) An exhibit space
(B) An information booth
(C) A clothing boutique
(D) A play area

82. Why does the speaker say, "Singer Jacob Keeve will be on site this Saturday"?

(A) To announce a concert
(B) To attract some shoppers
(C) To confirm some rumors
(D) To correct a mistake

GO ON TO THE NEXT PAGE

83. According to the speaker, what did the listener do?

(A) Published a story
(B) Asked for time off
(C) Returned from a trip
(D) Met with a supervisor

84. What must be completed by the end of the week?

(A) A business report
(B) A project proposal
(C) A movie review
(D) A magazine article

85. What is the listener told to give a colleague?

(A) Uncompleted drafts
(B) Contact details
(C) Office keys
(D) Itinerary information

---

86. What is taking place?

(A) A corporate gathering
(B) A teaching workshop
(C) A lecture series
(D) A college orientation

87. What is mentioned about the event?

(A) It was organized by students.
(B) It will be streamed online.
(C) It has been extended considerably.
(D) It will feature several presenters.

88. What does the speaker recommend the listeners do?

(A) Get a handout from a booth
(B) Select their own seats
(C) Register for a special event
(D) Ask questions during a talk

---

89. Who most likely is the speaker?

(A) A driving instructor
(B) A vehicle rental agent
(C) A car dealer
(D) An automobile mechanic

90. What does the speaker offer to do?

(A) Contact another auto repair shop
(B) Check a vehicle's oil quality
(C) Provide a service at a discounted price
(D) Order a part from a manufacturer

91. Why does the speaker say, "The whole operation should take around 30 minutes"?

(A) To point out that an engine is not operable
(B) To encourage the listener to approve a procedure
(C) To warn the listener against driving the car
(D) To suggest buying a replacement part

---

92. What has been planned for August 3?

(A) A gardening convention
(B) An annual banquet
(C) A grand opening
(D) A charity run

93. What can the listeners do online?

(A) Look up some directions
(B) Learn about a community project
(C) Complete a registration process
(D) Join an organization

94. According to the speaker, what are people able to do?

(A) Share ideas with city officials
(B) Support a cause financially
(C) Design some event flyers
(D) Encourage others to participate

Fanli Technologies
Staff directory

Extension	Name
1099	Peter Gold
1220	Laura Hargroder
1320	Sven Harma
1330	Margaret Carruth

95. According to the speaker, what is available online?

(A) Product information
(B) Billing support
(C) Purchasing assistance
(D) Telephone numbers

96. Look at the graphic. Who is on the corporate sales team?

(A) Peter Gold
(B) Laura Hargroder
(C) Sven Harma
(D) Margaret Carruth

97. According to the speaker, why should the listeners stay on the line?

(A) To check an order
(B) To submit a payment
(C) To reach an employee
(D) To leave a message

Aster Hatchback Lineup
Consumer Ratings

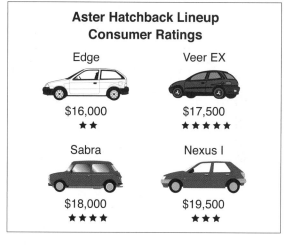

Edge
$16,000
★★

Veer EX
$17,500
★★★★★

Sabra
$18,000
★★★★

Nexus I
$19,500
★★★

98. According to the speaker, what was discussed in a letter?

(A) A newly launched lineup
(B) A firm's financial difficulties
(C) A company's expansion plans
(D) A quarterly profit goal

99. What is mentioned about Giselle Bram?

(A) She arranged a press conference.
(B) She was hired earlier this month.
(C) She hopes to hear from stakeholders.
(D) She is a business leader.

100. Look at the graphic. Which model is going to be eliminated?

(A) Edge
(B) Veer EX
(C) Sabra
(D) Nexus I

정답 p.166 / 점수 환산표 p.167 / 스크립트 p.222 / 무료 해석 바로 보기(정답 및 정답 음성 포함)

▮정답 음성(QR)이나 정답(p.166)을 이용해 채점하시기 바랍니다. 정답 음성에서 Boy는 (B)를, David는 (D)를 나타냅니다.
▮다음 페이지에 있는 Self 체크 리스트를 통해 자신의 문제 풀이 방식과 태도를 점검해 보세요.

Self 체크 리스트

TEST 10은 무사히 잘 마치셨죠?
이제 다음의 Self 체크 리스트를 통해 자신의 테스트 진행 내용을 점검해 볼까요?

1. 나는 테스트가 진행되는 동안 한 번도 중도에 멈추지 않았다.

   ☐ 예   ☐ 아니오

   아니오에 답한 경우, 이유는 무엇인가요?

2. 나는 답안지 표기까지 성실하게 모두 마무리하였다.

   ☐ 예   ☐ 아니오

   아니오에 답한 경우, 이유는 무엇인가요?

3. 나는 Part 2의 25문항을 푸는 동안 완전히 테스트에 집중하였다.

   ☐ 예   ☐ 아니오

   아니오에 답한 경우, 이유는 무엇인가요?

4. 나는 Part 3를 풀 때 음성이 들리기 전에 해당 질문과 보기를 모두 먼저 읽었다.

   ☐ 예   ☐ 아니오

   아니오에 답한 경우, 이유는 무엇인가요?

5. 나는 Part 4를 풀 때 음성이 들리기 전에 해당 질문과 보기를 모두 먼저 읽었다.

   ☐ 예   ☐ 아니오

   아니오에 답한 경우, 이유는 무엇인가요?

6. 개선해야 할 점 또는 나를 위한 충고를 적어보세요.

* 교재의 첫 장으로 돌아가서 자신이 적은 목표 점수를 확인하면서 목표에 대한 의지를 다지기 바랍니다. 개선해야 할 점은 반드시 다음 테스트에
  실천해야 합니다. 그것이 가장 중요하며, 그래야만 발전할 수 있습니다.

정답

점수 환산표

스크립트

Answer Sheet

《해커스 토익 실전 1000제 2 Listening》
무료 해석은 해커스토익(Hackers.co.kr)
에서 다운로드 받거나 QR 코드를 스캔하여
모바일로도 확인할 수 있습니다.

▋TEST 01

1 (C)	2 (A)	3 (D)	4 (D)	5 (C)
6 (C)	7 (C)	8 (B)	9 (A)	10 (C)
11 (A)	12 (C)	13 (A)	14 (B)	15 (C)
16 (A)	17 (B)	18 (A)	19 (C)	20 (B)
21 (C)	22 (C)	23 (A)	24 (C)	25 (B)
26 (C)	27 (B)	28 (B)	29 (B)	30 (A)
31 (C)	32 (B)	33 (D)	34 (B)	35 (D)
36 (C)	37 (A)	38 (D)	39 (B)	40 (D)
41 (D)	42 (D)	43 (C)	44 (C)	45 (A)
46 (A)	47 (C)	48 (C)	49 (D)	50 (A)
51 (D)	52 (B)	53 (D)	54 (A)	55 (B)
56 (D)	57 (C)	58 (A)	59 (B)	60 (A)
61 (D)	62 (D)	63 (D)	64 (A)	65 (D)
66 (A)	67 (D)	68 (C)	69 (A)	70 (A)
71 (B)	72 (D)	73 (C)	74 (B)	75 (A)
76 (D)	77 (C)	78 (A)	79 (D)	80 (D)
81 (B)	82 (A)	83 (D)	84 (A)	85 (B)
86 (B)	87 (B)	88 (C)	89 (C)	90 (D)
91 (A)	92 (C)	93 (D)	94 (A)	95 (B)
96 (C)	97 (A)	98 (D)	99 (A)	100 (A)

▋TEST 02

1 (D)	2 (C)	3 (B)	4 (C)	5 (B)
6 (A)	7 (A)	8 (B)	9 (C)	10 (B)
11 (C)	12 (B)	13 (A)	14 (B)	15 (C)
16 (A)	17 (C)	18 (B)	19 (B)	20 (B)
21 (C)	22 (A)	23 (A)	24 (B)	25 (C)
26 (B)	27 (A)	28 (C)	29 (B)	30 (B)
31 (C)	32 (D)	33 (B)	34 (C)	35 (C)
36 (D)	37 (C)	38 (D)	39 (A)	40 (B)
41 (D)	42 (C)	43 (C)	44 (B)	45 (B)
46 (C)	47 (B)	48 (C)	49 (B)	50 (B)
51 (C)	52 (D)	53 (B)	54 (C)	55 (B)
56 (D)	57 (D)	58 (C)	59 (D)	60 (B)
61 (C)	62 (D)	63 (B)	64 (A)	65 (D)
66 (B)	67 (B)	68 (C)	69 (D)	70 (A)
71 (B)	72 (D)	73 (C)	74 (B)	75 (B)
76 (D)	77 (A)	78 (C)	79 (B)	80 (B)
81 (D)	82 (A)	83 (B)	84 (A)	85 (B)
86 (C)	87 (B)	88 (D)	89 (C)	90 (D)
91 (B)	92 (D)	93 (C)	94 (B)	95 (D)
96 (C)	97 (A)	98 (B)	99 (B)	100 (C)

▋TEST 03

1 (B)	2 (A)	3 (C)	4 (B)	5 (D)
6 (C)	7 (B)	8 (C)	9 (C)	10 (B)
11 (A)	12 (A)	13 (B)	14 (A)	15 (B)
16 (B)	17 (A)	18 (C)	19 (B)	20 (C)
21 (B)	22 (A)	23 (A)	24 (B)	25 (C)
26 (C)	27 (B)	28 (B)	29 (C)	30 (A)
31 (C)	32 (A)	33 (C)	34 (B)	35 (D)
36 (B)	37 (C)	38 (A)	39 (A)	40 (B)
41 (A)	42 (B)	43 (C)	44 (D)	45 (C)
46 (D)	47 (B)	48 (C)	49 (B)	50 (C)
51 (C)	52 (A)	53 (A)	54 (B)	55 (B)
56 (D)	57 (A)	58 (B)	59 (A)	60 (B)
61 (C)	62 (B)	63 (A)	64 (C)	65 (B)
66 (D)	67 (D)	68 (C)	69 (C)	70 (B)
71 (A)	72 (C)	73 (D)	74 (C)	75 (B)
76 (B)	77 (A)	78 (D)	79 (B)	80 (C)
81 (C)	82 (A)	83 (C)	84 (B)	85 (B)
86 (C)	87 (B)	88 (C)	89 (A)	90 (B)
91 (B)	92 (D)	93 (B)	94 (D)	95 (D)
96 (C)	97 (C)	98 (D)	99 (B)	100 (C)

▋TEST 04

1 (C)	2 (B)	3 (A)	4 (C)	5 (D)
6 (D)	7 (A)	8 (A)	9 (C)	10 (A)
11 (A)	12 (B)	13 (B)	14 (C)	15 (C)
16 (B)	17 (A)	18 (C)	19 (B)	20 (A)
21 (A)	22 (A)	23 (B)	24 (A)	25 (B)
26 (C)	27 (A)	28 (B)	29 (A)	30 (C)
31 (B)	32 (A)	33 (C)	34 (A)	35 (D)
36 (C)	37 (B)	38 (D)	39 (B)	40 (B)
41 (A)	42 (B)	43 (C)	44 (B)	45 (D)
46 (B)	47 (C)	48 (B)	49 (D)	50 (D)
51 (C)	52 (B)	53 (D)	54 (A)	55 (D)
56 (D)	57 (C)	58 (D)	59 (D)	60 (B)
61 (B)	62 (D)	63 (A)	64 (A)	65 (C)
66 (D)	67 (C)	68 (B)	69 (C)	70 (D)
71 (B)	72 (C)	73 (A)	74 (D)	75 (B)
76 (B)	77 (B)	78 (A)	79 (C)	80 (D)
81 (C)	82 (A)	83 (A)	84 (A)	85 (D)
86 (D)	87 (C)	88 (D)	89 (D)	90 (D)
91 (B)	92 (C)	93 (B)	94 (B)	95 (B)
96 (B)	97 (C)	98 (B)	99 (C)	100 (A)

TEST 05

1 (C)	2 (B)	3 (D)	4 (B)	5 (B)
6 (A)	7 (C)	8 (B)	9 (B)	10 (B)
11 (C)	12 (B)	13 (A)	14 (B)	15 (A)
16 (C)	17 (B)	18 (A)	19 (B)	20 (A)
21 (B)	22 (A)	23 (C)	24 (C)	25 (B)
26 (B)	27 (A)	28 (B)	29 (A)	30 (C)
31 (B)	32 (C)	33 (C)	34 (A)	35 (C)
36 (B)	37 (D)	38 (B)	39 (C)	40 (A)
41 (D)	42 (B)	43 (A)	44 (C)	45 (B)
46 (B)	47 (A)	48 (B)	49 (D)	50 (C)
51 (D)	52 (C)	53 (D)	54 (B)	55 (A)
56 (B)	57 (C)	58 (D)	59 (D)	60 (A)
61 (B)	62 (A)	63 (C)	64 (D)	65 (B)
66 (D)	67 (B)	68 (D)	69 (C)	70 (A)
71 (A)	72 (C)	73 (B)	74 (C)	75 (B)
76 (C)	77 (D)	78 (A)	79 (B)	80 (B)
81 (C)	82 (D)	83 (D)	84 (C)	85 (B)
86 (D)	87 (C)	88 (D)	89 (B)	90 (D)
91 (C)	92 (C)	93 (C)	94 (B)	95 (D)
96 (B)	97 (C)	98 (B)	99 (B)	100 (A)

TEST 06

1 (B)	2 (A)	3 (C)	4 (B)	5 (B)
6 (D)	7 (B)	8 (C)	9 (B)	10 (A)
11 (C)	12 (A)	13 (C)	14 (A)	15 (C)
16 (A)	17 (B)	18 (B)	19 (A)	20 (B)
21 (B)	22 (A)	23 (B)	24 (B)	25 (B)
26 (A)	27 (C)	28 (B)	29 (C)	30 (C)
31 (B)	32 (A)	33 (C)	34 (A)	35 (A)
36 (C)	37 (D)	38 (A)	39 (D)	40 (D)
41 (D)	42 (C)	43 (D)	44 (D)	45 (D)
46 (B)	47 (C)	48 (D)	49 (A)	50 (B)
51 (C)	52 (B)	53 (D)	54 (D)	55 (C)
56 (D)	57 (A)	58 (B)	59 (A)	60 (B)
61 (C)	62 (D)	63 (C)	64 (D)	65 (C)
66 (D)	67 (D)	68 (B)	69 (C)	70 (A)
71 (D)	72 (C)	73 (D)	74 (C)	75 (A)
76 (D)	77 (B)	78 (C)	79 (B)	80 (D)
81 (C)	82 (A)	83 (B)	84 (C)	85 (D)
86 (C)	87 (A)	88 (D)	89 (D)	90 (C)
91 (A)	92 (A)	93 (D)	94 (B)	95 (A)
96 (B)	97 (B)	98 (A)	99 (D)	100 (B)

TEST 07

1 (B)	2 (D)	3 (A)	4 (C)	5 (C)
6 (D)	7 (A)	8 (A)	9 (B)	10 (C)
11 (A)	12 (B)	13 (B)	14 (C)	15 (A)
16 (C)	17 (B)	18 (C)	19 (B)	20 (C)
21 (C)	22 (B)	23 (A)	24 (C)	25 (A)
26 (B)	27 (A)	28 (C)	29 (B)	30 (A)
31 (C)	32 (B)	33 (C)	34 (D)	35 (A)
36 (C)	37 (A)	38 (A)	39 (B)	40 (A)
41 (B)	42 (D)	43 (A)	44 (D)	45 (C)
46 (B)	47 (A)	48 (B)	49 (C)	50 (A)
51 (D)	52 (C)	53 (C)	54 (D)	55 (B)
56 (B)	57 (D)	58 (B)	59 (C)	60 (B)
61 (A)	62 (A)	63 (C)	64 (A)	65 (C)
66 (D)	67 (C)	68 (A)	69 (D)	70 (C)
71 (D)	72 (B)	73 (B)	74 (B)	75 (A)
76 (C)	77 (B)	78 (D)	79 (B)	80 (C)
81 (A)	82 (B)	83 (A)	84 (C)	85 (D)
86 (B)	87 (C)	88 (C)	89 (B)	90 (D)
91 (C)	92 (A)	93 (D)	94 (B)	95 (D)
96 (D)	97 (A)	98 (B)	99 (C)	100 (A)

TEST 08

1 (A)	2 (B)	3 (B)	4 (C)	5 (B)
6 (D)	7 (A)	8 (A)	9 (C)	10 (A)
11 (B)	12 (A)	13 (C)	14 (A)	15 (C)
16 (B)	17 (C)	18 (B)	19 (A)	20 (C)
21 (C)	22 (A)	23 (B)	24 (B)	25 (C)
26 (B)	27 (B)	28 (A)	29 (B)	30 (C)
31 (B)	32 (D)	33 (A)	34 (C)	35 (D)
36 (B)	37 (A)	38 (A)	39 (B)	40 (C)
41 (D)	42 (B)	43 (C)	44 (D)	45 (B)
46 (C)	47 (B)	48 (B)	49 (A)	50 (D)
51 (B)	52 (C)	53 (C)	54 (A)	55 (D)
56 (D)	57 (C)	58 (B)	59 (B)	60 (C)
61 (C)	62 (A)	63 (B)	64 (B)	65 (A)
66 (B)	67 (C)	68 (B)	69 (A)	70 (A)
71 (D)	72 (D)	73 (C)	74 (A)	75 (B)
76 (C)	77 (D)	78 (B)	79 (C)	80 (A)
81 (B)	82 (D)	83 (D)	84 (B)	85 (C)
86 (C)	87 (D)	88 (D)	89 (A)	90 (C)
91 (A)	92 (C)	93 (B)	94 (D)	95 (B)
96 (B)	97 (D)	98 (B)	99 (A)	100 (B)

▌TEST 09

1 (B)	2 (B)	3 (A)	4 (C)	5 (A)
6 (B)	7 (C)	8 (A)	9 (A)	10 (C)
11 (A)	12 (B)	13 (A)	14 (B)	15 (C)
16 (A)	17 (A)	18 (C)	19 (C)	20 (B)
21 (A)	22 (A)	23 (B)	24 (B)	25 (C)
26 (C)	27 (B)	28 (C)	29 (C)	30 (A)
31 (A)	32 (B)	33 (C)	34 (D)	35 (C)
36 (B)	37 (A)	38 (C)	39 (B)	40 (A)
41 (C)	42 (B)	43 (A)	44 (B)	45 (D)
46 (A)	47 (A)	48 (A)	49 (B)	50 (A)
51 (D)	52 (B)	53 (B)	54 (A)	55 (C)
56 (D)	57 (C)	58 (B)	59 (C)	60 (D)
61 (B)	62 (B)	63 (C)	64 (C)	65 (C)
66 (B)	67 (A)	68 (D)	69 (B)	70 (D)
71 (C)	72 (B)	73 (C)	74 (D)	75 (A)
76 (C)	77 (D)	78 (D)	79 (A)	80 (A)
81 (C)	82 (B)	83 (C)	84 (D)	85 (B)
86 (C)	87 (B)	88 (D)	89 (B)	90 (C)
91 (A)	92 (A)	93 (D)	94 (C)	95 (C)
96 (B)	97 (D)	98 (D)	99 (C)	100 (A)

▌TEST 10

1 (D)	2 (A)	3 (B)	4 (B)	5 (A)
6 (D)	7 (C)	8 (A)	9 (C)	10 (B)
11 (C)	12 (A)	13 (A)	14 (C)	15 (B)
16 (B)	17 (C)	18 (B)	19 (A)	20 (A)
21 (C)	22 (A)	23 (B)	24 (B)	25 (C)
26 (C)	27 (A)	28 (C)	29 (A)	30 (B)
31 (B)	32 (B)	33 (C)	34 (D)	35 (D)
36 (A)	37 (A)	38 (D)	39 (A)	40 (C)
41 (C)	42 (A)	43 (D)	44 (B)	45 (C)
46 (C)	47 (D)	48 (C)	49 (B)	50 (B)
51 (D)	52 (C)	53 (A)	54 (C)	55 (A)
56 (B)	57 (A)	58 (D)	59 (C)	60 (C)
61 (A)	62 (D)	63 (C)	64 (C)	65 (B)
66 (A)	67 (C)	68 (B)	69 (A)	70 (D)
71 (D)	72 (B)	73 (A)	74 (A)	75 (B)
76 (D)	77 (C)	78 (D)	79 (A)	80 (C)
81 (D)	82 (B)	83 (B)	84 (D)	85 (A)
86 (C)	87 (D)	88 (A)	89 (D)	90 (C)
91 (B)	92 (D)	93 (C)	94 (B)	95 (A)
96 (B)	97 (D)	98 (B)	99 (D)	100 (A)

* 아래 점수 환산표로 자신의 토익 리스닝 점수를 예상해봅니다.

정답수	리스닝 점수	정답수	리스닝 점수	정답수	리스닝 점수
100	495	66	305	32	135
99	495	65	300	31	130
98	495	64	295	30	125
97	495	63	290	29	120
96	490	62	285	28	115
95	485	61	280	27	110
94	480	60	275	26	105
93	475	59	270	25	100
92	470	58	265	24	95
91	465	57	260	23	90
90	460	56	255	22	85
89	455	55	250	21	80
88	450	54	245	20	75
87	445	53	240	19	70
86	435	52	235	18	65
85	430	51	230	17	60
84	425	50	225	16	55
83	415	49	220	15	50
82	410	48	215	14	45
81	400	47	210	13	40
80	395	46	205	12	35
79	390	45	200	11	30
78	385	44	195	10	25
77	375	43	190	9	20
76	370	42	185	8	15
75	365	41	180	7	10
74	355	40	175	6	5
73	350	39	170	5	5
72	340	38	165	4	5
71	335	37	160	3	5
70	330	36	155	2	5
69	325	35	150	1	5
68	315	34	145	0	5
67	310	33	140		

※ 점수 환산표는 해커스토익 사이트 유저 데이터를 근거로 제작되었으며, 주기적으로 업데이트되고 있습니다. 해커스토익(Hackers.co.kr) 사이트에서 최신 경향을 반영하여 업데이트된 점수환산기를 이용하실 수 있습니다. (토익 > 토익게시판 > 토익점수환산기)

▌TEST 01 스크립트

PART 1

1   🔊 미국식 발음
(A) She's watering a plant.
(B) She's cooking a meal.
(C) She's wiping a stove.
(D) She's washing a dish.

2   🔊 캐나다식 발음
(A) One of the women is holding a document.
(B) There is a curtain covering a glass door.
(C) A man is reaching for a cup.
(D) There is furniture lined up against a wall.

3   🔊 영국식 발음
(A) Streetlights are being installed.
(B) Doors have been left open.
(C) Cars are stopped at an intersection.
(D) A parking space is unoccupied.

4   🔊 호주식 발음
(A) People are putting on work gloves.
(B) A flowerpot has been placed on a windowsill.
(C) People are moving monitors across the floor.
(D) Some chairs have been pushed in under the tables.

5   🔊 영국식 발음
(A) One of the women is looking out a window.
(B) They are standing in a lobby.
(C) The man is leaning on a bicycle.
(D) They are entering a building.

6   🔊 캐나다식 발음
(A) A power cord is being packed in a box.
(B) The man is operating a computer.
(C) A device is being disassembled.
(D) The man is repairing a lamp.

PART 2

7   🔊 캐나다식 발음 → 미국식 발음
Which printer should we buy?
(A) I printed out several copies.
(B) We may not return this purchase.
(C) Maybe the most expensive one.

8   🔊 영국식 발음 → 캐나다식 발음
Where can I register for the convention?
(A) The convenience store stocks thousands of products.
(B) Right at the information desk over there.
(C) I left my wallet at the cash register.

9   🔊 미국식 발음 → 호주식 발음
How do you feel about the new leave policy?
(A) It doesn't seem very fair.
(B) The manager is on sick leave.
(C) I feel excited about the project.

10   🔊 캐나다식 발음 → 영국식 발음
When is the next shipment scheduled for?
(A) It's the one next door.
(B) With a delivery company.
(C) It should have been here by now.

11   🔊 호주식 발음 → 영국식 발음
Didn't you stay longer after we left the library?
(A) I left about 10 minutes later.
(B) It was a long journey.
(C) My stay at this hotel was extended.

12   🔊 미국식 발음 → 호주식 발음
May I give you a call back after lunch?
(A) No, the lunch was canceled.
(B) A document was faxed yesterday.
(C) OK. I'm available after 1 P.M.

13   🔊 영국식 발음 → 호주식 발음
What was your favorite part of the show last night?
(A) I'd say the last five minutes.
(B) I personally prefer the latter one.
(C) Yes. It was a lot of fun.

14   🔊 캐나다식 발음 → 미국식 발음
Should I bring an umbrella?
(A) No, it's already raining outside.
(B) The forecast said there might be a shower.
(C) I've actually decided not to go.

15   🔊 호주식 발음 → 영국식 발음
It will be challenging to find a replacement for you.
(A) I can replace it for free.

(B) It somehow got lost.
(C) I am sure there is someone good.

16
Have you listened to Kendrick King's new song yet?
(A) It was on the radio a few minutes ago.
(B) I heard he performed here last year.
(C) There is a new musical I would like to watch.

17
When do you expect the article to be done?
(A) In the editorial section.
(B) By noon at the latest.
(C) Leave it in my office.

18
Should I submit my refund request online or call customer service?
(A) The Web site is down for maintenance.
(B) Incomplete requests will be rejected.
(C) I met with the client in person.

19
Can you finish the stock count before you leave today?
(A) I picked up all the leaves in the driveway.
(B) What are the best stocks to buy at the moment?
(C) Sure. It will only take a few minutes.

20
The new French restaurant on Wells Street is finally open, isn't it?
(A) I saw that on the bill.
(B) Since last Saturday, I think.
(C) I have not been to France.

21
Do you want to increase the employees' hours or hire someone temporarily?
(A) Lift the painting on your left a little higher.
(B) I had to wait for more than an hour.
(C) We can manage without anyone else.

22
Why has the blueprint not been approved yet?
(A) Print out a few more leaflets.
(B) Is your approval necessary?
(C) You have to ask Amy.

23
How much did you spend for the car repairs?
(A) It took my whole paycheck.
(B) We can look into some auto insurance plans.
(C) With my debit card.

24
What type of investments did you research for your assignment?
(A) I've already submitted an art portfolio.
(B) It took a while to finish the report.
(C) Mostly real estate.

25
Is Allan ready to give his speech?
(A) He will present an award to the CEO.
(B) He's still changing his clothes.
(C) I took several speech lessons.

26
Would you like to start with some drinks while you look at the menu?
(A) The drinking fountain is currently out of order.
(B) This place has the best dessert options in town.
(C) Actually, we are ready to order our food.

27
Do we have a large enough budget to install new computers?
(A) He is quite resourceful.
(B) We have the money for about 10.
(C) Yes, we've got some in the computer laboratory.

28
Who was your supervisor when you started at this firm?
(A) Starting my own company was hard.
(B) Mr. Brady was the manager then.
(C) My office is down the hall.

29
I am satisfied with the outcome of the sales meeting.
(A) We are holding our annual sale soon.
(B) I agree that it went well.
(C) There are three likely outcomes.

30
Is it wiser to wait for a better time to sell the house?
(A) Maybe try in a few months.
(B) The house is very spacious.
(C) I moved in just last week.

31
Do you plan on listing me as a reference?
(A) The contact information is listed online.
(B) I was thinking of citing your new research.
(C) If you recommend doing so.

PART 3

Questions 32-34 refer to the following conversation.

미국식 발음 → 캐나다식 발음

W: Good afternoon. I am here to check out your storage space options. Do you offer short-term rentals?

M: Yes, certainly. How long do you want to leave your belongings here?

W: I am renovating my house soon and need to store some furniture for at least two months.

M: If you are not absolutely sure, I would rent it for longer. You can always cancel your agreement with a 14 days' notice.

W: Oh, perfect. In that case, let's go with three months with the cancellation option you just mentioned. Could you show me what size options are available?

M: Sure, let me take you to the main storage area.

Questions 35-37 refer to the following conversation.

영국식 발음 → 호주식 발음

W: Oliver, thanks for helping me plan my brother's graduation party. Do you think you could pick a restaurant for the event? I don't eat out that often, so I'm not sure where to go.

M: Of course. How many guests have been invited?

W: There will be 22 people in total.

M: Hmm . . . La Casa could seat that many. It's a great Mexican restaurant and easily accessible from Oakwood Subway Station.

W: Uh, my brother lives in the suburbs.

M: I see. Then, how about BK Steakhouse? It is a little expensive and there's not a lot of parking, but it has large tables outside on its patio.

W: That'd be great. I'll make a reservation this afternoon.

Questions 38-40 refer to the following conversation with three speakers.

캐나다식 발음 → 영국식 발음 → 호주식 발음

M1: Welcome to the Collingwood Art Center. Are you here for the sculpture exhibit?

W: Yes. But I want to confirm one of your policies. Your Web site states that cameras are not permitted.

M1: That's right. We have a brochure that includes many images if you're interested.

W: Well, I was wondering if I would be allowed to shoot some photos for my university's newspaper.

M1: I bet we can make an exception for media representatives. Can't we, Arthur?

M2: Yes, but you'll need to fill out this application for a press pass. Why don't you do that now? Our manager will approve it in a few minutes.

W: I'll do that. Thanks.

Questions 41-43 refer to the following conversation.

영국식 발음 → 호주식 발음

W: Hi, Craig. I didn't expect you at today's team meeting. When did you return to the office?

M: Today, actually. I was in Amsterdam for a week to see my grandparents.

W: What a coincidence. I'm going there next month to meet with a client. Did you do much sightseeing?

M: A bit. I did a one-day tour of the old city center. We shopped at an outdoor market and went to some museums and galleries. I especially enjoyed the restaurant where we had lunch. It served traditional Dutch food.

W: That sounds great. What was the tour company called? I might have some free time when I'm there.

M: I'll e-mail you the link to its Web site.

Questions 44-46 refer to the following conversation.

캐나다식 발음 → 미국식 발음

M: What do you think of the candidate we just interviewed?

W: Well, I was impressed that she had experience working on advertising campaigns for Maxwell Clothing.

M: Me, too. Our agency will be doing several big-budget commercial projects for similar clients in a few weeks, so she would be a great help.

W: Right. Plus, her salary expectations are quite reasonable. But she has a month left on her current contract.

M: That's a good point. Then, could you also look through the other résumés we received? If you find any other qualified applicants, I'll schedule times to interview them.

Questions 47-49 refer to the following conversation with three speakers.

호주식 발음 → 캐나다식 발음 → 미국식 발음

M1: Raymond, have you finished your article on the city council's approval of funds for the new bridge construction? If you want it to appear in this month's edition of our magazine, you need to submit it by lunchtime tomorrow.

M2: Almost. I just need to print a hard copy to proofread. Unless there is a serious problem, I will make the deadline.

W: Oh, our printer is out of order. I've called a technician already.

M2: Really? When do you think it will be fixed?

W: He won't be able to come until tomorrow afternoon.

M1: Then, Raymond, why don't you use the design

department's printer?

M2: Sounds like a plan. I'll take my laptop upstairs.

Questions 50-52 refer to the following conversation.

[3)] 캐나다식 발음 → 미국식 발음

M: Sarah, did you read the e-mail that was sent to all employees this morning?

W: Yeah. Everyone needs to come in on Saturday to assist with the spring cleaning of the laboratory. I expected this . . . We do it every year around this time.

M: Right. I'm a little worried, though. I signed up for a cooking class on Saturday, and the fee is non-refundable. But I can't go if we have to clean that day.

W: Hmm . . . We weren't given much notice, so you can't be the only one who has plans this weekend. Why don't you speak with our manager about your situation?

M: Good idea. Let me call her right away.

Questions 53-55 refer to the following conversation.

[3)] 미국식 발음 → 호주식 발음

W: Thanks for coming, Jinsu. I asked you to stop by my office because I'm concerned about your team. Its sales declined significantly last quarter.

M: I know. But it's only a short-term setback. Our numbers should improve steadily.

W: That's a relief. By the way, what's the issue?

M: Two of my team's best salespeople are currently taking an extended period of leave. Umm . . . Matt has some health issues, and Abigail requested a month off to participate in a certificate program at Watterson College. But both will return next week.

W: I see. If you need extra hands before their return, let me know immediately. I'll assign someone to your team.

Questions 56-58 refer to the following conversation.

[3)] 영국식 발음 → 캐나다식 발음

W: You've reached the Eastern Lodge.

M: Hi. I reserved a room from June 15 to 19. My new mobile application will be introduced in the conference being held at your hotel's convention center.

W: I see . . . Um, is there a problem with your booking?

M: No. But your Web site states that the fitness center of the hotel will be closed on those dates. Is that correct?

W: Unfortunately, yes. We will be putting in some larger windows and light fixtures.

M: Are there any alternative options nearby?

W: Don't worry. We've arranged for guests to use the gym across the street. I'll give you a pass when you check in.

Questions 59-61 refer to the following conversation.

[3)] 미국식 발음 → 호주식 발음

W: Hello, David. It's Karen. I'm working on slide shows for a client meeting, but my work laptop keeps freezing. Have you encountered this problem before?

M: Um, did you try rebooting it?

W: Several times. It doesn't seem to be working.

M: Maybe you should ask for a new computer. Just bring a request form to the IT department's office.

W: It will take a couple of days to get a new one, but tomorrow is the due date for my first draft.

M: Why don't you make a request for deadline extension?

W: Well, I'd have to discuss that with our manager Ms. Harper, but she's in New York to meet with the CEO and won't be back until Tuesday.

M: You could always send her an e-mail.

Questions 62-64 refer to the following conversation and directory.

[3)] 호주식 발음 → 미국식 발음

M: Excuse me. I received an e-mail yesterday saying that I owe $4 for a book I returned late. I'd like to take care of that now.

W: OK. I'll need your library card and the payment. And just a reminder . . . I recommend visiting your account overview page on the library's Web site regularly to avoid similar problems in the future.

M: Got it. Um, one more thing . . . Does the library have a copy of a book called *Distant Horizons*?

W: Let me check . . . You're in luck. We received that novel yesterday, and no one has checked it out yet.

M: Thanks. I'll head to that section now.

Questions 65-67 refer to the following conversation and coupons.

[3)] 영국식 발음 → 캐나다식 발음

W: Hi, Steve. Mr. Harris asked me to prepare a written analysis comparing our promotional methods with those of our competitors. Do you mind if I ask you a few questions?

M: Of course not, Sally.

W: Thanks. As of last week, our main rival Syntek Appliances no longer charges for deliveries. Do you think that will cause any problems for us?

M: Not really. Our prices are still competitive.

W: That's good to hear. And we're offering four coupons to our customers, right?

M: Correct. However, the one with the highest minimum purchase amount will soon be replaced. It's rarely used because only a few of our products are more expensive than that price.

Questions 68-70 refer to the following conversation and map.

🔊 호주식 발음 → 미국식 발음

M: Beth, how are your preparations for the new recruits going?

W: I'm almost ready. I was surprised by the number of incoming employees. The size of our staff will almost double. We're really taking the firm to the next level.

M: It's very exciting. Oh, and I looked over the new employee training manual you created for the workshops. It was quite impressive.

W: Thanks. I put a lot of work into it. Um, have we found a new office yet?

M: Yes. It's on Jackson Avenue, right across from the Greendale Subway Station. I'm heading over there now. Would you like to come and see the space?

W: Sure. I'll just get my jacket.

PART 4

Questions 71-73 refer to the following talk.

🔊 영국식 발음

I hope everyone has been enjoying the tour of the Browning Library. Now, we're about to move on to the rare collections room. Here, you can browse our extensive collection of rare books, including first editions of novels and letters from famous writers. All of these materials are listed in our online catalog. Needless to say, you cannot take any items with you when you leave. While staying, please remain quiet at all times. If you need help with anything, the librarian at the desk over there will be happy to assist you.

Questions 74-76 refer to the following broadcast.

🔊 미국식 발음

Welcome back to YSJ Radio station. I am Francine Donaldson with your local news update. The Seattle Modern Art Institute, located downtown, is holding an opening celebration this weekend as it has finally finished its massive expansion project. It will specially open its doors to everyone for free and there will be plenty of activities indoors and in the sculpture garden. The big party will commence on Saturday at 10 A.M. and last until 8 P.M. The same hours will be observed on Sunday. Children will have lots of fun things to do. For adults, some live jazz will play during the evening hours.

Questions 77-79 refer to the following telephone message.

🔊 캐나다식 발음

Hi. This is Chris Vazquez from Magna Consultancy. I stopped by your studio to discuss professional headshots of my employees. Um, we agreed that my team would visit your place for a shoot on June 26th, but now it seems like we'll have to push back the date. Some of the employees and I are traveling to Portland next week to take a safety class at our company's office there. Our return flight is on June 30. Please contact me at 555-2938 to let me know your preferred date. Thank you.

Questions 80-82 refer to the following excerpt from a meeting.

🔊 호주식 발음

As you know, our team has been tasked with carrying out a detailed analysis of the company's finances. Some of you have expressed concern about completing this project by the deadline, especially since there have been major changes to the company's cash flow and assets this year. Fortunately, we'll have some help. I'd like to introduce Judith Walker. She was employed at our company's Birmingham branch for over 10 years before relocating to Essex last month to work with us. Um, I've asked her to take a couple of days to go over what we've accomplished with our report so far. When we meet again on Friday, she'll present her ideas to help speed up the process.

Questions 83-85 refer to the following advertisement.

🔊 미국식 발음

Get in shape without leaving your house using the new Bronze Gym Turbo. This machine allows you to do squats, pull-ups, and more to get a full-body workout. Best of all, the Turbo is easy to assemble and maintain, and it won't take up much space in your home. Since the Turbo was introduced last month, over 500,000 units have been shipped to our loyal customers around the world. In fact, it has become our best-selling machine ever. But don't just take our word for it. Visit our Web site to read testimonials from our many satisfied customers.

Questions 86-88 refer to the following excerpt from a meeting.

🔊 호주식 발음

The response to our latest advertisement, which aired during the American Football Championship, was extremely positive. Many people loved how funny it was. According to the search engine Viewpoint, there were over 600,000 searches for our new station wagon in the 24 hours after the ad aired. This is a noteworthy result. Um, we averaged about 50,000 per day last week. Now that we've got people's attention, I think it's important that we keep it by releasing more advertisements of the same type. By June, I think we should have three advertisements circulating.

영국식 발음

Welcome to Newman Medical Supplies' end-of-the-year party. Before we start, I'd like to share what we hope to accomplish over the coming year. After extensive preparations, the company is finally ready to expand into the European market. The first step will take place in February, when our offices in Manchester and Barcelona begin operations. Then, in September, construction of our new plant in Romania will finish. Um, it should be running at full capacity by the following month. I'm also excited to report that there will be opportunities for employees here to work overseas. The personnel department will be releasing a brochure on Monday morning with more details about the available positions, and I encourage everybody to check it out.

Questions 92-94 refer to the following telephone message.

캐나다식 발음

Good morning, Nina. It's Jack Benet from *Nature Monthly*. I was just reviewing the story you submitted for the March issue, and we have a problem. It exceeds the maximum word count by about 400 words. I realize the topic you chose is fairly complex, but the piece simply won't fit into the space we have set aside in the magazine. Please start the revisions right away. Our editor intends to review the article before the end of the week. Anyway, I was thinking that we could cut the interview with the representative of Bedrock Industries. If you could contact me by phone later today to discuss this matter, I would appreciate it.

Questions 95-97 refer to the following talk and schedule.

미국식 발음

I'd like to welcome all of you to Delta Shipping. Before we get started with the orientation, I have a quick announcement to make. I called the manager of our warehouse yesterday and asked him to show you around the facility today. Of course, this will result in a change to our schedule. We'll head over to the warehouse right after we eat, so the topic we were originally going to discuss during that session will be covered tomorrow. OK . . . We'll begin in about 15 minutes. If you haven't done so already, please ask the receptionist for your employee ID card. Her desk is the one closest to the main entrance.

Questions 98-100 refer to the following broadcast and flight schedule.

영국식 발음

For the second day in a row, the Midwest has been blanketed in snow. Weather forecasters are calling this storm one of the strongest in the past decade, with wind gusts of up to 40 miles per hour and 20 inches of snow in some areas. As a result, the airport in Detroit has been closed since January 1, and flights into the city have been canceled. Affected passengers should contact their airline to reschedule. Passengers at other airports, including Cleveland and St. Louis, should expect to face significant delays. A government official will hold a press conference tomorrow morning to present measures to assist those impacted by the storm.

PART 1

1 🔊 미국식 발음

(A) He's facing a closed window.
(B) He's painting a portion of the wall.
(C) He's repositioning a stepladder.
(D) He's extending his arms upward.

2 🔊 캐나다식 발음

(A) One of the women is cleaning a counter.
(B) One of the women is filling plates with cupcakes.
(C) One of the women is lifting a cup.
(D) One of the women is taking baked goods out of a kitchen.

3 🔊 영국식 발음

(A) A woman has her hand on a computer.
(B) They're studying X-ray images.
(C) A man is turning on a screen.
(D) Some people are filing a document.

4 🔊 호주식 발음

(A) She's paying for some jewelry at a checkout.
(B) She's trying on a necklace in a boutique.
(C) She's carrying a handbag on her shoulder.
(D) She's assembling one of the store shelves.

5 🔊 영국식 발음

(A) Umbrellas have been unfolded above the tables.
(B) A cruise ship has stopped in the harbor.
(C) A set of patio furniture is being placed on a vessel.
(D) Streetlamps circle an outdoor dining area.

6 🔊 캐나다식 발음

(A) A statue has been situated in a plaza.
(B) A group of people is sitting on the steps.
(C) A structure is being reflected in a window.
(D) A building is being constructed by a work crew.

PART 2

7 🔊 캐나다식 발음 → 미국식 발음

How many people are we expecting for our performances on Sunday?
(A) 100 for each show.
(B) They'll be here at 8.
(C) We've performed it many times.

8 🔊 영국식 발음 → 캐나다식 발음

Is this Mariah's computer bag?
(A) Please enter your password.
(B) She left it here yesterday.
(C) Yes, the scanner is working.

9 🔊 미국식 발음 → 호주식 발음

Who moved the boxes from the front door?
(A) I'm sure it's in the back room.
(B) I'll do it right after the snow stops.
(C) I saw Issac doing it this morning.

10 🔊 캐나다식 발음 → 영국식 발음

My medical checkup is at 4:40, but I won't finish work until 5 today.
(A) At Queens Hospital.
(B) That's a problem.
(C) You need to make sure you're qualified.

11 🔊 호주식 발음 → 영국식 발음

Would you prefer to rent a sedan or a larger vehicle?
(A) I've run out of gas.
(B) The rental fee is negotiable.
(C) We require a van to fit everyone.

12 🔊 미국식 발음 → 호주식 발음

Why has our director been out of the office all morning?
(A) Around seven o'clock.
(B) She's attending a workshop.
(C) Yes, your directions were useful.

13 🔊 영국식 발음 → 호주식 발음

Does the cleaning service send us monthly bills?
(A) Yes, on the 1st.
(B) It's fine to pay with a credit card.
(C) I spent $50 last month.

14 🔊 캐나다식 발음 → 미국식 발음

When do you want me to restock the shelves?
(A) No, I think it is on the bottom shelf.
(B) Before taking your lunch break.
(C) In the storage room.

15 [호주식 발음 → 영국식 발음]

How often do you go to Tokyo on business trips?
(A) It's an event occurring in Tokyo.
(B) An agent will plan the trip.
(C) We no longer have a branch in that city.

16 [미국식 발음 → 호주식 발음]

Who should I submit my employment application to?
(A) The woman behind the reception desk.
(B) You should include a résumé and cover letter.
(C) The position won't be vacant for another two weeks.

17 [영국식 발음 → 캐나다식 발음]

Why don't we ask the baker to recommend a high quality bread flour?
(A) No, we've already arrived.
(B) I bought some cakes.
(C) Yes, that would be helpful.

18 [미국식 발음 → 캐나다식 발음]

Would you organize the museum's charity luncheon?
(A) We received a generous donation.
(B) It would be my pleasure.
(C) No, I don't need a ride.

19 [영국식 발음 → 호주식 발음]

You've reserved your seat for the concert already, haven't you?
(A) I should be ready by 6 P.M.
(B) I'm going to do it now.
(C) No, it'll be my first time playing there.

20 [캐나다식 발음 → 영국식 발음]

What is the company's reason for recalling the vehicle?
(A) No, I didn't receive a full refund.
(B) Consumers are reporting faulty brakes.
(C) They should be brought back to the store.

21 [호주식 발음 → 미국식 발음]

The conference on business strategies is going to be postponed.
(A) Across from the convention center.
(B) That strategy was very effective.
(C) Oh, I didn't know that.

22 [캐나다식 발음 → 영국식 발음]

Where did you put our flight tickets to Vancouver?
(A) I left them in my desk drawer.
(B) We need to hurry to catch the flight.
(C) I made a reservation this morning.

23 [미국식 발음 → 영국식 발음]

Didn't the guests in Suite 234 request room service?
(A) The kitchen staff will know.
(B) They have checked in.
(C) It's bigger than I had expected.

24 [호주식 발음 → 미국식 발음]

Which shirts are currently on sale?
(A) Yes, 75 percent off.
(B) All of the ones on this rack.
(C) Let's go shopping at the Riverton Mall.

25 [캐나다식 발음 → 미국식 발음]

Why do you want to return this table?
(A) Thanks. I'll exchange it later.
(B) My turn is coming up next.
(C) It's too big for my living room.

26 [영국식 발음 → 캐나다식 발음]

I've decided which apartment I'm going to lease when I move to Madrid.
(A) I knew you were unhappy with your landlord.
(B) Great, that's one major decision.
(C) They're trying to sell their house.

27 [캐나다식 발음 → 미국식 발음]

Will my flight depart on time?
(A) There haven't been any delays.
(B) The altered project schedule.
(C) No, it arrived two days ago.

28 [호주식 발음 → 미국식 발음]

Should we stay at the beach or head back to the hotel?
(A) Some extra beach towels.
(B) OK, if you're done swimming.
(C) Let's relax here a bit longer.

29 [캐나다식 발음 → 영국식 발음]

Hasn't the technician fixed our network yet?
(A) We met him at the networking event.
(B) No, he's still working on it.
(C) I'm glad we solved it together.

30 [미국식 발음 → 호주식 발음]

Do you know who the woman delivering the welcome address is?
(A) Yes, it was delivered to my home last week.
(B) Her name is Kate Wong.
(C) I think it's on 17th Street.

영국식 발음 → 호주식 발음

The Boston Herald reports that the Eastwood Public Library is closed for renovations.
(A) Have you completed the report?
(B) I have to renew my card next month.
(C) Really? When will it reopen?

PART 3

Questions 32-34 refer to the following conversation.

미국식 발음 → 캐나다식 발음

W: Hello. My name is Vanessa Johnson, and I'm calling because I want to report an error in your newspaper.
M: What mistake did you discover, Ms. Johnson?
W: Well . . . I'm the owner of the vitamin and supplement store called Lancaster Health and Nutrition. Yesterday, you published an article about our new branch that's going to open in Dalton Plaza next week. But the article said it's opening next month.
M: Oh, I'm very sorry. I'll be certain to notify our news editor immediately. Once he verifies the misprint, I'm sure he'll arrange for a correction to be posted in tomorrow's edition.

Questions 35-37 refer to the following conversation.

영국식 발음 → 호주식 발음

W: It appears that we need more meals for tonight's year-end, corporate dinner party. Seven of our employees brought additional guests, but the cooks only prepared enough food for the confirmed number of guests.
M: Hmm, that's odd. I was in charge of keeping track of the guest list, and just one person contacted me today to say that he was bringing an extra person with him.
W: Maybe some of them changed their minds at the last minute. Anyway, could you ask the chef to make a few more dishes?
M: Sure. I'll head to the kitchen and find out if he can do that.

Questions 38-40 refer to the following conversation.

캐나다식 발음 → 영국식 발음

M: Shannon, I noticed that you ride your bike to work. Did you know that some of the people in our department have formed a bicycle group?
W: Really? I hadn't heard that. Can you tell me more about it?
M: Well, we meet every Saturday and go on long rides together. Some of us just enjoy the workout, while others are training for competitive events. Of course, participating in these races isn't a requirement for club members.

W: That's a relief. I'm not very experienced. But I do like the idea of getting some exercise. How do I join?
M: I'll e-mail you the registration form this afternoon.

Questions 41-43 refer to the following conversation.

캐나다식 발음 → 미국식 발음

M: After this morning's new recruit orientation, you said that you'd provide me with a list of the names of the new employees from each department. But the one you sent me was from the last orientation instead.
W: Sorry about that. Is it OK if I get you the correct one later? I must go to an important lunch meeting with the funders of our new building project right now, so I don't have enough time at the moment.
M: That's fine. Just remember to get it to me before you leave the office today. I'll need to enter their contact information into our database before I publish the new employee directory on Wednesday.
W: I won't forget.

Questions 44-46 refer to the following conversation.

호주식 발음 → 영국식 발음

M: You want to see me, Ms. Collins?
W: Yes. Many customers have provided negative feedback about the XLNC solar clocks. I'm a little worried. They say their machines aren't charging properly, which causes them to stop functioning after just a few days.
M: Bill Johnson from our engineering team and I recently tested 200 random units. They all worked perfectly. So, my guess is that consumers aren't using the devices properly. I think we need to clarify our user manual.
W: I see. We should also post information about it on our Web site. Can you please make a draft of that?
M: OK. When do you want this done by?
W: Early enough so that I can skim through it before my shift ends today.

Questions 47-49 refer to the following conversation with three speakers.

미국식 발음 → 호주식 발음 → 캐나다식 발음

W: All right, we are about to begin our promotion. There are many stores in this building, and although we are allowed to walk around, we should not enter any of them. Please approach shoppers in a friendly manner, and use the script word for word.
M1: Are we supposed to hand out the chocolates before or after we talk to them?
W: Do it simultaneously, Robert. Also, please make sure to tell everyone where our store is located in the mall. Any other questions?
M2: I heard that John Pence is covering the event and that he asked for some photos for his article.

Should we do anything specific?

W: No. Just let him follow you around.

Questions 50-52 refer to the following conversation.

🔊 캐나다식 발음 → 미국식 발음

M: Hello. I read about the fitness courses your business offers in a flyer. I'm interested in the weight-training class. When is it held?

W: That one is held once a week on Saturday, from 9 A.M. to 1 P.M. in our largest room. We used to offer a second session at 7 P.M., but not many people signed up, so we decided to cancel it.

M: Oh, that's OK. I wasn't planning on coming in then, anyway. The earlier option should work for me. So, I'd like to know a bit more about the details of the session.

W: Would you like me to grab you an informational pamphlet? It'll explain everything you need to know.

Questions 53-55 refer to the following conversation with three speakers.

🔊 호주식 발음 → 영국식 발음 → 미국식 발음

M: Excuse me. I've come to your office because I received a service request from Sarah Long.

W1: Yes. Um . . . her desk is next to mine. Sarah, the repairperson from Raymond is here to fix the water cooler.

W2: Oh, sorry. I was just finishing up a conference call. Anyway, the cooler is right here behind my desk.

M: Water is leaking from the device's spout, right?

W2: Yeah. I noticed it dripping this morning.

M: Hmm . . . the spout isn't working correctly and needs to be replaced.

W2: OK. However, before you begin, I've got to notify the building manager that a repair is going to be made. Janice, what is Mr. Renner's extension?

W1: It's 6849. I'll call him and tell him for you.

W2: Great. I appreciate it.

Questions 56-58 refer to the following conversation.

🔊 영국식 발음 → 캐나다식 발음

W: Hello. My name is Annabel Christiansen. I'm here to check in for the 5:40 P.M. flight to London. I have my passport and ticket here.

M: I'm sorry. You've arrived too late, Ms. Christiansen. Check-in for that flight closed 20 minutes ago. There won't be enough time for you to reach the gate before takeoff.

W: Oh, no. I was worried this was going to happen, seeing as my taxi was stuck in traffic on the way here. Are there any other flights today that I can take instead?

M: Yes, we still have seats available on the one that leaves at 10:30 P.M. For a $100 fee, I can update your reservation and issue you another ticket.

Questions 59-61 refer to the following conversation.

🔊 캐나다식 발음 → 영국식 발음

M: Hello, Ms. Law. My name is Lance Graner, and I am organizing a conference in April for young professionals who are just entering the field of finance. As you are an investment consultant for a respected firm, I am calling to offer you a paid speaking opportunity at the conference.

W: Well, I'll be unavailable in early April as I'm planning to visit one of our offices abroad during that time. However, as long as the event takes place after April 15, I can participate.

M: Hmm . . . It'll be held on April 4. But I'll contact you if we have other speaking opportunities in the future.

Questions 62-64 refer to the following conversation and schedule.

🔊 캐나다식 발음 → 미국식 발음

M: Beverly, it's Stewart. I won't be leaving with you for the airport anymore. I still have a few things to finish, so I'll see you at the gate. What time is our departure?

W: Ten minutes after 8. By the way, do you want some food for the flight? I'm thinking of buying some before I get there.

M: Hmm . . . I'd love a sandwich or anything quick. Thank you. Oh, if possible, why don't we sit next to each other? I think I am currently sitting behind you.

W: I am sure we can get someone to change one of our seats. We have a lot to decide, and it would be nice to discuss them on the flight.

Questions 65-67 refer to the following conversation and program.

🔊 호주식 발음 → 영국식 발음

M: The restaurant's opening week was rather successful, wouldn't you say?

W: Absolutely. We exceeded our expected guest numbers, and the restaurant was fully booked last weekend.

M: Yeah. And many of the people who came said they were going to post about our restaurant on their social networking pages. That's great publicity.

W: Also, our publicist, Harold Newman, will be appearing on *Morning Buzz* tomorrow. That will be sure to help us gain even more positive public attention.

M: That's great. A lot of people in the area watch that program. We should get a lot of new customers.

Questions 68-70 refer to the following conversation and map.

🔊 호주식 발음 → 미국식 발음

M: Hello. My name is Frank Lott, and I am reporting for my first shift.

W: Great! I was expecting you. You've been hired as one of our security guards.

M: Yes. I received training for three weeks. Is there anything in particular that I should be aware of?

W: Umm . . . As you will be assigned to the ceramics area, it is important to make sure that no one touches the artwork. By the way, do you have your uniform with you?

M: I've heard that there's one in the locker.

W: Okay. I'll call my boss and let him know that you've arrived.

PART 4

Questions 71-73 refer to the following telephone message.

[3·I] 영국식 발음

Good afternoon, Mr. Jackson. This is Claudia Omar, from Proactive Insurance, responding to the voice mail you left me yesterday. You mentioned you'd like to learn more about motorcycle insurance. Well, our most popular plan is the Platinum Protection package, which provides you up to $250,000 in coverage, and I think it would be your best choice. The premium for the plan varies considerably depending on the motorbike you have, so I'll need to know the brand and model of your bike before I can give you an accurate quote. Please call me back today with those details if you can. Thanks.

Questions 74-76 refer to the following talk.

[3·I] 미국식 발음

I appreciate you joining us at Fradston Pharmaceuticals' media event. I'm delighted to be here today, as Fradston's newly appointed chief executive officer, to announce our intention to build a new research center in downtown Atlanta. This center will serve as the hub for all of our medical research and is scheduled to open in nine months. The facility is expected to contribute to the creation of over 200 new jobs. More details about these will be posted on our Web site at a later date. We at Fradston hope that this development will solidify the company's position as the nation's top provider of pharmaceutical products.

Questions 77-79 refer to the following recorded message.

[3·I] 캐나다식 발음

You have reached Cedar Kitchen, Houston's number-one spot for contemporary dining. As our staff is participating in the Southwestern Food Festival June 8 and June 9, we will be closing at 1 P.M. each day. Our normal hours of operation of 11 A.M. to 10 P.M. will resume on Wednesday, June 10. We greatly appreciate your patience in this matter. For details about menu offerings, please press "one." For reservations, press "two" and record your contact information and desired reservation time after the tone. Specific details regarding the Southwestern Food Festival may be obtained by visiting our Web site.

Questions 80-82 refer to the following telephone message.

[3·I] 호주식 발음

Hi, Ms. Wheeler. This is Jeff Perkins from Best Cut Electronics. We have fully assessed the health of your laptop, and found significant damage to its hardware. Well, this model is five years old. Unfortunately, you are no longer covered by warranty. If we go ahead with the repair, it would set you back $400. Just be aware that the newest model costs $500. Why don't you stop by sometime soon so we can discuss all your options? We would be able to retrieve all of your files from your old computer. That would be free of charge if you buy a new device.

Questions 83-85 refer to the following talk.

[3·I] 미국식 발음

Hello, and welcome to our annual two-day seminar on project management. This year's event promises to be very special as we have a wide range of speakers. Now, I'd like to give you some information about our schedule. We are going to focus on planning and implementing projects for the first day and on evaluating results for the second. Both days will follow the same basic pattern. The mornings are going to begin with presentations by experienced project managers and end with panel discussions and question-and-answer sessions. In the afternoons, we'll break into small groups to develop action plans for specific projects. OK . . . my assistant will now hand out information packets that contain details about what will be covered during the seminar.

Questions 86-88 refer to the following broadcast.

[3·I] 호주식 발음

In business news, the multinational technology company Core Resources has announced that its CEO, Kerry Rose, will be stepping down from her position at the end of May. Under Ms. Rose's leadership, the company grew to be the world's third-largest software developer. It had under 8,000 workers when she started, while it currently employs about 15,000 staff members. Although Core Resources has yet to release her replacement's name to the public—and most likely won't do so until closer to Ms. Rose's departure—some analysts are speculating about who the next leader of the company might be. One widely discussed candidate is Dale Fenny, the company's current chief financial officer.

Questions 89-91 refer to the following advertisement.
🔊 캐나다식 발음

If you're tired of shoveling snow from your driveway or sidewalk, then contact Harford Snow today. For a flat monthly fee, you will never have to worry about doing this again. At Harford, we pride ourselves on our efficiency and reliability, which is why we guarantee that the snow will be removed from your property within four hours after a snowfall ends. If our workers ever arrive late, you will not be charged for that month. And for a small additional fee, we will use salt to get rid of the ice on all your walkways. Visit us at www.harfordsnow.com for a list of the areas that we operate in and over 100 testimonials from satisfied customers.

Questions 92-94 refer to the following speech.
🔊 미국식 발음

Let me begin by thanking the Silver Screen Academy for granting me this Best Young Director Award. While I suspected that *The Time Was Then* was going to do well, I never guessed it would break international box office records. The incredible team that worked on the film deserves a huge amount of credit. What's more, I want to give a special thanks to Gabriela Hernandez, who taught me everything I know about this art form. Gabriela has worked on hundreds of projects, and I aspire to achieve such a long career. Moving forward, I can only promise to bring an equal amount of passion to my future movies, including *Staying Warm*, which begins production in August. Again, thank you.

Questions 95-97 refer to the following excerpt from a meeting and graph.
🔊 호주식 발음

Since you are all in charge of designing our firm's digital cameras, I must share some feedback about the model we launched in May. This graph shows the results of a recent customer survey. As you can see, the model in question got the worst satisfaction score. According to respondents, this is largely because they found the camera's button layout to be confusing. While a few people voiced concerns before the release, this seems to be a much larger issue than anyone anticipated. I know it's going to be a hassle, but I want to redesign the model and then relaunch it later this summer.

Questions 98-100 refer to the following telephone message and schedule.
🔊 영국식 발음

Hello. My name is Alice Warren, and I'm registered for the student employment workshop that will be held at the Westwood Employment Center on Saturday. I'm very excited about this because I plan to begin searching for a summer internship in early May, once I've finished my final exams at the end of April. But there's one problem . . . I have to meet with my professor to discuss an assignment that day. Um, it slipped my mind when I signed up for the workshop yesterday. Would it be a problem if I skipped one of the sessions? I would leave at noon and be back just after two. Please call me at 555-4938 to let me know if this is allowed. Thanks.

PART 1

1 3ⁿ 미국식 발음
(A) She's removing her glasses.
(B) She's looking at a laptop.
(C) She's writing on a piece of paper.
(D) She's clearing off a table.

2 3ⁿ 캐나다식 발음
(A) The man is shoveling some snow.
(B) The man is closing a car hood.
(C) A vehicle is being parked.
(D) A tire is being replaced.

3 3ⁿ 영국식 발음
(A) Some people have placed notepads on a table.
(B) Some people are raising their hands.
(C) Some people are seated in a circle.
(D) Some people are rearranging furniture.

4 3ⁿ 호주식 발음
(A) The man is playing a violin.
(B) The woman is showing the man an instrument.
(C) A lamp is shining light toward some people.
(D) Some wood is being carved.

5 3ⁿ 영국식 발음
(A) The office is being cleaned.
(B) Chairs are stacked in a work area.
(C) A curtain is covering a window.
(D) Desks are lined up in rows.

6 3ⁿ 캐나다식 발음
(A) Pedestrians are walking across a bridge.
(B) Cars are parked beside a road.
(C) Traffic cones are positioned on a street.
(D) Vendor stalls are set up in a market.

PART 2

7 3ⁿ 캐나다식 발음 → 미국식 발음
Where is this shipment of printer paper going?
(A) Ship it by today.
(B) A local school.
(C) To shop at a store.

8 3ⁿ 영국식 발음 → 캐나다식 발음
When do you need the sales analysis?
(A) Yes, I did.
(B) Sales have gone up considerably.
(C) By the end of the workday.

9 3ⁿ 미국식 발음 → 호주식 발음
Who signed up for tomorrow's workshop?
(A) From 10 A.M. to noon.
(B) As long as it works properly.
(C) Everyone in my department.

10 3ⁿ 캐나다식 발음 → 영국식 발음
Could you ask the staff to gather in the lobby in 15 minutes?
(A) Sure, they'll be able to lift it.
(B) I'll make an announcement.
(C) An hour after it started.

11 3ⁿ 호주식 발음 → 영국식 발음
Why can't gym members use the pool right now?
(A) It's being cleaned.
(B) Swimming is a great exercise.
(C) Because she's a member.

12 3ⁿ 미국식 발음 → 호주식 발음
Should we consult with a lawyer before signing the contract?
(A) Yes, I think so.
(B) Did he sign the agreement?
(C) I received his autograph too.

13 3ⁿ 영국식 발음 → 호주식 발음
What's the name of the neighborhood where Neil will be moving to in November?
(A) This area gets quite busy.
(B) Maybe Susan remembers.
(C) The product hasn't been named yet.

14 3ⁿ 캐나다식 발음 → 미국식 발음
How far does this beach extend?
(A) About half a mile or so.
(B) No, I've never visited this beach.
(C) Let's put on our sunglasses.

15 [3n] 호주식 발음 → 영국식 발음
Have all the clients taken their seats?
(A) Each has been installed.
(B) A few still haven't arrived.
(C) My seat is over there.

16 [3n] 미국식 발음 → 호주식 발음
Why did you switch the brown sweater for another one?
(A) Then we'll find another location.
(B) It was too small for me.
(C) Brown is my favorite color.

17 [3n] 영국식 발음 → 캐나다식 발음
Should beverages be served at 5 P.M., or should we wait until after the performance?
(A) Earlier would be better.
(B) Our waiter is very friendly.
(C) We should make a donation.

18 [3n] 미국식 발음 → 캐나다식 발음
You already watched our training video, didn't you?
(A) That train already departed.
(B) Yes, I'm enjoying the job.
(C) About a month ago.

19 [3n] 영국식 발음 → 호주식 발음
Where did you work before this?
(A) See you after the show.
(B) I interned at a laboratory.
(C) From some corporate leaders.

20 [3n] 캐나다식 발음 → 영국식 발음
Is $500 too much for this painting, or is it a fair price?
(A) I'll check the receipt.
(B) You're going to love the museum.
(C) That seems overpriced.

21 [3n] 호주식 발음 → 미국식 발음
Does the pamphlet you're making for our company explain our ongoing projects?
(A) Yes, but it's not my container.
(B) I made sure to include that information.
(C) Most of the brochures can be recycled.

22 [3n] 캐나다식 발음 → 영국식 발음
Are you satisfied with your raise?
(A) Yes, I really appreciate it.
(B) It'd be nice to increase productivity.
(C) They were sent to the payroll department.

23 [3n] 미국식 발음 → 영국식 발음
Didn't you see the warehouse when you were shown around our facility?
(A) I was told we had to skip it.
(B) Let's store those goods too.
(C) Both tour times work for me.

24 [3n] 호주식 발음 → 미국식 발음
I had a difficulty logging in to the wireless network.
(A) I couldn't find the venue either.
(B) It's been unreliable lately.
(C) Thanks for solving the problem.

25 [3n] 캐나다식 발음 → 미국식 발음
Would you like to borrow my phone charger?
(A) Try dialing the number again.
(B) When did you lend them to Paul?
(C) Sure. I'll give it back soon.

26 [3n] 영국식 발음 → 캐나다식 발음
How many rehearsals are left before the first performance?
(A) The car performed well.
(B) We're looking forward to the play.
(C) This is the second-to-last.

27 [3n] 캐나다식 발음 → 미국식 발음
Cassie will be on sick leave for the rest of the month.
(A) I was ill last December.
(B) Who will handle her duties?
(C) An updated calendar.

28 [3n] 호주식 발음 → 미국식 발음
We should conduct a focus group on our new laptop, shouldn't we?
(A) Since the company grew larger.
(B) I doubt we have the funds to do that.
(C) Yes, most of the participants.

29 [3n] 캐나다식 발음 → 영국식 발음
The chef prepared this complimentary dessert for you.
(A) I'm well prepared for the interview.
(B) Tell them it will be served soon.
(C) Wow. It looks delicious.

30 [3n] 미국식 발음 → 호주식 발음
Are there any rental cars available that can fit six people?
(A) This SUV can accommodate seven passengers.
(B) Customers are charged extra for gas.
(C) Many drivers find the congestion frustrating.

31 영국식 발음 → 호주식 발음

For $50 more, I can give you an extended warranty.
(A) There are fewer models than expected.
(B) Great. I'll be sure to delete it.
(C) OK. Charge it all to my credit card.

PART 3

Questions 32-34 refer to the following conversation.

미국식 발음 → 캐나다식 발음

W: Hi, Mark. I heard you were asked to travel with the marketing and sales team members to Tokyo next week.

M: That's right. Our CEO thinks we may have to make a few last-minute changes to the contract with the local company that will distribute our products. So, he wants someone from the legal department to go along. Oh, that reminds me . . . I paid for my flight and hotel with my personal credit card. Do you know where I can get information about the reimbursement process?

W: You should read the guide posted on the company intranet by the accounting team. It includes detailed instructions.

M: Thanks. I'll do that right away.

Questions 35-37 refer to the following conversation with three speakers.

영국식 발음 → 캐나다식 발음 → 호주식 발음

W: Mitch, aren't you in charge of conducting an inventory count at our store?

M1: Normally, I am. However, Ben took care of it yesterday since it was my first day back after returning from vacation. If you have any questions about our stock levels, he's right behind you.

W: Oh, excuse me, Ben. I have a question for you about our inventory. How many XR monitors do we have in stock? Our database says that we have two left, but I can't find any on the shelf.

M2: That's odd. We should indeed have two left. Let me look in the warehouse.

W: I have a customer on hold, so let me know as soon as possible.

Questions 38-40 refer to the following conversation.

호주식 발음 → 영국식 발음

M: Excuse me. I watched a play here on May 19, and I believe I left my watch in the bathroom. I took it off when I was washing my hands. Has anyone turned one in?

W: Actually, yes. But I need to confirm that you are the owner. Um, could you tell me what your watch looks like?

M: Sure. It has a steel case and a leather strap. And, uh, if you look at the back, you will see that my name is inscribed . . . um, James Higgs.

W: Well, Mr. Higgs, you are in luck! If I can just see your driver's license or another piece of photo ID, I can give you your watch back.

Questions 41-43 refer to the following conversation with three speakers.

캐나다식 발음 → 미국식 발음→ 영국식 발음

M: Elena, Patricia! It's so nice to see you both. You're a bit early, though. Dan's birthday party doesn't officially begin until 4 P.M.

W1: We know it's only 3 o'clock, but we thought we would come a bit early to lend a hand.

W2: Yeah. We figured you might need some help preparing food and decorating. Hopefully, we're not intruding.

M: Not at all! In fact, I'm glad you're here. I'm running a bit behind, so this is great.

W2: Well, what can we do?

M: Why don't you two chop up the tomatoes and onions in the kitchen for fresh salsa? While you do that, I'll set the table.

Questions 44-46 refer to the following conversation.

영국식 발음 → 호주식 발음

W: Thanks for inviting me today. The Stallions are my favorite baseball team, but I rarely get a chance to go to their games. This is a lot of fun.

M: My pleasure. A coworker of mine has season tickets for all of the home games. He's out of town this weekend, so he gave me his tickets.

W: That was very generous of him. Well, I'm going to grab some snacks. Do you need anything?

M: I've got a hot dog and soda.

Questions 47-49 refer to the following conversation.

호주식 발음 → 미국식 발음

M: Bellport Florist, Gerald speaking. How can I help you today?

W: I'm interested in buying flowers for a coworker. She's been selected as the employee of the month and will be presented with an award during a ceremony tomorrow morning. So, I need to pick the flowers up this afternoon.

M: That shouldn't be a problem. Is there a particular kind of flower you'd like to get?

W: Yes. Orchids are her favorite flower, so a bouquet of those, please.

M: Oh . . . I'm very sorry, but we ran out of those this morning. We don't expect another shipment until Saturday. However, our branch in Hereford might have some available. I suggest that you give them a call.

Questions 50-52 refer to the following conversation.

캐나다식 발음 → 미국식 발음

M: I have a suggestion for decorating this lobby. Why don't we choose furniture that complements the blue and green wallpaper we have used throughout the hotel?

W: Good idea. We'll definitely need several couches. And they should be made of leather as that material is very durable. Why don't we look at some from West Loop?

M: West Loop mostly sells items that are suitable for private residences. But, um . . . Bently Furniture specializes in commercial furniture.

W: Yeah, I suppose so. In that case, I'll call that store to find out whether they have any leather sofas in stock.

Questions 53-55 refer to the following conversation.

미국식 발음 → 호주식 발음

W: Hello, sir. How can I help you this morning?

M: I need to travel to Berlin. I know a train on the Red Line regularly heads there from Bonn. When does the next one leave?

W: The next one won't leave for about two hours.

M: I'd like a ticket for that one. I can call some of my clients while I wait.

W: Certainly. It'll be €75. By the way, I encourage you to make use of our lounge. It offers comfortable chairs, free wireless Internet, and vending machines. It's just down the hallway to your left.

Questions 56-58 refer to the following conversation.

영국식 발음 → 캐나다식 발음

W: I'm glad I've bumped into you. I'm wondering how the report you're working on is coming along. The one about the risk analysis of the South American consumer markets that we're considering entering.

M: I finished it two hours ago.

W: Could you e-mail it to me, then? Tomorrow, I'll be meeting with Fred Diamond, a major investor in our clothing firm. He wants to discuss our plan.

M: Actually, I already sent it. I figured you already knew.

W: Oh, I must have overlooked that e-mail. I'll check for it again and contact you if I have questions about the report.

Questions 59-61 refer to the following conversation.

호주식 발음 → 미국식 발음

M: Mayor Lamar, thank you for joining me on this episode of *Happening Today*. We'll spend most of the hour talking about your work as a civil rights lawyer before being elected earlier this year. However, I believe you have some news to share before we get into that.

W: Yes. I'm very pleased to announce that, after working with the city council, I've been able to secure over $5 million in additional funding for the city's schools next year. It's my first major accomplishment as the mayor of Chicago.

M: And how will the funds be used?

W: City schools will be getting additional books, art materials, and furniture.

Questions 62-64 refer to the following conversation and highway map.

미국식 발음 → 호주식 발음

W: Paul, it's Wendy. I'm wondering how far away you are from the office. The gathering to welcome our new branch manager doesn't start for another hour, but I'd like to talk to you about the training workshop we're holding for the accounting staff next week.

M: Not too far. I just pulled off the highway, and I am passing Sun Market now. I should be there in 15 minutes or so.

W: OK, great. That'll give us a chance to chat beforehand.

M: Sounds good. By the way, do you need me to get any last-minute supplies? Are there enough drinks for everyone?

W: Thanks, but that's not necessary.

Questions 65-67 refer to the following conversation and shelving unit.

캐나다식 발음 → 영국식 발음

M: Pardon me. I'd like to buy my nephew a laptop. He's going to college soon, and he'll need one to write papers.

W: Sure thing. Are there any particular features you have in mind?

M: I know he likes to have many windows open at once, so a wider screen would be best. I'm leaning toward the C34, but I'm not certain.

W: While the C34 is a great model, it's intended for video editing. I'm guessing it's more powerful than necessary.

M: Yeah, good point.

W: However, the device just below that one is the same size. Although less powerful than the C34, it's ideal for running word processing programs. It's also much cheaper.

Questions 68-70 refer to the following conversation and sign.

호주식 발음 → 미국식 발음

M: Charlotte, did you hear that our IT company will be hosting a volunteer day? Management is hoping it'll attract some positive media attention, and all of the technicians are encouraged to participate. I'm really looking forward to it.

W: Yeah, me too. I guess we'll be tutoring students at local schools.

M: It's a great idea, but I'm a bit surprised by some of the goals. Uh, 20 people from our newest office are expected to take part, but there are only 30 employees.

W: I'm sure that office will meet its goal. And I'm going to sign up now. I want to make sure that our branch has enough volunteers.

M: Good point. I'll join you.

PART 4

Questions 71-73 refer to the following announcement.

영국식 발음

May I have your attention, please? This is just a reminder that, as Greenway customers, you do not have to pay for parking in the grocery store's parking lot, provided you spend at least $20 in the store. When you leave our parking facility, simply show your sales receipts to the attendant at the gate. In addition, please note that the parking spaces beside the elevators on all levels of the facility are reserved for the physically disabled. Individuals wishing to park in these spaces must have a valid government permit clearly displayed in the window of their vehicles.

Questions 74-76 refer to the following telephone message.

호주식 발음

Ms. Sandberg, this is Carter Malek calling from your bank. I'd like to notify you that you qualify for a new credit card. Based on your account activity and income level, we'd like to offer you the Gold Card with a $10,000 limit. Apart from the limit, it provides you with 3% cash back on every purchase. Also, you will be eligible for exclusive sales from our wide range of partners. This includes the Grandor Hotel Group and Americana West Airways. All we need is your authorization, and you will receive the card within five business days. You've been pre-approved for this process. Please call me back at 555-5044. Thank you.

Questions 77-79 refer to the following introduction.

캐나다식 발음

How's everyone enjoying the music so far? Um, our next performer is making his second appearance at the Salem Blues Festival. He was here seven years ago—the very first time this event was held—and his performance was one of the festival's highlights. At that time, Philip Waterfield was accompanied by five bandmates, but today he'll be appearing on stage all by himself to promote his record, which came out in April.

He doesn't play live much anymore, so this is certainly a special occasion. Ladies and gentlemen, put your hands together for Mr. Waterfield.

Questions 80-82 refer to the following telephone message.

호주식 발음

This message is for Blong Vang in response to his recent inquiry regarding his reservation with StarQuest Voyages. Mr. Vang, our records indicate that there might be a problem with the cruise you booked for June 14 to 21. You asked for a Standard cabin, which includes a twin-size bed. However, in the "special request" section, you left a note saying that you require a queen-size mattress. Well, Premier cabins include queen-size beds. Images of these accommodations are included in the digital brochure e-mailed to you last week. If this cabin type is satisfactory, please let us know as soon as possible so that your booking and billing statement can be updated.

Questions 83-85 refer to the following announcement.

미국식 발음

Attention, please. Due to technical difficulties with our sound system, there's going to be a change to today's main event at the Recreational Fishing Expo. Shawn Murray, the host of the television show *Catch and Release*, will still appear at the scheduled time of 2:30 P.M. However, his talk on the impact of technology on amateur fishing will be taking place in the ballroom rather than the auditorium. If you want to get a seat, you may want to head to the ballroom 10 or 15 minutes beforehand. Otherwise, there should be plenty of standing room. Thanks for your understanding.

Questions 86-88 refer to the following recorded message.

호주식 발음

You've reached Enderby Ice Rink after regular business hours. If you'd like to use our facility for ice skating, we are open to the public daily between 1 P.M. and 4 P.M. If you don't have your own skates, you can pay $5 an hour to use a pair. Those under the age of 12 can enter at no charge. To hear when the high school hockey matches will be held at our facility throughout the month, please press one now. Otherwise, have a pleasant day.

Questions 89-91 refer to the following radio broadcast.

영국식 발음

Hello, and welcome to *Science Nation* on Radio 109. For today's episode, I'll be talking to Lucy Mayfield, a marine biologist and this year's winner of the prestigious Research Foundation Prize. Ms. Mayfield is here to discuss her research on the impact of warming oceans on ocean life. Specifically, she will explain the various ways that warmer water is harming the coral and fish species that live there. It should be a very educational conversation. Ms. Mayfield will also take questions from the audience, though only a few. She'll be leaving at noon to give a seminar. Okay. Here we go!

Questions 92-94 refer to the following talk.

3▥ 캐나다식 발음

OK, everyone, please gather around. This room marks the final portion of your tour of author Leo Edmund's house. As you can see, this was his personal office, and he completed a fair amount of his writing here. As with the living room, bedrooms, and dining room, this is a very modest space considering Mr. Edmund's wealth. The only exception is the fine leather armchairs, which are actually quite famous. They were gifted to Mr. Edmund by King Ferdinand in 1877. Now, on the desk under some protective glass, you'll notice a few pages from Mr. Edmund's journal. I suggest taking a look at them.

Questions 95-97 refer to the following telephone message and map.

3▥ 미국식 발음

Hello, Mr. Franklin. This is Trina Johnson calling from Streubl Dentistry. I'd like to confirm your appointment with Dr. Streubl at 9:30 A.M. tomorrow. We are located downtown at 733 North Monroe Street, right across from the park. Please arrive at least 20 minutes early so you have enough time to fill out all the necessary forms. We advise taking public transportation as it's quite challenging to find a parking spot around our building. Also, please bring your insurance card with you. If you have any questions, call us at 555-0498. Thank you.

Questions 98-100 refer to the following excerpt from a meeting and list.

3▥ 호주식 발음

Next Sunday is our art gallery's 20th anniversary, and I want to celebrate this milestone by honoring artists who have been crucial to our success along the way. That's why we'll be hosting a temporary exhibit that day. It'll feature pieces from the first people who showed their work here. I've already coordinated with the artists, and aside from Lola Hays's piece, all of their work has been delivered to our facility, including paintings and sculptures by Mark Rubin and others. I, uh, plan to put up an announcement about the event on our Web site this afternoon. I'm hoping for a large turnout.

TEST 04 스크립트

PART 1

1   캐나다식 발음

(A) He is washing some clothing.
(B) He is emptying some cabinets.
(C) He is bending toward some dishware.
(D) He is closing a machine door.

2   영국식 발음

(A) They are conversing in a gallery.
(B) They are admiring some artwork.
(C) They are painting on a canvas.
(D) They are pointing at a picture.

3   미국식 발음

(A) An aircraft is on a runway.
(B) Some passengers are boarding an airplane.
(C) An airport is being renovated.
(D) Some people are standing in an auditorium.

4   호주식 발음

(A) Trees are being planted in large pots.
(B) Bricks are stacked near an entrance.
(C) Furniture is positioned outside a building.
(D) Umbrellas are being installed on tables.

5   캐나다식 발음

(A) A woman is fixing a wheelbarrow.
(B) A woman is pulling on a handle.
(C) A woman is chopping some wood.
(D) A woman is reaching into a shed.

6   미국식 발음

(A) An outdoor patio area is being used.
(B) A hallway leads to a kitchen.
(C) Some coffee mugs are in a sink.
(D) Some cups have been set on shelves.

PART 2

7   호주식 발음 → 미국식 발음

Who is the vice president going to be replaced by?
(A) Someone from another branch.
(B) Edwin Jones is on my team.
(C) It's time to replace this computer.

8   영국식 발음 → 캐나다식 발음

Where should I take this business suit to have it dry-cleaned?
(A) Our hotel has a laundry service.
(B) I'm not sure which jacket to buy.
(C) The room will be thoroughly cleaned.

9   호주식 발음 → 영국식 발음

When are you going to get your passport renewed?
(A) By transferring at Boston International Airport.
(B) Please write down the password.
(C) Hopefully, sometime this week.

10   미국식 발음 → 캐나다식 발음

Did Mr. Mason check the loading dock for the delivery?
(A) He's down there now.
(B) Yes, it was nice to meet you.
(C) For moving the heavy box.

11   영국식 발음 → 호주식 발음

Are you ready to go for a cup of coffee?
(A) No. I need a few more minutes.
(B) That comes to $3.99.
(C) OK, I'll prepare the report.

12   영국식 발음 → 캐나다식 발음

Where did you meet Professor Klein?
(A) A university instructor.
(B) We became acquainted at a conference.
(C) Wherever you want to dine.

13   호주식 발음 → 미국식 발음

Why do I need to take the stairwell to the second floor?
(A) The building has nine floors.
(B) Maintenance is being done on the elevator.
(C) You don't have to stay for the meal.

14   캐나다식 발음 → 영국식 발음

Do you want to receive a discount today or a voucher to use later?
(A) Yes. It's valid until July 30.
(B) Not for quite a while.
(C) I'll go with the second option.

15. 미국식 발음 → 캐나다식 발음

How likely is it that the flight to Singapore will be canceled?
(A) It's not on our route.
(B) That's what I like about her.
(C) At this point, it's almost certain.

16. 호주식 발음 → 영국식 발음

Will a technician move our fax machine later today?
(A) Some of their equipment was sent back.
(B) He should arrive soon.
(C) Tomorrow is supposed to be quite nice.

17. 호주식 발음 → 미국식 발음

Where can I get some advice about investment strategies?
(A) I'd recommend looking online.
(B) Yes, you should invest.
(C) The bank manager took them.

18. 캐나다식 발음 → 미국식 발음

How about postponing the presentation until the CEO arrives?
(A) No, I didn't hear the phone ring.
(B) I printed handouts for everybody.
(C) OK. I'll begin when she gets here.

19. 영국식 발음 → 호주식 발음

I'd like to incorporate a slide show presentation into my speech.
(A) The keynote speaker was excellent.
(B) A projector will have to be set up.
(C) For a major corporation.

20. 미국식 발음 → 캐나다식 발음

Manufacturing our clothing in America would be more expensive than importing it from China, right?
(A) I haven't analyzed the difference.
(B) While reading the export agreement.
(C) Well, you should try them on first.

21. 미국식 발음 → 호주식 발음

Aren't the interns attending a training session tomorrow afternoon?
(A) Have they been notified?
(B) It is a three-month internship.
(C) The training was a success.

22. 캐나다식 발음 → 미국식 발음

Cameron is studying to become an accountant, isn't he?
(A) That's right.
(B) I lost count.
(C) Check your account balance.

23. 영국식 발음 → 호주식 발음

Should I start working as a freelancer, or should I remain at my current company?
(A) As long as it's for free.
(B) Being self-employed can be stressful.
(C) You should promote him.

24. 캐나다식 발음 → 영국식 발음

When would you like me to schedule your next appointment?
(A) How about one week from now?
(B) Make a point of stopping by soon.
(C) No, at Dr. Blaise's clinic.

25. 미국식 발음 → 캐나다식 발음

I seem to have misplaced my office security badge.
(A) Set it down any place you want.
(B) You might want to let our supervisor know.
(C) The guard was hired in April, I believe.

26. 미국식 발음 → 호주식 발음

Would you hold the front door open for me?
(A) Once I get back from Spain.
(B) I've got a strong grasp of the subject.
(C) Sure, let me give you a hand.

27. 호주식 발음 → 영국식 발음

I'm trying to find my way to Grosvenor Station.
(A) Let me point it out on this map.
(B) Just leave it on the train.
(C) Thanks for dropping me off.

28. 영국식 발음 → 캐나다식 발음

Should I order protective equipment for the new workers?
(A) I don't think they were locked.
(B) Yes, after finding out their sizes.
(C) The amounts were almost equal.

29. 미국식 발음 → 호주식 발음

Mr. Richter is taking inventory of our surplus merchandise, isn't he?
(A) That's usually done on Sundays.
(B) These necklaces are selling quite well.
(C) Oh, any extra funding will be saved.

30. 캐나다식 발음 → 미국식 발음

How many hours did you spend practicing with the choreographer?
(A) We're scheduled to arrive this evening.
(B) Only two of the trainers could come.
(C) Honestly, I haven't been keeping track.

31 3⃞ 영국식 발음 → 호주식 발음

Are insurance policies for motorcycles available through this agency?
(A) A list of procedures is hanging in the break room.
(B) We cover every kind of personal vehicle.
(C) Throughout most of King National Park.

PART 3

Questions 32-34 refer to the following conversation.

3⃞ 캐나다식 발음 → 미국식 발음

M: Congratulations on completing your training period, Fiona. Everyone at the health center appreciates all the effort you've put in over the past month. How are things going from your perspective?

W: Thanks, Mr. Simmons. I'm quite happy, actually. The environment here is much more relaxed than the law office I worked at previously.

M: Great. That brings me to my other question . . . Would you be willing to do some overtime next month? Jack has booked some vacation time, so we need another receptionist to cover for him on Saturdays.

W: Um, that might be OK. I'll let you know for sure tomorrow.

Questions 35-37 refer to the following conversation.

3⃞ 호주식 발음 → 영국식 발음

M: Hello, welcome to Rick's Car Lot. How can I help you?

W: Um . . . I'm looking for a new vehicle that can accommodate my family. I have four children.

M: We definitely have cars that meet your needs. This right here is a Newman station wagon, which has six seats. It also has a four-wheel drive system.

W: How many miles per gallon does it get?

M: About 30, which is pretty good for this type of car.

W: That sounds fine. Do you think I could take it for a short test drive?

M: Of course. Please just give me a moment, and I'll be back soon.

Questions 38-40 refer to the following conversation with three speakers.

3⃞ 미국식 발음 → 호주식 발음 → 영국식 발음

W1: Welcome to the Easton Electronics Service Center.

M: Hi. The lens on my digital camera is cracked, and I'd like to get it fixed. I bought it last June.

W1: OK. But as the one-year warranty has expired, you'll have to pay for the full cost of the repairs.

M: Really? Yesterday, I stopped by the store I bought

it from, and I was assured that it was still under warranty.

W2: Excuse me, but did you say you bought it last June?

M: Yes.

W2: Then it is still covered. We offered a two-year extended warranty for that model as a special offer last year.

W1: Oh, I didn't realize that. In that case, sir, I'll just need you to complete this form.

Questions 41-43 refer to the following conversation.

3⃞ 미국식 발음 → 캐나다식 발음

W: Don Stevens from the IT department just told me that a new operating system will be installed on all company computers next Thursday beginning at 10 A.M.

M: How long will the work take?

W: About an hour . . . We'll need to find something for our team members to do during that period.

M: I'll schedule a training workshop for that morning in the conference room.

W: Thanks. One more thing . . . Mr. Stevens asked that everyone disable their computer passwords so that his technicians can access the devices.

M: OK. I'll send an e-mail now to the people on our team telling them to do this.

Questions 44-46 refer to the following conversation.

3⃞ 호주식 발음 → 영국식 발음

M: So, Ms. Greenly, where would you like me to take you next?

W: 449 King Street. I have an 11 A.M. appointment scheduled with a few SoundDrive executives to talk about a series of television commercials they want to create.

M: I'll head there right away. And would you like me to wait in front of the building until you're done?

W: No. You can take your lunch break as I expect to be there for a few hours. I'll call you as soon as I'm finished, and you can return for me then.

Questions 47-49 refer to the following conversation with three speakers.

3⃞ 호주식 발음 → 영국식 발음 → 미국식 발음

M: Do you think we chose the right wallpaper? The walls seem a little dark now. Our client wants this room to be bright and cheerful.

W1: I think it'll be fine once we install the new lights. What about you, Anne?

W2: I agree. And this project is over budget anyway, so we can't make any unnecessary changes. By the way, do either of you know where my tape measure is?

W1: It's in the bedroom.

W2: Thanks. I want to double-check the width of this window before we order the curtains.

M: Good idea. While you do that, I'll visit the furniture store. We still need to find a couch to put in the living room.

Questions 50-52 refer to the following conversation.

캐나다식 발음 → 영국식 발음

M: Anita, a man told me he's having trouble using one of the gas pumps. Could you provide him with some assistance? He's wearing a brown coat. I need to stay at the cash register.

W: I was going to put some bags of chips on the shelves, but I can do that afterward. Did the man give you any more specific information about his issue?

M: He's having trouble paying with his credit card. My guess is that he's putting it in backwards. Why don't you try swiping it one more time? If that doesn't work, then maybe the card's magnetic strip is damaged.

Questions 53-55 refer to the following conversation.

호주식 발음 → 미국식 발음

M: Mandy, do you have any plans for Saturday evening? The Milford Cinema is showing Paul Dorn's latest movie.

W: That sounds wonderful. What time do you want to meet? I'm supposed to go to a museum with a friend from 3 to 5 P.M., but I'll be free after that.

M: I was thinking of going at 8 P.M. I'm having dinner with some colleagues that night, but we should be finished before then.

W: OK. I'll meet you at the theater at that time. And don't worry about the tickets . . . I'll order them online today. You paid when we went to the amusement park last month, so it's my treat.

Questions 56-58 refer to the following conversation.

미국식 발음 → 캐나다식 발음

W: Jordan, you know you're responsible for making a chocolate cake, right? Some very important customers have made a reservation for tonight, and they've requested a fresh cake be prepared.

M: Yes, I know. I measured the sugar, butter, salt, and cocoa powder a few minutes ago. However, the flour jar on the counter is empty, so I can't finish preparing the ingredients.

W: There's a bag in the pantry. You'll see it just to the right of the door.

M: Oh, OK. Since I'm new here, I wasn't sure where to look. I'll go get it now.

Questions 59-61 refer to the following conversation.

호주식 발음 → 영국식 발음

M: Welcome to Central Hardware. Can I help you find anything?

W: Yes. I have a wood fence around my property, and I would like to coat it with something to protect it from the rain. Do you have any suggestions?

M: Colman Wood Stain is a good brand. It's easy to apply and not very expensive.

W: Great. Um, I don't know how much to buy, though. I wrote down the fence measurements in a notebook, but I forgot it at home.

M: We're open until 7, so you have time to go home and get it. Once I know the size of the fence, I can tell you how much of the product you'll need.

Questions 62-64 refer to the following conversation and flowchart.

영국식 발음 → 캐나다식 발음

W: Sorry I'm late. Todd Benson from Prime Appliances phoned to ask when he can expect to receive his next shipment of microwaves from us. Anyway, what do you want to talk about?

M: Our factory's quality-control protocol. Numerous managers have complained that the process takes too long. This flowchart breaks down the various steps involved.

W: Hmm . . . How might we improve it?

M: I think random product sampling is unnecessary. Any problems discovered during this stage would be found during performance testing anyway.

W: That's true. Let's get rid of that step, then. I'll announce the change later this morning when I tell employees about the new warehouse that will be built next year.

Questions 65-67 refer to the following conversation and seating chart.

캐나다식 발음 → 미국식 발음

M: There's been a last-minute change to our seating chart for tonight's Writer's House Award Ceremony.

W: How come?

M: Apparently, Gregory Grimes, the director of the Writer's House Foundation, recently sprained his ankle. He has asked to be seated at a table that is easy to access.

W: OK. I will move him from the one directly in front of the stage to the one closest to the entrance.

M: Yes, that'll definitely be more convenient.

W: Right. Now, I need you to wait near the entrance. When Mr. Grimes arrives, please tell him about the relocation once he has a chance to check his coat.

3ᵢₗ 영국식 발음 → 호주식 발음

W: Mr. Rolling just informed me that one of our training sessions tomorrow has to be moved to the afternoon so the new staff can take a tour of the factory.

M: I say we reschedule the session beginning at 9 o'clock. The material is quite complicated, and we would have more time to cover it if we held the workshop later in the day.

W: I was thinking we should postpone the one on warehouse regulations, but we can go with your suggestion. On a side note, did you make the instructional booklet for the quality-control session?

M: Yeah. It's in my office.

W: Excellent. Please go and get it now. I'll wait for you in the conference room.

PART 4

Questions 71-73 refer to the following talk.

3ᵢₗ 호주식 발음

Hello, everyone. Now that we've departed from Vancouver, I'd like to quickly explain some things to you all. Our ferry ride to Sydney is going to last about an hour and a half. Passengers are asked to remain on the second level of the ferry, where there is plenty of seating. The tour bus will be parked on the lower parking level, but won't be accessible during the ferry trip. Now, keep your eyes open for humpback whales while we travel. Over 100 live in the area, so you're likely to see at least one.

Questions 74-76 refer to the following excerpt from a meeting.

3ᵢₗ 미국식 발음

Next on the agenda for this month's meeting is the issue of package deliveries. As you all know, our apartment building will soon be changing its security policy, and delivery people will no longer be allowed to go past the lobby. Consequently, a new system is needed to make sure you all get your packages. Beginning next month, our daytime receptionist will accept parcels on everyone's behalf and leave a slip in individuals' mail slots notifying them about the delivery. Items can be retrieved at the front desk at residents' convenience.

Questions 77-79 refer to the following announcement.

3ᵢₗ 캐나다식 발음

Hey, everyone. Can I have your attention for a moment? I want to let you know that workers will be stopping by our law firm to make some repairs. After Sandra Boyd cleared out her belongings in preparation for her move to our Dallas branch, some water damage was discovered in her old office. Anyway, the workers will locate the source of the leak, and replace a section of a wall. The work will likely be very noisy, so we have scheduled it for Saturday afternoon.

Questions 80-82 refer to the following telephone message.

3ᵢₗ 호주식 발음

Andrew Cummings, my name is Matthew Schmitt, and I'm contacting you on behalf of Gladstone Bank. Two weeks ago, we mailed you a notice about your car loan, but you missed your scheduled monthly payment of $220. As a result, a surcharge of $20 will be added to the fee. Please pay the new total by this Friday. You can do so online or over the phone. Meeting this deadline will prevent further penalties. If you have any questions about the matter, you can reach me directly at 555-8342. Thank you.

Questions 83-85 refer to the following introduction.

3ᵢₗ 미국식 발음

That was a wonderful speech that Jason Ferguson just gave. Um . . . the next part of tonight's program is the presentation of the Career Achievement Award. Each year at this gathering, we honor a member of our industry who has raised the standards of journalism through many years of hard work. This year, our association has decided to recognize an individual who started out as a reporter and went on to write articles for news magazines. Please congratulate the winner, Emmanuel Walker.

Questions 86-88 refer to the following telephone message.

3ᵢₗ 캐나다식 발음

Good morning, Ms. Prescott. It's Adam Morris from Oakridge Pools calling. Sorry for not returning your call yesterday, but I was tied up preparing a site for a final inspection. Anyway, I want to let you know about a change related to your pool. Last Wednesday, I told you I need to put off the project because the tiles for the pool's edge weren't available until next month. Well, there was a miscommunication with my supplier. The shipment is scheduled to arrive tomorrow. If you're okay with it, my crew members will head over to your property on Thursday morning. One of them will give you the initial invoice.

Questions 89-91 refer to the following report.

3ᵢₗ 영국식 발음

In sports news, the Bridgeport Rockets will play the Greenville Tigers at 4 P.M. on August 18 in the championship game of the New England Soccer League Finals. There's a lot of interest in this match, and it has already sold out. During an interview on *Weekly Sports Update* last week, David Polanski, the coach of the Rockets, said that his team has signed several highly skilled players this season, which will give it an advantage. I will talk a bit about them after a brief message from our sponsor. Stay tuned.

Questions 92-94 refer to the following advertisement.

[3] 호주식 발음

Do you experience frequent fatigue or stress? Try AdaptoPro, a newly released protein powder from Superherbal. Its name comes from a powerful herb called Adaptogen, which provides both mental and physical benefits. That's why the powder has gotten favorable reviews from a variety of health magazines and Web sites. For a limited time, this product is available for 40 percent off. On top of that, all of our other protein powders are also 10 percent off during the month of June. Take advantage of this offer while supplies last. This will not happen again for a while.

Questions 95-97 refer to the following excerpt from a meeting and chart.

[3] 영국식 발음

The latest version of the MarbleBot is our best-selling smartphone ever. Like our previous models in this line, it has a fast processor and an advanced camera. But customers have been really impressed by the new fingerprint sensor. They also appreciate the long battery life. Even our device's main competitor only has an active battery life of about 15 hours, so we're well ahead in that respect. And for those who haven't heard, GadgetAssessor.com recently released its latest series of product ratings. Among a list of a dozen cell phones, the MarbleBot was ranked No. 1. The technology blog is highly respected, so this is great news. Let's figure out some creative ways to publicize this achievement.

Questions 98-100 refer to the following telephone message and inspection report.

[3] 캐나다식 발음

Ms. Witten, it's Ryan Tumbler from Lyndale Automotive. Since your family plans to drive from Phoenix to Las Vegas tomorrow, we're prioritizing repairs to your vehicle. As suspected, the exhaust pipe had a hole in it, and the brake pads were worn down. We've replaced those items, as you already said that was fine. Unfortunately, we discovered that another part needs to be replaced. However, the work will be quite costly, so I want to explain the problem to you. After that, you can decide if you want to proceed with repairs. Please call us back at your earliest convenience.

PART 1

1   영국식 발음
 (A) A woman is putting on a hat.
 (B) A woman is relaxing beneath some trees.
 (C) A woman is jogging along a trail.
 (D) A woman is skiing on the snow.

2   호주식 발음
 (A) The women are sipping their drinks.
 (B) The women are posing for a picture.
 (C) One of the women is setting up camera equipment.
 (D) One of the women is unwrapping a gift.

3   캐나다식 발음
 (A) Some people are exiting a greenhouse.
 (B) Bouquets are being sold at an outdoor market.
 (C) A customer is talking with a florist.
 (D) Women are browsing plants.

4   영국식 발음
 (A) An apron is hanging from a hook.
 (B) Shelves have been stocked with merchandise.
 (C) The man is buying items at a cash register.
 (D) The man is removing jars from a basket.

5   캐나다식 발음
 (A) Vehicles are on display at a dealership.
 (B) A multi-level structure surrounds a parking lot.
 (C) Windows overlook a garden area.
 (D) Water is spraying from a fountain.

6   미국식 발음
 (A) Some people are sitting on stones.
 (B) One of the people is walking up a hill.
 (C) An airplane is taking off from a runway.
 (D) Some pedestrians are photographing the jets.

PART 2

7   미국식 발음 → 캐나다식 발음
 When are you planning to revise the schedule?
 (A) If you can help me.
 (B) A daily work plan.
 (C) Later this afternoon.

8   영국식 발음 → 캐나다식 발음
 Who posted the recent announcement?
 (A) About a meeting.
 (B) The secretary did.
 (C) Yes, it's on the bulletin board.

9   호주식 발음 → 미국식 발음
 How do you usually get to the mall?
 (A) Only about 30 minutes.
 (B) I take a taxi.
 (C) To return some shoes.

10   영국식 발음 → 호주식 발음
 Excuse me. Is this seat taken?
 (A) It's not very comfortable.
 (B) I don't think so.
 (C) Please take only one pamphlet.

11   캐나다식 발음 → 미국식 발음
 A holiday promotion is being offered now, right?
 (A) The correct confirmation code.
 (B) Yes, I was promoted.
 (C) No, it starts this weekend.

12   영국식 발음 → 캐나다식 발음
 Where is the new art gallery going to be opened?
 (A) We close daily at 10 P.M.
 (B) In SoHo, most likely.
 (C) Art school was a great experience.

13   미국식 발음 → 호주식 발음
 How long are these batteries supposed to last?
 (A) Up to four months.
 (B) No, it was the first one I bought.
 (C) For my digital camera.

14   캐나다식 발음 → 미국식 발음
 Can you meet Mr. Lee at the train station?
 (A) You'd better hurry then.
 (B) Sorry, but my car is out of gas.
 (C) We trained for six weeks.

15   호주식 발음 → 영국식 발음
 What company are you writing for now?
 (A) The Leland Publishing Firm.
 (B) I sent him an e-mail about that.
 (C) I'm not sure they received the letter.

16 [캐나다식 발음 → 영국식 발음]

Have you been to the Thai restaurant next to the subway station?
(A) Sure. I can recommend several.
(B) A chef will be arriving shortly.
(C) Not yet, but I'd like to go.

17 [호주식 발음 → 미국식 발음]

Why aren't employees getting bonuses this quarter?
(A) Yes, sometime in December.
(B) Because the company can't afford it.
(C) A promotion as well.

18 [캐나다식 발음 → 영국식 발음]

When do you expect to begin staff evaluations?
(A) Oh, probably not until next Monday.
(B) I'll be leaving at 7 o'clock.
(C) We don't expect any problems.

19 [미국식 발음 → 캐나다식 발음]

Who was the keynote speaker at the agricultural conference?
(A) Mr. Lowe is talking to some clients.
(B) The owner of an organic farm.
(C) At an agricultural association.

20 [영국식 발음 → 호주식 발음]

The flavors in the main dish are a bit too strong.
(A) I agree. They're not to my taste.
(B) These dishes must be rinsed off very well.
(C) When will you graduate from culinary school?

21 [캐나다식 발음 → 미국식 발음]

When did you begin accepting applications for the analysis job?
(A) Through the newspaper review.
(B) Not long ago.
(C) An important research grant.

22 [호주식 발음 → 미국식 발음]

This business plan summary turned out extremely well.
(A) Yes, it's very thorough.
(B) Why does it keep turning off?
(C) The planning committee is running late.

23 [영국식 발음 → 캐나다식 발음]

Why don't we have the staff outing at the end of May?
(A) We didn't take any time off.
(B) Have they handed them out yet?
(C) I think we should have it later.

24 [미국식 발음 → 호주식 발음]

Hasn't the museum put up some additional displays?
(A) I've never seen this play.
(B) This is a great exhibition.
(C) They're being set up at the moment.

25 [호주식 발음 → 영국식 발음]

The ferry departs from the pier at 5 P.M. precisely.
(A) You'll have to ask the ticketing agent.
(B) That's only an hour from now.
(C) An announcement for passengers.

26 [캐나다식 발음 → 영국식 발음]

The benefit concert was quite impressive, wasn't it?
(A) I'm looking forward to it also.
(B) It was well-organized.
(C) We are concerned about it too.

27 [미국식 발음 → 캐나다식 발음]

Are we hiring a photographer for the product demonstration event?
(A) Do you think we need one?
(B) We'll need more projectors.
(C) You can find additional products on the shelves.

28 [호주식 발음 → 영국식 발음]

Can I get you anything to eat or drink?
(A) On the back of the menu.
(B) Actually, I'll wait until my friend arrives.
(C) No, the lounge was very neat.

29 [호주식 발음 → 미국식 발음]

Has the supply store's delivery van been repaired?
(A) Yes, and it is already being used again.
(B) It has lots of storage space.
(C) Well, delivery will cost extra.

30 [캐나다식 발음 → 영국식 발음]

We need to hire professionals to clean the windows.
(A) They sent us a billing statement.
(B) Hang the sign a bit higher.
(C) I'll inquire about services.

31 [미국식 발음 → 호주식 발음]

Can you speak with Ms. Tanner, or should I call her?
(A) I can't remember what it's called.
(B) I think I'll just send her an e-mail.
(C) The contract information is in this file.

## PART 3

Questions 32–34 refer to the following conversation.

캐나다식 발음 → 영국식 발음

M: Good morning. I don't have a reservation, but I would like to rent a car for a couple of days. Do you have anything available?

W: We do. What size car are you looking for?

M: Something spacious enough for four people. Also, is it possible to get a vehicle with a large trunk? We have quite a bit of luggage.

W: Of course. The CX2 sedan seats five people comfortably and has plenty of storage space. If you're interested in that vehicle, we can begin filling out the necessary paperwork. I'll just need to see your credit card and driver's license in order to proceed.

Questions 35–37 refer to the following conversation.

미국식 발음 → 캐나다식 발음

W: Spectrum Color Services. This is Danielle, what can I do for you today?

M: Hello, I was wondering if you could tell me how much you charge to paint a living room.

W: That would depend on the size of the room and the type of paint you choose. If you can give me that information, I could provide you with an estimate.

M: Well, I just want basic white paint, but I'm not certain about the size of the room. I'll go measure it right now and call you back in about 10 minutes.

Questions 38–40 refer to the following conversation.

호주식 발음 → 미국식 발음

M: Welcome to the Coleman Community Center. How may I help you?

W: Hi. I'm interested in entering the center's annual writing competition. Um, in the short story category . . .

M: Okay. I should mention that the submission deadline has been moved ahead to June 7.

W: Oh, no. This is my really busy season. I doubt if I can make some time for this.

M: You might want to find some time anyway. The winning story will be published in *New Fiction*, and that magazine is sold across the country.

W: That does sound like a great opportunity. I'll think about it.

Questions 41–43 refer to the following conversation.

영국식 발음 → 호주식 발음

W: I'd like to discuss a recent assignment that you collaborated with the marketing team on.

M: No problem. Is there something specific you'd like to discuss?

W: Yes, there is. You included an incorrect location in this online advertisement. It states that there will be a sale at our Seattle branch on July 22. However, the sale is actually going to be at our Portland branch.

M: Really? I'm so sorry about that! I must have missed that while proofreading the advertisement. I will make the necessary changes to the advertisement immediately.

Questions 44–46 refer to the following conversation with three speakers.

영국식 발음 → 캐나다식 발음 → 미국식 발음

W1: Hey, Randy. Doesn't your shift start at 9 o'clock?

M: Yeah, I came in early this morning to unpack the Digi 5 game consoles. They just arrived, and we need to get them on the shelves.

W1: I see. Here . . . I'll help.

W2: Sorry to interrupt. I know we don't open for five more minutes, but some customers have already started to form a line at the door. They're here for the Digi 5.

W1: I was going to keep stocking the shelves after we opened, but we'd better finish soon if people are lined up.

M: Maybe one of us should ask Richard to give us a hand.

W2: I can do that.

M: Thanks. He should be in the storeroom.

Questions 47–49 refer to the following conversation.

미국식 발음 → 캐나다식 발음

W: Colson, the Winchester branch of our cinema will need more personnel for the summer. Maybe we should hire three additional employees for the evening and weekend shifts.

M: Yeah . . . This is the busiest time of the year. Could you make a job posting? Just include a brief description of the position and list our required qualifications.

W: Sure. I'll try to finish it before I break for lunch.

M: That'd be ideal. I'll review it when you are finished, and then add it to our company Web site later this afternoon.

Questions 50–52 refer to the following conversation.

호주식 발음 → 영국식 발음

M: Hello, I'm calling to reserve three tickets for the Wild Animals guided tour at Jungle Wonderland this coming Saturday. How much will that cost?

W: It's $40 per person. The tour begins at 9 A.M. and will last two and a half hours.

M: Hmm . . . That's higher than I had expected. Have your rates changed recently? My friend went on the same tour last month, and she said it cost $32 per person.

W: She must have our Jungle Wonderland Annual Pass Card. Cardholders automatically receive a 20 percent discount on admission and tours in the wildlife preserve for a year.

Questions 53-55 refer to the following conversation.

3)) 캐나다식 발음 → 미국식 발음

M: Erin, I met up with our realtor a few hours ago. He showed me a vacant space that would be perfect for our recording studio.

W: Was the unit in a building on Ferguson Avenue? If so, I received an e-mail from him about the vacancy last night.

M: Yes, that's the one. The space has a very practical layout. Plus, there is enough room for a reception area and a private office. I was even introduced to the owner of the building, Janet Davidson. She was quite welcoming and professional.

W: That sounds promising. Would you arrange another showing for tomorrow? I'd like to see the property too.

Questions 56-58 refer to the following conversation.

3)) 호주식 발음 → 미국식 발음

M: Have you loaded the scuba gear into the boat yet? We need enough equipment to take 10 people on a diving trip.

W: Yeah, but I discovered a crack in one of the masks.

M: Really? That's a problem since the other dive group has taken all the spare ones with them.

W: Hmm . . . Splash World, the dive supply shop, is really close to here. If they have any in stock, I can go pick one up. Why don't you give them a call and see if they have what we need?

M: Good idea! I'll get right on that. Only . . . do you know the store's phone number?

W: No, but I bet Reggie does.

Questions 59-61 refer to the following conversation with three speakers.

3)) 호주식 발음 → 미국식 발음 → 캐나다식 발음

M1: Marian and Steven, we're getting fewer and fewer customers every month. We need to do something about our restaurant.

W: Well, I think we should introduce some vegetarian dishes. A lot of people are concerned about their health, and there are no nearby restaurants offering vegetarian options.

M2: I agree. Everything we serve has meat.

M1: Okay. I'll talk to our chefs to start gathering ideas for new dishes. Then, Steven, can you review the results of the questionnaire we asked our customers to fill out last month?

M2: Sure. I remember that there were some

suggestions about ingredients we should use.

W: I can help you with that.

Questions 62-64 refer to the following conversation and map.

3)) 영국식 발음 → 캐나다식 발음

W: Josh, I'm sorry, but I forgot the lawn chairs. I thought they were in my car, but I must have left them at home.

M: Then, why don't we sit in front of the musical fountain instead of in the picnic area? I saw some benches there that we could use.

W: Good idea. I really don't want to sit on the grass.

M: Me neither. Um, before we head over there, I'll stop by the information center to find out what time the fireworks start. It's right beside the parking lot.

W: Okay. While you do that, I'll buy us some bottles of water.

Questions 65-67 refer to the following conversation and building directory.

3)) 미국식 발음 → 호주식 발음

W: Excuse me. I'm scheduled to meet with Harvey Pinkerton. However, the office listed for him on the directory here in the lobby is incorrect. I went up to the second floor, but someone else was using that office.

M: Oh, I'm very sorry for the inconvenience. Mr. Pinkerton was recently transferred from marketing to sales, so he moved to another floor.

W: I see . . . Well, where is his new office?

M: He's in Mr. Olsen's old office, which is down the hall and to the right.

W: OK, I'll head there now. Thanks.

Questions 68-70 refer to the following conversation and floor plans.

3)) 캐나다식 발음 → 영국식 발음

M: I'm very happy to have you join our engineering firm, Ms. Doyle. You have a lot of experience designing Web sites, so I'm sure you will play an important role in our upcoming projects.

W: Well, I very much look forward to working here too.

M: Regarding your new office, we currently have four available spaces that you can choose from. Do you have any particular requirements for your workspace?

W: Well, I plan to hold regular meetings in my office with my team, so the bigger the better . . . Plus, a window would be nice.

M: We have one that should meet your needs. You can move your things in after I show you around our headquarters.

## PART 4

Questions 71-73 refer to the following advertisement.

[3ʷ] 미국식 발음

Join us at the Suarez Performing Arts Center for a one-evening performance by world-renowned violinist Wan Cheol Shin. Mr. Shin will perform an evening of classical pieces and modern works accompanied by the San Bernardo Symphony Orchestra. Recordings of Mr. Shin's music will be available for purchase after the concert. Doors for the concert open at 7:20 P.M. tomorrow, April 9. For tickets and reservations, please call the box office at 555-7219. Don't miss out on your chance to see Wan Cheol Shin performing live. Make your reservations today!

Questions 74-76 refer to the following announcement.

[3ʷ] 영국식 발음

Hi, everyone. As you may already know, we are closing down Bedford Tower next Friday. Several tenants of the building have complained about issues with ants and other insects, so we've hired a pest control company to perform the necessary work on that day. Since the building will be closed, only a few staff members will have to come into work that day. I will be here along with my assistant, who will accompany the workers throughout the building. Also, the maintenance staff will need to come in to clean up at the end of the day. The rest of you are in luck. I'll provide more details later today.

Questions 77-79 refer to the following talk.

[3ʷ] 영국식 발음

Good morning, and welcome to this seminar on European clothing trends. I will be your lecturer today. My name is Caroline LeGrand, and I head the design department at Tyler Sharp Apparel. I'm delighted to see such a large turnout here today, as I will be discussing a very interesting topic that affects everyone within the fashion industry. All of you were handed a copy of today's program, which outlines everything that will take place. The lecture should last about two hours and take us right into lunch at noon. Then, the afternoon session will get underway at 1 o'clock. For that segment, another fashion designer, Liv Holbein, will give a slide show presentation. OK, now let's begin.

Questions 80-82 refer to the following announcement.

[3ʷ] 미국식 발음

I have a quick announcement. After receiving a few complaints, I had a technician look at our old shredder this morning. It appears that there is a serious problem with its cutting blades, and it has effectively stopped working. I know this is a major inconvenience for you

all. However, I've contacted Mellor Supplies, and a delivery will be made this week. If you need to shred anything in the meantime, just use the one in the accounting department's office on the third floor. Staff there have been notified that some of you may make use of the machine. All right, that's all for now.

Questions 83-85 refer to the following telephone message.

[3ʷ] 캐나다식 발음

Hello. This is Tyrone Dyson calling from the city of Dallas's Department of Parks and Recreation. I received your message yesterday about possibly reserving the main room at the Pointer Park Community Center for a gathering on Saturday, September 2. Unfortunately, another group has already booked the space for that specific date you requested. However, I've contacted Dallas's other community center near Gleeson Park and was informed that they do have a space available at that time. If you are interested in booking that room, let me know. You can check out details and photos of the space by visiting www.dallasrecreation.gov. Thanks, and have a great day.

Questions 86-88 refer to the following talk.

[3ʷ] 호주식 발음

My name is Samir Nasser, and I'm a consultant and motivational speaker. I've been invited here by your employer to speak about how developing strong communication skills can improve your work life. As telemarketers for a software company, your ability to communicate with customers is obviously an essential part of your job. It enables you to express your thoughts clearly and concisely, which will in turn improve clients' confidence in you. But communication skills are not only important when it comes to increasing sales. They're also crucial for fostering healthy work relationships. In fact, the number one cause of workplace conflict is poor communication. To help prevent such issues, I'd like us all to participate in some activities together aimed at strengthening interactions between colleagues.

Questions 89-91 refer to the following news report.

[3ʷ] 영국식 발음

My name is Anita Busby, and you're tuned in to Channel 9 News. Today's top story is on Williamton's Citizen of the Year Award. This year's recipient is Maude Evans, owner of Gately Automotive Dealership right here in Williamton. Ms. Evans has been selected for the award in recognition of her charitable work in the Williamton community. Over the previous six months, she has devoted much of her personal time to collecting donations for Memorial Hospital and raising money to establish the city's first performing arts center. The award will be presented to Ms. Evans on September 22 at a dinner hosted by the Williamton City Council. The event will be attended by community leaders and city government officials.

Questions 92-94 refer to the following telephone message.

[3ᴗ] 호주식 발음

Sally, it's Richard Holsten. We need to find a location for our department's Christmas party. This morning, I called Golden China—the restaurant we discussed yesterday—but the manager said that 30 seats are not available on that day. They could host us if we broke up into smaller groups . . . but that's not really a good option. It'd be great if you could call the new place that opened on Jefferson Street—Jacob's Steak House. I heard they have a private party room. I'd contact the place myself, but I'm headed to the airport now. With the event coming up in only three weeks, we need to make a reservation as soon as possible.

Questions 95-97 refer to the following talk and illustration.

[3ᴗ] 영국식 발음

I'd like to share the latest updates regarding our fast food restaurant. For starters, we recently hired celebrity chef Dawn Rather to team up with our corporate chefs in order to improve our existing menu. As a result of the partnership, we've decided to offer preset food combinations to customers. Each one will feature a burger and a side dish. Of course, people can mix and match the burger styles and side options. For instance, they can change the barbecue burger and onion rings pairing to a barbecue burger and garden salad. Another important announcement is that we plan to redesign our logo. A replacement will be unveiled in July.

Questions 98-100 refer to the following broadcast and schedule.

[3ᴗ] 캐나다식 발음

Welcome to *Entertainment News*. The organizer of the annual Calgary Music Festival has announced an interesting addition to the lineup of daily headliners. The press release from Lisa Gomez, who is in charge of booking acts, stated that international superstar DJ James Money will join his former partner Karl Slocum for the first time in over a decade at the festival. This is very exciting news for local music lovers. Viewers interested in attending should purchase tickets soon, as they are likely to sell out quickly. A pass for the entire festival costs $49, while tickets for individual concerts cost $30. And remember, half of the proceeds will be donated to a local orphanage, so you will be supporting a worthy cause while enjoying some great music.

TEST 06 스크립트

* QR 코드로 바로가기

PART 1

1 🔊 캐나다식 발음
(A) She's taking off a face mask.
(B) She's examining a document.
(C) She's picking up an item from a desk.
(D) She's hanging up a phone.

2 🔊 미국식 발음
(A) Two people are working in a kitchen.
(B) One of the men is sharpening a knife.
(C) One of the men is opening a fridge.
(D) Two people are placing buns on a pan.

3 🔊 호주식 발음
(A) Trucks are parked in front of a building.
(B) Lines are being painted on a street.
(C) A cone is being set up on a road.
(D) A sign is attached to a vehicle.

4 🔊 영국식 발음
(A) The man is holding a paintbrush.
(B) A canvas has been put on an easel.
(C) A painting is being displayed in a gallery.
(D) They are writing on a blackboard.

5 🔊 미국식 발음
(A) The man is getting on a bicycle.
(B) Trees are growing along a path.
(C) Leaves are falling onto a trail.
(D) The man is putting on gloves.

6 🔊 호주식 발음
(A) Curtains are covering the windows.
(B) Cushions have been thrown on the floor.
(C) Lights have been fastened to the wall.
(D) Pictures are hanging above a couch.

PART 2

7 🔊 호주식 발음 → 영국식 발음
Is your train ticket still valid?
(A) I passed the shop yesterday.
(B) No, I need a new one.
(C) At the train station.

8 🔊 캐나다식 발음 → 미국식 발음
Why did you leave the second page of the report empty?
(A) It is five pages long.
(B) Sorry. The second floor is already occupied.
(C) I will finish it later.

9 🔊 영국식 발음 → 캐나다식 발음
Should I check on the patient now?
(A) The check is on the desk.
(B) Please. I don't have time myself.
(C) Yes, you seem to be getting better.

10 🔊 영국식 발음 → 호주식 발음
When can I expect the latest draft from you?
(A) By the end of the day.
(B) I expected worse.
(C) I was a bit late for the show.

11 🔊 미국식 발음 → 호주식 발음
How can I access the file on my phone?
(A) By charging it regularly.
(B) She already called back.
(C) Just install a mobile application.

12 🔊 캐나다식 발음 → 미국식 발음
Did you find out whom to contact regarding the travel expenses?
(A) I still haven't.
(B) Mr. Lee likes to travel by himself.
(C) I lost the keys yesterday.

13 🔊 영국식 발음 → 캐나다식 발음
How did you manage to get into the party?
(A) At a party planning service.
(B) Thank you for inviting me.
(C) We were on the guest list.

14 🔊 호주식 발음 → 미국식 발음
Who is responsible for the coffee machine maintenance?
(A) Ask Deborah on the third floor.
(B) One with some sugar.
(C) She is the main focus of the article.

15 캐나다식 발음 → 영국식 발음

Posting on social media might not result in enough publicity.
(A) I will go to the post office later.
(B) It's technically a social gathering.
(C) Why don't we talk to the chief marketing officer?

16 미국식 발음 → 캐나다식 발음

Isn't the executive team going to announce our new CEO today?
(A) Yes. At the shareholders' meeting.
(B) He definitely is a board member.
(C) It wasn't useful at all.

17 호주식 발음 → 영국식 발음

Could you help me with my presentation at some point today?
(A) Was Sally present at the meeting?
(B) I have some time after lunch.
(C) That's a good point.

18 캐나다식 발음 → 미국식 발음

Which song will you perform first at the concert tonight?
(A) The performance runs for 30 minutes.
(B) It's a top secret.
(C) Through a management firm.

19 호주식 발음 → 영국식 발음

The book will be translated into several languages, won't it?
(A) It has yet to be decided.
(B) I am currently enrolled in a Japanese class.
(C) Yes, it's the second edition.

20 영국식 발음 → 호주식 발음

Do you prefer a buffet, or would you rather have the meals served to your guests?
(A) Send me the list of preferences.
(B) I think the former is too casual.
(C) Their food is always the best.

21 미국식 발음 → 캐나다식 발음

Why hasn't Olivia responded to my message yet?
(A) Have you considered changing your phone case?
(B) She must be very busy this morning.
(C) Yes, I responded right away.

22 영국식 발음 → 미국식 발음

How many times have you revised the contract so far?
(A) I did not change anything after our last meeting.
(B) By following the revision guidelines.
(C) The lawyer will visit me soon.

23 호주식 발음 → 캐나다식 발음

What event venue do you like most?
(A) It's for an upcoming seminar.
(B) The one with the high ceiling.
(C) That's up to the event organizer.

24 미국식 발음 → 호주식 발음

What do you say to hiring additional part-timers for the weekends?
(A) But she doesn't have the proper degree.
(B) We're running short of budget.
(C) I don't really want to cook on Sundays.

25 영국식 발음 → 캐나다식 발음

The new advertising campaign will be revealed at the press conference.
(A) We produce two campaigns per year.
(B) Do you know who the presenter will be?
(C) I attended the conference last week.

26 호주식 발음 → 영국식 발음

Should I help you prepare the survey questions?
(A) I'd appreciate that.
(B) He was not prepared for the delay.
(C) I provided some detailed answers.

27 미국식 발음 → 호주식 발음

When do you land in Singapore exactly?
(A) That's what the captain just said.
(B) Roughly about a thousand dollars.
(C) The itinerary says midnight.

28 캐나다식 발음 → 영국식 발음

I am curious to hear the result of our new product test.
(A) They will certainly be put to the test.
(B) I'm honestly a little bit nervous.
(C) Were you satisfied with the results?

29 호주식 발음 → 미국식 발음

Could we add some more fashion influencers to the invitation list?
(A) The decision was influenced by a study.
(B) The fashion collection is out now.
(C) Just give me the names.

30 영국식 발음 → 캐나다식 발음

Where did you see the notice first?
(A) In the morning.
(B) I didn't notice a difference, actually.
(C) On a bulletin board downstairs.

🎧 캐나다식 발음 → 미국식 발음

Will the editorial be published both online and in print?
(A) Print three copies of the document.
(B) We are thinking of it as an online exclusive.
(C) By the editorial board.

PART 3

Questions 32-34 refer to the following conversation.

🎧 미국식 발음 → 호주식 발음

W: Hello, Mr. Yu. This is Brenda from the *Daily Denver Times* newspaper. At present, you only get our newspaper on the weekend. Are you interested in receiving it during the weekdays as well?

M: No. I barely even read the one on the weekend. I'm quite busy these days.

W: How about switching to the online version? You will get access to all the articles as well as premium content. It will cost you $2 more, but you can get two months for free.

M: That sounds like a great deal. But I recently got a new credit card, so I'll need to change my payment details. Can you do that for me now?

Questions 35-37 refer to the following conversation with three speakers.

🎧 캐나다식 발음 → 호주식 발음 → 영국식 발음

M1: I just spoke with a representative of the company we hired to renovate our gym. The work will take place from June 1 to 7.

M2: So we'll close for a week? We'd better give our members a discount to avoid any complaints.

W: I agree with you. But the new exercise machines we ordered won't arrive until June 10 . . . three days after the remodeling work finishes.

M2: That means we'll have to close again to install them.

W: Maybe we should postpone the renovation work so that the machines get here before we reopen. What do you think, Brandon?

M1: Good idea. Let me ask them if that is possible.

Questions 38-40 refer to the following conversation.

🎧 호주식 발음 → 미국식 발음

M: Do you have any brochures for local attractions?

W: Of course. They're on the rack behind you, right next to the tour map on the wall.

M: Thanks. I was planning to visit the National Museum this afternoon, but it seems to be closed. I thought it was open on holidays.

W: It usually is, but there's a fundraiser tonight. The museum employees need time to set everything up.

The exhibits will be open to the public again tomorrow, though.

M: I fly back to Boston in the morning. Um, can you recommend something fun to do around here?

W: Why don't you visit the market? It's just down the street.

M: That sounds interesting.

Questions 41-43 refer to the following conversation.

🎧 캐나다식 발음 → 영국식 발음

M: So, the sales department is looking to fill its manager position and would like us to find a suitable candidate.

W: Is there a chance of promotion from within the department, or are we expected to hire externally?

M: They want us to find someone new as soon as possible—by the end of the month, actually.

W: We may need more time.

M: They were pretty clear about the deadline. Maybe we should get our department head's opinion on the matter.

W: All right. Ms. Lewis just got back from a meeting, so she's probably in her office right now. Let's go talk to her.

Questions 44-46 refer to the following conversation.

🎧 미국식 발음 → 호주식 발음

W: Hi, Tom. This is Angela calling from the public relations department. I would like to get an update on the product launch. Is everything still set for next week?

M: Yes. I don't expect any delays. But, um, I'm worried about the lack of media interest. Do you think we should hold a launch party?

W: That's a good idea. I'll get Polly Mitchell to arrange it. She has a lot of experience with these types of events, so I'm sure it will be a success.

M: Great. And when her statement for the media is ready, please e-mail me a copy to review. Thanks.

Questions 47-49 refer to the following conversation.

🎧 캐나다식 발음 → 영국식 발음

M: Kathy, a customer asked me to order an out-of-stock printer, but I can't do that because I haven't been shown how. It's only my second day working at this store.

W: I'll take care of it. What's the name of the model?

M: It's the Lyson 635. She also mentioned that this product is advertised as being 15 percent off.

W: Right. But the sale ends tomorrow, so she needs to pay for the device now to get the discount. Um, tell her we'll deliver it to her home without any delivery fee and she can track the order online. If she has any questions, just let me know.

Questions 50-52 refer to the following conversation.

미국식 발음 → 호주식 발음

W: Hi, my name is Camilla Robertson. I'm here to pick up a new debit card. My old one expired last week.

M: Sure thing. Oh, and I should let you know that we are now offering the Gavin Premium Credit Card to our loyal customers. As long as you pay the full balance by the due date each month, you'll be exempted from interest for three months on new purchases. Are you interested?

W: It's a tempting offer, but I already have a credit card that I'm happy with.

M: No problem. But please consider taking one of the booklets about the credit card to look through at your convenience. Wait here, and I'll be back with your card.

Questions 53-55 refer to the following conversation.

호주식 발음 → 영국식 발음

M: Are all of the art pieces ready for the event?

W: Yes. I'm optimistic that the attendees will be eager to bid on them. We'll likely raise a lot of money from the sale of these works for the aid agencies we support.

M: That's good to hear. I'm worried about how much we're spending on catering and entertainment, though.

W: It's necessary to draw people to our event. Oh, that reminds me . . . Ms. Holmes has agreed to deliver the opening address.

M: Wonderful. She's such a talented artist, so people will be interested in hearing what she has to say.

W: I agree. I'll add this information to the event's homepage now.

Questions 56-58 refer to the following conversation with three speakers.

영국식 발음 → 캐나다식 발음 → 호주식 발음

W: I'm a little concerned about the Very-Berry soda our company released last month.

M1: It's a great beverage. I'm not sure why sales have been so low. What do you say, Brad?

M2: I'm pretty sure it's because of our TV commercial. It isn't really effective at attracting the attention of consumers.

M1: That would explain why we haven't seen more visitors to our official Web page or consumer reviews.

M2: Maybe we should consider using social media to promote our products rather than relying on TV ads.

W: That's going to be a major shift. Let's gather extra customer feedback before making a decision.

Questions 59-61 refer to the following conversation.

영국식 발음 → 캐나다식 발음

W: Did you ever contact Wave Seafood Restaurant about hosting our annual corporate party?

M: Yes. I called there this morning. The person I spoke with was very helpful. She said they can accommodate our anticipated headcount of 100 people, although that's their maximum capacity.

W: Well, 125 people are now expected to attend. I'm sorry, but you'd better keep looking.

M: Oh, I see. That's OK. I'm sure there are other places in Tampa that would work.

W: Also, Richard Seymore is coming. He has invested a lot of money into our technology firm. He is a vegetarian, so I want to make sure that special arrangements are made for him. Please don't forget.

Questions 62-64 refer to the following conversation and table.

미국식 발음 → 호주식 발음

W: Excuse me. A business class I enrolled in is only offered online. One of my friends suggested that I get a tablet computer for it.

M: Well, Wind SG is our best seller. It comes with a wireless charging pad.

W: Actually, I don't really care about that accessory. But I definitely need both a stylus and a detachable keyboard.

M: Then this one is perfect for you. And it's currently available at a 10 percent discount.

W: Great. Um, I saw a sign near the store entrance about getting a free pair of headphones with each purchase . . .

M: Unfortunately, this model doesn't qualify for that promotion. It's only for certain laptop brands.

Questions 65-67 refer to the following conversation and map.

영국식 발음 → 캐나다식 발음

W: Hi. My flight has been pushed back until tomorrow morning due to the typhoon. One of the airline employees said I should ask for a hotel recommendation at this information desk.

M: Sure. As you can see on this map, there are four in the area.

W: The Skyway Hotel and the Express Hotel seem to be the closest ones.

M: Hmm . . . do you have a car? Both are quite distant to walk to from here.

W: No. I already returned my rental.

M: In that case, I would suggest that you stay at the one farthest from the airport. It has a free shuttle bus. Just go through that door, and you will see the bus waiting.

W: Great. Thanks a lot.

Questions 68-70 refer to the following conversation and bill.

[3)] 영국식 발음 → 호주식 발음

W: Can I bring you anything else? Maybe some dessert?

M: No, thanks. I just need the check, please.

W: Of course. Here you go. I hope you enjoyed your meal this evening.

M: I did. I especially appreciated the jazz band that was playing. They made the dining experience very relaxing.

W: I'm glad you liked them. And keep in mind that we will be opening our patio for the summer soon. There is a great view of the river from there.

M: Thanks for letting me know. Oh, hold on . . . There seems to be an error with my bill. I didn't order a beverage.

W: I'm sorry, sir. I will remove that charge right away.

PART 4

Questions 71-73 refer to the following talk.

[3)] 영국식 발음

I'd like to begin by welcoming all of you to Whiteford Investment's 10th anniversary celebration. As the founder of this firm, I'm pleased to announce that we are finally going forward with our plan to open new branches in San Francisco. This expansion is the result of our success, which I believe is due to the great effort we make to serve our clients. And no one has demonstrated this commitment to our customers more than the head of our sales department, Michael Pearson. Before the food is served, he will say a few words about our plans for the coming year. Now, let's welcome him to the stage.

Questions 74-76 refer to the following advertisement.

[3)] 캐나다식 발음

Are you a business owner looking for a commercial space in downtown Houston? If so, consider Ventra Tower. Located on Briarwood Street right across from the Plaza Subway Station, this 15-story office building includes an underground parking facility and a state-of-the-art security system. The units come in sizes of up to 2,000 square meters and feature large windows and central air conditioning. Best of all, sign a five-year lease agreement, and you won't have to pay rent for the first two months. If you are interested, contact Ventra Management at 555-9029. Don't delay, though. We are already accepting applications.

Questions 77-79 refer to the following advertisement.

[3)] 미국식 발음

Travelers looking for inexpensive flights to destinations throughout the Western United States now have a new option! Rocky Mountain Air began providing service to 15 major population centers on June 10. Our goal is to provide our customers with amazing service at an affordable price. And to commemorate our first step, we are offering a 20 percent discount on all flights for the remainder of the summer. This offer will end on August 31, so don't miss out! To find out more about our company and to receive updates on fares and schedules, download our smartphone app today.

Questions 80-82 refer to the following telephone message.

[3)] 호주식 발음

Hi, Ms. Stevenson. It's Gareth Freemont from Freemont Brokerage. As we discussed in our meeting last weekend, we need to make an adjustment since there have been no responses to the listing of your business at $225,000. The EZ Clean on Elma Street sold for $190,000. If you are willing to make changes to the price, I believe we could find a buyer within a month or so. I have several potential buyers in my database who initially were interested. Let me know what you think. Thanks.

Questions 83-85 refer to the following talk.

[3)] 캐나다식 발음

Thank you everyone for coming today. Our hospital has always been a leader in medical education. To expand on this tradition, we will begin having our interns and residents participate in both theoretical and practical learning sessions under the direct supervision of department heads. Therefore, each of you will be personally responsible for creating a series of workshops and practice sessions. This will provide more direct opportunities for our new talent to learn. Please start brainstorming about what you would like to teach, and send me an outline next Monday. I will be around a bit longer for questions.

Questions 86-88 refer to the following announcement.

[3)] 미국식 발음

May I have everyone's attention, please? Unfortunately, the audition for the role of Peter Thompson in HFG Studio's film *Days of Summer* will start a bit later today than planned. I apologize for the delay, but we are experiencing technical difficulties with the sound system. Fortunately, it should be fixed by noon, so we will proceed as planned right after lunch. While we wait, I would like all of you to head upstairs. There, a photographer will take several pictures of you. The director asked to be provided with recent pictures of everyone to help him make a final decision.

Questions 89-91 refer to the following introduction.

[音] 영국식 발음

Welcome to Focus Incorporated's booth at the Delaware Technology Conference. I'd like to now introduce our company's latest product, the XPro II controller. Compatible with most console and PC games, this wireless device features completely programmable buttons and very responsive joysticks. In addition, we signed an agreement with Balefire Software last month to provide a free copy of Speed Run, their popular racing game, to anyone who purchases an XPro II. Visit www.focusincorporated.com to place an order. We guarantee that you will be satisfied with this controller. If not, don't worry. We are now offering a 15-day no-questions-asked return period. There's no risk involved.

Questions 92-94 refer to the following telephone message.

[音] 미국식 발음

Hello, Mr. Potter. This is Lydia Downing calling from Green Shields. We recently acquired Biomed Group and have been examining the insurance records of our new customers. Our goal is to ensure that everyone gets the best deal possible. As you often purchase short-term travel insurance, you are eligible to receive 20 percent off our Global Insurance Package. It provides comprehensive coverage in 33 countries for an entire year. If this appeals to you, consider checking a number of reviews from satisfied clients on our online page. If you have any questions or would like to sign up, you can reach me at 555-3939. Thank you.

Questions 95-97 refer to the following talk and catalog.

[音] 캐나다식 발음

I hope all of you enjoyed your visit to the museum and the art gallery this morning. You will now have about 30 minutes to buy some souvenirs. This gift shop offers a wide variety of items to remind you of your trip to Quebec. And if you are looking for a great gift for a friend or family member back home, I suggest buying one of the coffee mugs with the Canadian flag on it. They are very popular. Once you have paid for your purchase, head back to the bus in the parking lot. Um, we have a reservation at a traditional Canadian restaurant at 1 P.M., and we shouldn't be late.

Questions 98-100 refer to the following announcement and map.

[音] 호주식 발음

Attention, Oxlade Crossfit members. As workers will be repainting the walls, our gym's underground parking facility will be closed on May 15. Please note that other workout facilities will be accessible. To minimize the inconvenience, we have made an agreement to allow our customers to use a nearby parking lot. Simply show your membership card to one of the employees at our information desk to receive a complimentary parking pass. Then, give it to the parking attendant when you leave the lot. Keep in mind that the pass is only valid for May 15. The parking lot is located right next to Winston Bank, where Green Street and 8th Avenue intersect. Thank you.

TEST 07 스크립트

* 무료 해석은 해커스토익(Hackers.co.kr)에서
다운로드 받을 수 있습니다.

* QR 코드로
바로가기

PART 1

1 미국식 발음
   (A) She is giving a menu to a guest.
   (B) She is setting a table for a meal.
   (C) She is pouring water into a glass.
   (D) She is flipping a light switch.

2 호주식 발음
   (A) Some people are removing their hats.
   (B) Some people are filling up a basket.
   (C) One of the people is moving a food stall.
   (D) One of the people is kneeling on the sand.

3 캐나다식 발음
   (A) Some rope is hanging from a cliff.
   (B) Some people are camping near a mountain.
   (C) Climbing gear is being purchased.
   (D) A man is resting his hand on a rock.

4 영국식 발음
   (A) Reading materials have been placed on a rack.
   (B) A man is holding a pair of scissors.
   (C) One of the women is trimming a client's hair.
   (D) One of the women is sitting under a dryer.

5 호주식 발음
   (A) A road sign extends over multiple lanes.
   (B) Vehicles have been left in a parking lot.
   (C) A median divides a highway.
   (D) Traffic cones have been lined up along the street.

6 미국식 발음
   (A) The man is carrying some hand tools.
   (B) The man is digging a hole with a shovel.
   (C) Farming equipment is being put away.
   (D) There are structures at the edge of a field.

PART 2

7 캐나다식 발음 → 미국식 발음
   It isn't time for the training session yet, is it?
   (A) We have another half an hour.
   (B) Ms. Rodriguez is leading it.
   (C) I believe it's in the meeting room.

8 미국식 발음 → 캐나다식 발음
   Would you mind trading seats with me?
   (A) Sure, no problem at all.
   (B) Oh, up near the stage.
   (C) For a trading firm.

9 미국식 발음 → 호주식 발음
   What do you want me to bring you from the cafeteria?
   (A) I enjoy working as a cook.
   (B) Whatever you're eating.
   (C) I brought it back yesterday.

10 캐나다식 발음 → 미국식 발음
   Have you decided on a venue for the marketing convention?
   (A) The market is a major tourist attraction.
   (B) Yes, but not very much.
   (C) I can't find anything suitable.

11 영국식 발음 → 호주식 발음
   Do you know when our rehearsal is supposed to begin?
   (A) We'll start at noon.
   (B) The lead actress is Julie Stone.
   (C) It will be our rehearsal.

12 캐나다식 발음 → 미국식 발음
   Haven't you worked as a corporate lawyer?
   (A) Where is the law office?
   (B) Only for a few years.
   (C) Let's visit the headquarters.

13 영국식 발음 → 호주식 발음
   Who do I need to speak with about canceling my reservation?
   (A) The resort was just opened.
   (B) You need to call our booking department.
   (C) I have confirmed your stay.

14 캐나다식 발음 → 영국식 발음
   Why is the videoconference equipment turned on?
   (A) It was a very informative conference.
   (B) For another couple of hours.
   (C) The IT team is conducting a test on it.

15 ⟨♪⟩ 호주식 발음 → 영국식 발음
Where should I go to photocopy these forms?
(A) The print shop down the block.
(B) They need 10 pages.
(C) No, sign on the dotted line.

16 ⟨♪⟩ 미국식 발음 → 호주식 발음
Which cities will Ms. Arden be visiting during her upcoming trip?
(A) At a recent meeting.
(B) Everyone had a lot of fun.
(C) I haven't seen her itinerary.

17 ⟨♪⟩ 영국식 발음 → 캐나다식 발음
How did you learn to speak German so well?
(A) The speaker was very engaging.
(B) By taking classes in college.
(C) We didn't earn much.

18 ⟨♪⟩ 호주식 발음 → 영국식 발음
Where do you want to store these boxes of paper?
(A) For the office printers.
(B) I sent out for them.
(C) In the reception area for now.

19 ⟨♪⟩ 캐나다식 발음 → 미국식 발음
When should I print out the contract for you to review?
(A) He will sign the contract.
(B) Anytime this afternoon.
(C) No problem, just pick it up.

20 ⟨♪⟩ 호주식 발음 → 영국식 발음
These tables will have to be set for the banquet.
(A) Yes, I'm planning to come.
(B) Try adjusting the settings.
(C) How long will that task take?

21 ⟨♪⟩ 미국식 발음 → 캐나다식 발음
Aren't you conducting a safety inspection next week?
(A) Yes, we got a good evaluation.
(B) He works as a conductor.
(C) I'll have to check my schedule.

22 ⟨♪⟩ 영국식 발음 → 호주식 발음
Amy Tran is planning to travel overseas to consult clients, isn't she?
(A) He's our most loyal client.
(B) That's right. She's going to Chile.
(C) The test results still haven't come.

23 ⟨♪⟩ 캐나다식 발음 → 미국식 발음
I can drop you off at the airport this weekend.
(A) Only if it's convenient for you.
(B) Yes, from my travel agent.
(C) The files are quite important.

24 ⟨♪⟩ 호주식 발음 → 미국식 발음
We require receipts for all exchanges.
(A) To inquire about an event.
(B) You'll be pleased with this item.
(C) OK. I have mine with me.

25 ⟨♪⟩ 영국식 발음 → 호주식 발음
Do you want help analyzing the data you collected?
(A) No, Pete took care of that yesterday.
(B) Mr. Mack will distribute the programs.
(C) They're from the questionnaires.

26 ⟨♪⟩ 캐나다식 발음 → 영국식 발음
Why did you decide to rename your company?
(A) Customers really like that product.
(B) The previous name seemed outdated.
(C) It sells custom jewelry.

27 ⟨♪⟩ 미국식 발음 → 캐나다식 발음
Should I close the window, or do you want it open?
(A) Well, it is quite hot in here.
(B) I want to see it too.
(C) It's very close to my apartment.

28 ⟨♪⟩ 영국식 발음 → 호주식 발음
Could you put together a short presentation for the auto expo?
(A) The car is fully automatic.
(B) Just put them in the showroom.
(C) I think so, but not until Monday.

29 ⟨♪⟩ 미국식 발음 → 캐나다식 발음
What did the realtor say about the condominium?
(A) A property management firm.
(B) No serious offers have been made on it.
(C) The one located in Woodrow Tower.

30 ⟨♪⟩ 호주식 발음 → 미국식 발음
When is the office dress code going to go into effect?
(A) Let's discuss that at the morning meeting.
(B) Salespeople must wear black shirts.
(C) Our business address has not changed.

31 ⟨♪⟩ 영국식 발음 → 캐나다식 발음
The warehouse equipment has to be upgraded soon.
(A) They know where to go.
(B) The show should begin soon.
(C) But the forklift is only a year old.

PART 3

Questions 32-34 refer to the following conversation.

영국식 발음 → 호주식 발음

W: Good morning. Do you know who's responsible for editing our company's brochure for the upcoming trade fair? The manager wants to change some of the contact information in it, and he asked me to pass on his request to whoever is working on it.

M: Sorry, I'm not sure. But you should talk to Sun Nam. She's overseeing the team that will be attending the fair, so she can provide you with that information.

W: All right. I believe she will be out of the office until the early afternoon, but I'll speak with her once she returns. Thanks.

Questions 35-37 refer to the following conversation.

캐나다식 발음 → 미국식 발음

M: Hello. I purchased this set of plates here on Monday. When I got home and took them out of the box, I noticed that one of them is broken.

W: I can assist you with that. If you can provide proof of purchase, I would be happy to replace the set or give you a refund. Which would you prefer?

M: I'd like to get another set. However, before you complete the transaction, can I grab some wine glasses that I want to purchase as well?

W: Certainly. Just come back to the customer service desk once you're ready to check out.

Questions 38-40 refer to the following conversation.

영국식 발음 → 호주식 발음

W: Dennis, how much longer will it be until the entrées for Table 5 are ready?

M: At least 15 minutes. I'm . . . ah . . . I'm struggling to keep up with orders since we're short-staffed today.

W: I know it's not your fault, but the customers have been waiting for almost an hour . . . One of them just left.

M: Sorry, but I don't know what to tell you. I'm doing the best I can.

W: In that case, I think we'd better give them a discount to make up for the delay. I'll see if our manager is fine with that.

M: OK. I'll inform you as soon as the food is ready.

Questions 41-43 refer to the following conversation with three speakers.

영국식 발음 → 미국식 발음 → 캐나다식 발음

W1: Wilma, I think our nonprofit organization needs a more effective fund-raising method.

W2: Did you have something in mind?

W1: What about an online campaign?

W2: I'm not sure. Marcus, what do you think about changing to online fund-raising?

M: We could do that. Web-based campaigns cost very little, so it could save money. I'm sure it would be better than hosting fund-raising dinners like we do now.

W2: I see. Well . . . I'm open to the idea. However, I'm unfamiliar with the steps we'd need to take.

M: I organized some campaigns at my previous job that were very successful. If you want, I can make an initial strategy proposal for you to review.

W1: Would you? That'd be helpful.

Questions 44-46 refer to the following conversation.

영국식 발음 → 캐나다식 발음

W: Hello, this is Angela calling. I've got some bad news. I might not be able to join you at the Autumn Festival next Saturday. As it turns out, I have conflicting engagements.

M: I'm sorry to hear that. What do you have to do on Saturday?

W: I just found out that some of my relatives will be in town then. I have to entertain them during their visit.

M: Well, you're welcome to bring them along. I'm sure they would enjoy the experience, as the festival has a lot of fun activities. Last year, I even harvested my own pumpkin to carve!

Questions 47-49 refer to the following conversation.

미국식 발음 → 호주식 발음

W: Mr. Warner, I'm wondering if I could have the day off on Thursday. I need to go to the dentist for a checkup.

M: That's not a good day for you to be gone, as we're having a public relations workshop then. Everyone in our department is required to attend. You'd better possibly schedule your appointment for Friday or next Monday.

W: That's right! I completely forgot. In that case, I can call the clinic and ask if they have an opening on Friday instead. I'm sure they will be able to accommodate my request.

Questions 50-52 refer to the following conversation.

캐나다식 발음 → 미국식 발음

M: Ms. Bont, this is Maurice Martin from Red Publishing.

W: Good morning, Mr. Martin. Are you calling about my manuscript?

M: Yes. I read over it last month, and it has a lot of potential. We received hundreds of submissions, but have chosen your book for publication.

W: Oh, that's great to hear! I'm so honored!

M: However, despite our interest, there are some problems that must be addressed. Nothing too major—mostly stylistic issues.

W: OK. Would you like to meet and further discuss

things?

M: Yes. Are you available next Tuesday at 1 P.M.? There's a quiet café across the street from my office where we could meet. It's called The Oxford Club.

W: Wonderful. See you then.

Questions 53-55 refer to the following conversation with three speakers.

[3에] 캐나다식 발음 → 영국식 발음 → 호주식 발음

M1: Gary and Veronica, We need to organize the inventory of our grocery store's cold storage on Saturday. Would both of you be interested in working overtime that day?

W: I'm available. I don't have any plans for the weekend.

M1: What about you, Gary? Can you help on Saturday?

M2: I'm really sorry. I'm going to the doctor for my annual health checkup.

M1: No problem. Hmm . . . But we still need two more people. Maybe we can get others to help out.

W: The rest of the staff is stocking the shelves in the bakery section right now. I'm heading that way, so I'll check and see if anyone else is available.

Questions 56-58 refer to the following conversation.

[3에] 호주식 발음 → 미국식 발음

M: Hello, my name is Raj Shan. I'm calling because there's an issue with my credit card. Its . . . magnetic strip is worn, and scanners can't read it. So, I need a replacement.

W: Certainly, Mr. Shan. To get one, you must fill out the necessary form on our Web site.

M: Can't we take care of that over the phone?

W: I'm afraid not. We have a strict procedure for such requests.

M: Oh, I see.

W: Just go to our Web site and then click on the card replacement link. You'll find the necessary instructions there.

M: OK. By the way, can I adjust the card's credit limit on the Web site too?

W: Yep, you'll be able to do that as well.

M: Great. Thanks for the information.

Questions 59-61 refer to the following conversation.

[3에] 캐나다식 발음 → 영국식 발음

M: Eva, are you still looking for a programmer to help you develop that new accounting program?

W: Hi, Brian. Yes, I am. I received some applications, but all of the candidates seem to prefer working from home.

M: Well, I have a friend who might be able to help. Her name is Donna Phillips, and she has over five years

of experience developing computer programs. Not only that but she just moved into a house close to your office.

W: All right. Could you ask her to e-mail me her résumé? I can check it out after lunch.

M: I'll tell her to do that right now.

Questions 62-64 refer to the following conversation and schedule.

[3에] 영국식 발음 → 캐나다식 발음

W: You've reached the Wilson Language Academy.

M: Hello. I'm interested in taking Spanish lessons with a private tutor once a week.

W: Have you studied Spanish before?

M: Yes, but I need to improve my business vocabulary. My company merged with a firm in Madrid, and I'll be inspecting its factory next month. I need to be able to communicate with the people showing me around the plant.

W: I see . . . Which day do you want to meet with a tutor?

M: I'm usually busy from Monday to Thursday, so Friday evenings would be best.

W: OK. If you could give me your e-mail address, I'll send you some details about the available tutor and the cost of the lessons.

Questions 65-67 refer to the following conversation and graph.

[3에] 호주식 발음 → 미국식 발음

M: I finally had a chance to meet with the president and tell her about our new advertising idea for smartphone applications.

W: And? How did it go?

M: Not as expected. She feels that the message of the advertisement is too complex. She wants us to make it more straightforward and easy to understand.

W: That seems reasonable. Well, maybe we can make it more like the one from the campaign we launched earlier this year. You know—the previous advertisement that was released in the month in which we had more than 11,000 views for the first time this year.

Questions 68-70 refer to the following conversation and calendar.

[3에] 캐나다식 발음 → 영국식 발음

M: Hello. I'm calling because I heard you're holding special events at your botanical garden in July. Is that correct?

W: Yes. The tour of the facility is especially popular. It's conducted by Myra Lawrence . . . um, an assistant botany professor from a local university.

M: Actually, I'd like to take one of the classes. However,

given my work hours, I'll only be able to attend one on the weekend.

W: Certainly. But you'll need to sign up ahead of time on our Web site. Simply click on the day you'd like to attend, and you'll be directed to the registration page.

PART 4

Questions 71-73 refer to the following talk.

[3] 영국식 발음

Welcome to the Masami Teahouse in Kyoto, Japan. The teahouse was built in the late 1700s and originally served as a private club for prestigious members of society. As you can see on this map, the complex includes a large dining area, kitchen, ceremonial rooms, garden, and even sleeping quarters for guests. Moreover, the teahouse was also used for numerous special occasions, including weddings, political gatherings, and receptions for members of the royal family. It now functions as a popular tourist site.

Questions 74-76 refer to the following advertisement.

[3] 호주식 발음

Whether you are decorating a reception hall or looking for a simple gift, Green Solutions has the perfect floral arrangement for you! That's because we are one of Edinburgh's largest floral shops. In fact, we have over 3,000 square meters of showroom space full of beautiful plants and vases. To view our huge selection of premade arrangements, come to our store at 341 Vincent Street. Customers who mention this advertisement to one of our cashiers will qualify for a 5 percent discount on any purchase.

Questions 77-79 refer to the following telephone message.

[3] 캐나다식 발음

Hello. My name is Kenneth Ambrose, and I'm the owner of Ambrose Gallery on Shaker Street. Last Sunday, I had the pleasure of seeing your art on exhibit at the Castillo Park Art Fair. I was very impressed by how lifelike your portraits are. The reason I'm calling is that I'd like to invite you to display your pieces in my gallery. You would benefit greatly from doing this. Um, it's in a busy location. If you accept my invitation, I propose that we hold a large reception to celebrate the opening of your exhibit. I could invite people I know in the art industry and publicize the event through the media. Please call me back at 555-3586.

Questions 80-82 refer to the following news report.

[3] 미국식 발음

In other news, transportation officials in Austin have temporarily halted construction of the SwiftRail commuter train system. The interruption comes amid criticism from a group of local citizens. Residents from the Kingfield neighborhood are claiming that rail lines are being built too close to their homes. Mary Stenos, the head of the transportation department, held a press conference on Wednesday regarding the matter. She stated that residents' complaints were being taken seriously and that work on the SwiftRail would be stopped until the issue is resolved. She also said that updates will continue to be posted at www.swiftrail.gov to keep the public informed on the progress of construction.

Questions 83-85 refer to the following advertisement.

[3] 호주식 발음

If you are looking to hire trained security personnel to protect your home or business, contact Ace Solutions today. We can provide access to over 10,000 trained guards throughout the country who are available for employment on a permanent or short-term basis. All of the individuals we represent undergo a rigorous screening process to confirm their work experience, educational history, and professional certification. This means that you do not have to worry about searching for qualified applicants. In addition, if you sign up for a membership before April 2, you will receive 50 percent off your first month of service. Don't miss out on this great opportunity! Please feel free to call our customer service hotline for more information.

Questions 86-88 refer to the following excerpt from a talk.

[3] 영국식 발음

I'd like to thank Littleton Books for inviting me here this evening. And I'm also grateful to everyone in the audience for showing up. Today, I'll be sharing several excerpts from my latest book, *Tiger in the Night*. This work is an autobiography based on my experiences in a South African town, including my troubled teenage years and my struggles in becoming a published writer. If you like what you hear, the book is currently 10 percent off. Copies have been placed in the back of the room.

Questions 89-91 refer to the following speech.

[3] 캐나다식 발음

I am honored to be here on behalf of Lifan Industries at this year's Consumer Electronics Show. Lifan Industries was founded over 25 years ago as a supplier of plastic parts to television manufacturers. Over time, however, we have produced increasingly high-tech products.

Today, Lifan has exclusive contracts to produce LED screens and chipsets for major corporations such as Silverstar, Vivica, and PTF. What's more, I'm pleased to announce that Lifan Industries will begin producing consumer electronics under its own brand next year. If you'll all turn your attention to the screen here, I'll give you a glimpse of some of the products that we plan to launch in January.

Questions 92-94 refer to the following telephone message.

[3)) 미국식 발음]

Good morning, Mr. Parker. This is Akita Kang from Goldman and Associates. I'm interested in having you audition for a movie that my agency has been hired to do the casting for. I was going to speak to your agent about this, but she is apparently on vacation until next month. So, I decided to contact you directly. Anyway, it is a supporting role in a romantic comedy. I know . . . Most of your parts have been in action movies. But it's a great opportunity to expand your résumé and try something new. You have several days to make a decision. I'll send you a preliminary copy of the screenplay to look over. Let me know what you think.

Questions 95-97 refer to the following talk and floor plan.

[3)) 호주식 발음]

Thank you all so much for joining our annual job fair. Your participation will be especially appreciated by our students. Many of them have experienced problems finding companies interested in hiring recent college graduates during this recession. We're happy to welcome many new corporate partners this year, including our sponsor, Global Education. Just one quick note. There has been a switch in the room assignments. We originally planned to have representatives from engineering companies in Hall B, but more of these types of firms sent workers than expected, so we've decided to let them use the larger space next door. OK, feel free to set up your display booths. You have an hour before people start arriving.

Questions 98-100 refer to the following telephone message and receipt.

[3)) 영국식 발음]

Good afternoon. This is Beverly Gilder. I stayed at the . . . um . . . Presidential Palace for the first time when I was in Manila last week. While I enjoyed the experience, I've run into a problem. I didn't closely examine my bill upon check-out, and I just noticed an error. I was charged for laundry services that I did not use. I would like you to review your billing records, refund me the amount in question, and e-mail me a corrected bill. This needs to be done as soon as possible because I have to turn in my final expense report on Friday. Thank you.

▌TEST 08 스크립트

* 무료 해석은 해커스토익(Hackers.co.kr)에서 다운로드 받을 수 있습니다.

• QR 코드로 바로가기

PART 1

1 　캐나다식 발음
   (A) They are traveling along a road.
   (B) They are removing their backpacks.
   (C) They are biking down a path.
   (D) They are walking near some trees.

2 　영국식 발음
   (A) A man is typing on a keyboard.
   (B) A man is leaning on an armrest.
   (C) A woman is pushing a chair.
   (D) A woman is pointing at a monitor.

3 　미국식 발음
   (A) Some dirt is piled next to a shed.
   (B) A worker is spraying a stream of water at the ground.
   (C) A gardener has grasped a hose with both hands.
   (D) A gardener is rinsing a tool near a flower bed.

4 　호주식 발음
   (A) Some trucks are being loaded with goods.
   (B) A garage door is being closed.
   (C) Some lights are attached to the ceiling.
   (D) A vehicle window is damaged.

5 　영국식 발음
   (A) A river connects to a larger body of water.
   (B) Both sides of a canal are bordered by structures.
   (C) A boat is sailing under a footbridge.
   (D) People are lined up to board a vessel.

6 　캐나다식 발음
   (A) A fence blocks the entrance to a building.
   (B) All pedestrians have cleared out of a public square.
   (C) A group has gathered at the base of a lamppost.
   (D) Some bicycles have been left unattended.

PART 2

7 　호주식 발음 → 미국식 발음
   Who can register for the business Spanish class?
   (A) Anyone interested may sign up.
   (B) It's right by the cash register.
   (C) Kendra is our newest instructor.

8 　캐나다식 발음 → 영국식 발음
   Which of our clients will have to pay increased fees?
   (A) They all will.
   (B) I processed the payment.
   (C) Because of rising costs.

9 　미국식 발음 → 영국식 발음
   Have you considered switching to a different bank?
   (A) Just a $50 cash withdrawal, please.
   (B) You'd better let the accountant know.
   (C) I like my current one well enough.

10 　캐나다식 발음 → 미국식 발음
   Let's take a walk through the park.
   (A) I'll go grab my jacket.
   (B) It's underneath that tree.
   (C) About two miles.

11 　영국식 발음 → 캐나다식 발음
   I don't know how to fill out the new time sheet.
   (A) I think I saw it on your desk.
   (B) Ask Sue to give you a hand.
   (C) My friend showed me around.

12 　호주식 발음 → 미국식 발음
   Where did you decide to hold the fundraising banquet?
   (A) A few options are being discussed.
   (B) Most of the guests have arrived.
   (C) It will take place next Saturday.

13 　영국식 발음 → 캐나다식 발음
   How much will it cost to have this skirt altered?
   (A) That color suits you.
   (B) All items of clothing are on sale.
   (C) There's no charge for that.

14 　호주식 발음 → 영국식 발음
   Is North Road closed off for street repairs?
   (A) Yes, until next week.
   (B) No, the shop is on Leland Drive.
   (C) That is the quickest route.

15 [3n] 미국식 발음 → 캐나다식 발음

Wouldn't you rather have a first class seat for the flight?
(A) No, I wanted coffee instead.
(B) I've already arrived at the Gimpo airport.
(C) Yes, but it's too expensive.

16 [3n] 호주식 발음 → 미국식 발음

Why are you dissatisfied with these eyeglasses?
(A) We manufacture commercial lenses.
(B) Don't you think the frames are too large?
(C) Customers seem to be happy with the results.

17 [3n] 영국식 발음 → 호주식 발음

Is the new line of sportswear going to be launched on schedule?
(A) About two months ago.
(B) It is very popular with consumers.
(C) The launch has been pushed back.

18 [3n] 미국식 발음 → 캐나다식 발음

Apparently, Abby from the human resources department was promoted.
(A) I hadn't heard about the outing.
(B) Mr. Richard has named her regional director.
(C) They're promoting a new product.

19 [3n] 호주식 발음 → 영국식 발음

Where do you want to get together to plan our backpacking trip?
(A) I don't have a preference.
(B) Our gear must be packed.
(C) Don't you think we should camp for a few nights?

20 [3n] 캐나다식 발음 → 미국식 발음

Why don't we carpool to the office from now on?
(A) I usually drive to work.
(B) There are vehicles parked along the street.
(C) That would save us gas money.

21 [3n] 영국식 발음 → 캐나다식 발음

When will my raise go into effect?
(A) I'd like to go in, too.
(B) The show begins at 5 P.M.
(C) Within a week or so.

22 [3n] 미국식 발음 → 호주식 발음

Aren't suitcases supposed to be stored in overhead compartments?
(A) Small ones can be kept under the seats.
(B) The airline has misplaced my luggage.
(C) The store is still open.

23 [3n] 호주식 발음 → 영국식 발음

Employees receive a commission on every appliance that they sell.
(A) That model is one of our top sellers.
(B) That's a great incentive for workers.
(C) Actually, we visited a local dealership.

24 [3n] 미국식 발음 → 캐나다식 발음

How long can I use this transit pass?
(A) You can buy it at the ticket office.
(B) It's good for two more weeks.
(C) Transfer at Stanford Station.

25 [3n] 호주식 발음 → 캐나다식 발음

Has anyone confirmed tonight's dinner reservations at Denarii Bistro?
(A) Sure, I can make some food for us.
(B) The restaurant on Elm Street.
(C) Didn't your secretary contact the restaurant?

26 [3n] 영국식 발음 → 호주식 발음

The CEO offered you a position as a sales manager, didn't she?
(A) I really appreciate your offer.
(B) No, that's just a rumor.
(C) I plan to host the corporate executives.

27 [3n] 캐나다식 발음 → 미국식 발음

What time will the volunteers show up for the event?
(A) At the main entrance.
(B) I'll have to check with Ann.
(C) There are 30 expected guests.

28 [3n] 영국식 발음 → 캐나다식 발음

Please set up two additional workspaces.
(A) I'll take care of that now.
(B) OK, but subtract the sum from the bill.
(C) Everyone had his or her own station.

29 [3n] 호주식 발음 → 미국식 발음

Whose fountain pen is sitting on the front desk?
(A) Sign your name on the register.
(B) I've never seen it before.
(C) You may sit anywhere you'd like.

30 [3n] 영국식 발음 → 캐나다식 발음

Are you going to paint the kitchen yourself or hire a contractor?
(A) The same color as the living room.
(B) Put it next to the refrigerator.
(C) I'm too busy these days.

31 호주식 발음 → 미국식 발음

Did you buy the watch we saw at the department store yesterday?
(A) I will deliver it soon.
(B) I couldn't resist.
(C) Yes, I thought it was.

PART 3

Questions 32-34 refer to the following conversation.

미국식 발음 → 호주식 발음

W: Good afternoon. I'm here to drop off the car I rented for the weekend. The vehicle is an SXA 390 sedan, and my name is Jenna Clarkson.

M: OK. I'd just like to ask you a couple of questions regarding the vehicle. First, was the car scratched or otherwise damaged while you were using it? Also, did you refill the gas tank prior to dropping it off, as is stipulated in the rental agreement?

W: The car is undamaged, but I unfortunately wasn't able to put gas in the tank before coming here.

M: Oh, then I'll have to charge you an additional fee. Please wait a moment while I make the adjustment to your bill.

Questions 35-37 refer to the following conversation.

영국식 발음 → 캐나다식 발음

W: It seems like the book fair went well overall.

M: For the most part. However, fewer people showed up than expected. That was a bit of a letdown.

W: Yeah, I was a little disappointed by that as well. Personally, I think we should have better advertised the event in order to attract more participants.

M: I suggested running an online marketing campaign a few months ago. I'm not sure why our boss, Ms. Gabbert, never followed up on my recommendation.

W: I think she couldn't allocate any more money for the fair because our advertising budget had already been used for other projects.

Questions 38-40 refer to the following conversation.

호주식 발음 → 미국식 발음

M: Susan, I was very impressed with the article you handed in last Thursday about popular Kentsville dining spots. Also, a lot of people have posted on social media about one of the restaurants you mentioned. Uh, Lima Kitchen, the Peruvian restaurant that opened just recently . . .

W: Thanks, Chris. It's nice to hear that the public is pleased with what I wrote.

M: Given the positive feedback, maybe you should do something similar. You could write a piece about

another new dining establishment in the area.

W: I've been asked to do just that, actually. I'm about to go to our head editor's office to discuss that assignment right now.

Questions 41-43 refer to the following conversation with three speakers.

캐나다식 발음 → 호주식 발음 → 영국식 발음

M1: There isn't enough space in our garage to do all the repair work that we have been getting. Allen, do you think we need a larger facility?

M2: Hmm . . . I'm not sure. Our customers might not know where our new location is. I'm worried our competitors might get some of our business if we move.

W: Actually, the vacant lot next door was just put up for sale. If we acquire it, we could have a bigger facility constructed on the land. That way, we would be able to expand right here.

M1: That would be perfect! Let's start by determining how much the parcel of land is being sold for.

Questions 44-46 refer to the following conversation.

영국식 발음 → 호주식 발음

W: Stan, I just watched the promotional video you put together for our bakery.

M: What do you think of it?

W: It looks good, but I'm worried because the sale we're having on cream-filled donuts isn't mentioned in it.

M: Unfortunately, the advertisement only runs for 30 seconds, so I couldn't include everything.

W: In that case, could you take out the part at the end that shows the interior of our shop?

M: Remove the final segment? You specifically asked for that content to be included.

W: I know. But providing information about the sale is more important at this point.

M: OK. I understand now. I'll make those changes this afternoon.

Questions 47-49 refer to the following conversation.

캐나다식 발음 → 미국식 발음

M: Hello. This is Danny Martinson calling from Westend Boutique. I'm sorry, but the evening gown you ordered online was returned to our shipping facility as the address you entered was inaccurate.

W: I apologize for that. Could you please resend it? I live at 3258 Pleasant Avenue, Denver, Colorado.

M: Certainly. It'll take about five days to reach you.

W: OK, that's acceptable. While I have you on the phone, can you explain how to use discount coupons on your Web site? I've had trouble with them in the past.

M: Before you complete your order, click the green

"Promotions" button on the bottom of the page. Then, type the coupon code into the box that appears to apply the discount, and click "Submit."

Questions 50-52 refer to the following conversation.

호주식 발음 → 영국식 발음

M: OK, Ms. Kelly, what seems to be the problem with your wrist?

W: Well, it's been bothering me a lot at my job lately. I bend my right wrist repetitively at work, so I think that might be the cause of the pain. I work in a shoe manufacturing facility, and I'm often pulling levers on massive equipment.

M: I see. In that case, I'll prescribe you some pain-killing medication. However, I recommend you speak with your boss about ways to ensure that the constant motions aren't causing you any injuries in the meantime.

Questions 53-55 refer to the following conversation.

캐나다식 발음 → 미국식 발음

M: Candace, we've been advertising the programmer position for three weeks, but very few people have applied. Plus, none of the candidates have enough relevant work experience.

W: Hmm . . . I'll tell representatives from the recruitment Web site to run the advertisement for another week. Also, I think we should consider placing the job posting on some social media sites to attract applicants.

M: I agree. Dylan Marks from the human resources department is familiar with those types of sites. After our 10 A.M. staff meeting, I'll ask which ones he feels are most effective.

W: If he offers specific suggestions, can you let me know after lunch? That way I can upload the posting this afternoon.

Questions 56-58 refer to the following conversation with three speakers.

미국식 발음 → 호주식 발음 → 캐나다식 발음

W: Did you see the weather report? A blizzard with at least six inches of snow is expected tonight.

M1: That will be dangerous for our emergency patients. They could slip and fall if the walkway leading to the entrance of the hospital is covered in snow.

W: Right. We need to make sure that any snow is cleared right away. Do we have shovels, by the way?

M2: No, we don't. There's a hardware store less than a mile away. Could you drive there and buy some, Shawn? I'll reimburse you.

M1: Sure, I can do that.

W: Great. In the meantime, I'll write an announcement on our Web site telling people to be cautious when coming here.

Questions 59-61 refer to the following conversation.

캐나다식 발음 → 영국식 발음

M: You're watching Priority Home Shopping. Today, I'll be talking to Madeline Hartman about her firm's best-selling product.

W: That's right. Braxton Industries' ES32 is the first suitcase with a magnetic luggage tag, a protective cover, and a removable travel pouch.

M: Amazing! This item certainly offers some great features.

W: We've even added a built-in battery charger. With this suitcase, travelers can charge their phones on the go.

M: Wow! Is it available now?

W: Yes. And we are offering it to Priority Home Shopping viewers at 50 percent off its regular price. Interested shoppers should order soon, however, as this discount will be applicable for a limited time.

M: When, exactly, will the sale end?

W: On October 1.

Questions 62-64 refer to the following conversation and schedule.

미국식 발음 → 캐나다식 발음

W: Excuse me. I bought a ticket for one of today's screenings at the film festival, but I seem to have lost it.

M: Well, if you paid by credit card, I can print you a replacement.

W: I did . . . Um, here is my card.

M: Great. Now, just to confirm . . . The film you want to watch is *Low Horizon*, right?

W: That's correct.

M: OK, here is your ticket. Is there anything else I can help you with?

W: Actually, there is. I parked my car on the street next to the theater. How long can I leave it there?

M: Oh, you should move it. Parking is not permitted there. I suggest using the garage across the street.

Questions 65-67 refer to the following conversation and receipt.

호주식 발음 → 미국식 발음

M: Hello, and welcome to Engel's Department Store. Is there anything I can help you with?

W: There is. I recently purchased some clothing here, and I noticed this pair of shoes was incorrectly scanned in as the more expensive deluxe version of the Wriggly line.

M: Let me confirm the error quickly . . . Yes, you're right. I apologize for the mistake. I can give you a slip indicating store credit for the difference.

W: That'll do. Oh . . . by the way, I wanna return this

shirt, which I purchased at the same time.

M: Sorry, but sale items can't be refunded.

W: Actually, this one wasn't discounted.

Questions 68-70 refer to the following conversation and map.

[음성] 캐나다식 발음 → 영국식 발음

M: Good morning, Casey. Can you tell me exactly where the meeting will be? I will be taking the metro.

W: Get off at Greenwood Station. The building is on Humphrey Avenue, right across the street from the hospital. I will wait for you in the lobby.

M: Thanks. Oh, and unfortunately, I can't attend the lunch with the new clients afterward.

W: That won't be a problem. I'll take care of that. What are you planning to do, though?

M: Mr. Chen wants to meet me to sign some paperwork for my upcoming promotion. I am really excited about it.

W: Congratulations! It's about time, and you absolutely deserve it.

PART 4

Questions 71-73 refer to the following talk.

[음성] 캐나다식 발음

I'm very excited to be here at the National Restaurant Association's annual trade show at the Brighton Exhibition Hall, and I'd like to take this opportunity to tell you about Vend Corporation's newest commercial dishwasher, the Clear Flow XS. Made almost entirely of stainless steel, the Clear Flow XS is durable and easy to clean. In addition, because of its innovative design, this appliance uses significantly less power than other models, which saves money and benefits the environment. And, of course, it is covered by Vend Corporation's comprehensive, five-year warranty. Now, I'm sure many of you are wondering about cost, and I'll go over that in detail soon. But first, I'd like to give a brief demonstration of this amazing product in action.

Questions 74-76 refer to the following telephone message.

[음성] 호주식 발음

Hi, Ryan. It's Martin Dickey from the International Business Institute. I just received a copy of the speech you plan to give for our lecture series on infrastructure investment and overseas development. Overall, I'm very pleased with it. However, I do have a recommendation. You might want to use visual materials to illustrate the data in your report—photographs or charts, for example. One other thing . . . I just found out

that Carol Wilkins has to give her lecture on Friday given her travel plans. So, regarding your talk, June 15 works best for us. I'm hoping that will be fine since you said you'll be in New York City through Sunday.

Questions 77-79 refer to the following advertisement.

[음성] 미국식 발음

If you're planning on building your own home, then now is the time to buy property! Silver Property Management is selling a large number of undeveloped, one-acre lots along Lake Brandon at reasonable prices. These lots have spectacular views and ample space for a range of landscaping possibilities. Another advantage is that while these properties have never had homes erected on them, they are ready to be connected to Hartford County's water, electric, and sewer systems. There is a great deal of interest in these lots, and we expect them to sell out quickly. Don't miss out on this great opportunity! If you would like someone to show you around our site on Lake Brandon, call our office at 555-9000 to make an appointment.

Questions 80-82 refer to the following talk.

[음성] 호주식 발음

As the volunteer coordinator, I'd like to welcome you to the Fairfield Senior Center. Our facility is on a tight budget, so your assistance is greatly appreciated. First, I would like to briefly explain your duties. You will be expected to organize activities, which means, you'll be tasked with scheduling and setting up events at our facility. These activities are aimed at helping residents improve their mental and physical health. OK, if anyone wants to ask me anything, now is a good time. Otherwise, we'll head to the lounge to watch a short video detailing past activities we've arranged at our center.

Questions 83-85 refer to the following talk.

[음성] 미국식 발음

Before we get started, let me just remind you of one thing really quickly. An extra rehearsal for our orchestra will be held tonight. Please note that the current seating arrangement will stay the way it is until tomorrow. Also, please come to the hall with two copies of the musical score in case something happens. We need to keep in mind that everything must go as smoothly as possible. This season's gala show will be attended by our main donors. If you still have questions, come see me in my office. Let's get started now.

Questions 86-88 refer to the following talk.

[3) 영국식 발음

As you know, the Star Resort chain is planning to develop several sites throughout the country next year. And this will open up management positions at the new hotels. I received an e-mail from the CEO this morning stating that he would prefer to promote existing employees to fill these roles. He wants each hotel to implement a mentorship program for employees who demonstrate leadership skills. This will guarantee a large pool of suitable management candidates. To begin with, I would like each of you to provide a list of employees in your departments that have management potential. Um, e-mail it to me by Wednesday.

Questions 89-91 refer to the following radio broadcast.

[3) 호주식 발음

You're listening to *Melbourne Today* on 103.9 FM. My guest this afternoon is Marsha Summers, a world-renowned explorer who has been featured on the Adventure Channel and the Outdoor Channel, as well as in countless magazines and newspapers. For the past year, she's been making her way across the world in a privately owned sailboat with a crew of only three people. She landed in Australia two days ago and departs for Thailand tomorrow. I plan to ask Ms. Summers about Marine Protectors, a nonprofit organization she founded that is dedicated to protecting the wildlife in the world's oceans. We urge all of our listeners to support this group's efforts. Information on how to make a contribution is available at www.marineprotectors.com.

Questions 92-94 refer to the following talk.

[3) 영국식 발음

Everyone, please gather round. I have a few details to share about today's plan before leading you on your Norwegian Heritage Tour. Please note that there's been a small change to our plan. Ottosen Castle was supposed to be our first stop, but the building was badly damaged in a recent storm. However, we can begin our morning with a stop at an old fishing village nearby called Anker Village. Then, we'll make our way to Oslo City Hall, which is known for its incredible wall paintings. We'll easily be able to spend a couple of hours at that site alone. All right, let's walk over to the shuttle bus. We've got a great day ahead of us.

Questions 95-97 refer to the following announcement and schedule.

[3) 미국식 발음

Attention, passengers. We have been notified that Highway 45 has been closed due to a collision involving several automobiles. It had been announced that the road would be reopened at noon, but that now looks unlikely. As a result, the bus that departs at 10:40 is expected to run behind schedule. We apologize for any inconvenience this may cause, and will update you on the new departure time as soon as possible. While you wait, we would like to remind all passengers that the transit lounge opened on the second floor of the terminal. It includes free Wi-Fi, comfortable seating, and a café. Make sure to check it out.

Questions 98-100 refer to the following telephone message and sign.

[3) 캐나다식 발음

Hi, Sandra. I got your message about the team-building exercise you're arranging for our department. I really like your idea of playing a soccer game at a park. Actually, there's a great spot where we can play just a few miles from our workplace—Berkley Park. Maybe you've heard of it? It has a large field that can be reserved in advance. The only downside is that there's very limited parking. People will have to use the nearby East Street Garage. We'll probably only play for an hour, but I imagine we'll want to hang out a bit afterward, so people will have to pay for two hours. Hopefully, that won't be an issue.

▌TEST 09 스크립트

PART 1

1   ᠔⍰ 캐나다식 발음

(A) The woman is folding a document.
(B) The woman is operating a machine.
(C) The woman is installing equipment.
(D) The woman is reading a newspaper.

2   ᠔⍰ 미국식 발음

(A) The man is plugging in a cord.
(B) The man is handling a power tool.
(C) A hard hat is sitting on a shelf.
(D) Tiles are being laid on the floor.

3   ᠔⍰ 호주식 발음

(A) A customer has approached a check-in counter.
(B) A customer is unpacking a suitcase.
(C) Ticketing agents are stationed across from each other.
(D) Ticketing agents are inspecting some baggage.

4   ᠔⍰ 영국식 발음

(A) Curtains are hanging from both walls.
(B) A stage is prepared for a concert.
(C) Chairs are arranged in a classroom.
(D) A microphone is being set up at a podium.

5   ᠔⍰ 미국식 발음

(A) The man is crouching on the ground.
(B) The man is adjusting the handlebars.
(C) The woman is walking along the road.
(D) A helmet is lying on the pavement.

6   ᠔⍰ 호주식 발음

(A) A vendor is pushing a fruit cart in front of a shop.
(B) Some produce has been put on display.
(C) A salesperson is assisting a customer at a market.
(D) Some baskets have been stacked in a truck.

PART 2

7   ᠔⍰ 호주식 발음 → 영국식 발음

How far is the drive to Los Angeles?
(A) I've lived there for a long time.
(B) We decided to ride together.
(C) It's about 50 kilometers from here.

8   ᠔⍰ 캐나다식 발음 → 미국식 발음

What assignment were you given?
(A) Proofreading some articles.
(B) Sam was appointed to the position.
(C) There is still a lot to do.

9   ᠔⍰ 미국식 발음 → 캐나다식 발음

Will there be an additional charge for a large group?
(A) The venue adds an extra 10 percent to the bill.
(B) No, the large size will be too big.
(C) We're making an addition to our team.

10   ᠔⍰ 영국식 발음 → 호주식 발음

Where will the workshop be conducted?
(A) Right after lunch.
(B) Yes, I thought it was interesting.
(C) In meeting room four.

11   ᠔⍰ 미국식 발음 → 호주식 발음

Is Ms. Landrey going to wait for us in the lobby or come up to the office?
(A) I think she'll meet us in the lobby.
(B) The lady in the blue jacket.
(C) She can ask the waiter about the specials.

12   ᠔⍰ 캐나다식 발음 → 미국식 발음

I was wondering if you have an available room for two nights.
(A) Yes, this is the hotel's Web site.
(B) There are no more vacancies, sorry.
(C) To pay for the accommodations.

13   ᠔⍰ 영국식 발음 → 캐나다식 발음

Would you like to go on an island tour?
(A) That would be a lot of fun.
(B) We walked down the beach.
(C) They should take the boat.

14   ᠔⍰ 호주식 발음 → 미국식 발음

Who can I talk to about this faulty product?
(A) What's the phone number?
(B) I'll call a manager over.
(C) All our devices come with a warranty.

15 ③ 캐나다식 발음 → 영국식 발음

Is Ms. Yoon going to make an announcement?
(A) I already told her about them.
(B) No, someone else made the coffee.
(C) Yes, within the next hour.

16 ③ 미국식 발음 → 캐나다식 발음

I should talk with a financial advisor.
(A) I can recommend someone to you.
(B) It was a profitable investment.
(C) Let's talk about the party later.

17 ③ 호주식 발음 → 영국식 발음

Why did the organizer cancel the seminar?
(A) Not enough people signed up.
(B) He'll need to get a refund.
(C) Two weeks after the event.

18 ③ 캐나다식 발음 → 미국식 발음

This is the final edition of the journal, isn't it?
(A) Yes, we finally arrived.
(B) A new addition to the team.
(C) Yes, it's the last one.

19 ③ 호주식 발음 → 영국식 발음

When does your new fitness class start?
(A) I witnessed an accident.
(B) At Macy's Gym.
(C) I decided not to take it.

20 ③ 영국식 발음 → 호주식 발음

How many of these files do you need to copy?
(A) Just fill out this information card.
(B) All of them, actually.
(C) No, it's the original copy.

21 ③ 미국식 발음 → 캐나다식 발음

Wouldn't it take less time if we sent the letters by courier?
(A) Yes, but have you considered the cost?
(B) I'm sending them the goods.
(C) They only have carry-on luggage.

22 ③ 영국식 발음 → 미국식 발음

The last article Michael wrote was very entertaining.
(A) I can't wait to read the next one.
(B) Yes, I can write that story for you.
(C) It only lasted a few minutes.

23 ③ 호주식 발음 → 캐나다식 발음

How much do opera tickets cost on the opening day?
(A) Some tickets are still available on the Web site.
(B) They're twice as expensive as usual.
(C) The theater will remain open until 10 P.M.

24 ③ 미국식 발음 → 호주식 발음

Don't you normally use a travel agent to arrange business trips?
(A) No, it has been canceled.
(B) I usually book tickets online.
(C) To inspect the new production plant.

25 ③ 영국식 발음 → 캐나다식 발음

Have you been to the company's new offices yet?
(A) We have been to that cinema.
(B) These records are old.
(C) I visited them yesterday.

26 ③ 호주식 발음 → 영국식 발음

Would you like some help with your suitcase, ma'am?
(A) I'll help Matt around noon.
(B) Be sure to bring enough clothes.
(C) That won't be necessary.

27 ③ 미국식 발음 → 호주식 발음

As far as I know, this lot doesn't require a parking pass.
(A) Why are there markings on the contract?
(B) Really? I always thought it did.
(C) The valet is retrieving your vehicle.

28 ③ 캐나다식 발음 → 영국식 발음

How did the new employees' training go for everyone?
(A) Because it's raining outside.
(B) To learn about our computer systems.
(C) There haven't been any problems yet.

29 ③ 호주식 발음 → 미국식 발음

Do you need someone to pick you up at the airport?
(A) I picked out a second necktie.
(B) No, the flight was very affordable.
(C) Oh, I'll just find a taxi there.

30 ③ 영국식 발음 → 캐나다식 발음

Where can I sign up for the tour?
(A) Do you mean the one of the factory?
(B) Sign at the bottom of the contract.
(C) We should hire a guide.

31 ③ 캐나다식 발음 → 미국식 발음

The Spanish clothing firm requested more marketing services, right?
(A) Isn't the company based in Portugal?
(B) The fashion show features new designers.
(C) We have fewer staff now than before.

해커스 토익 실전 1000제 2 Listening

PART 3

Questions 32-34 refer to the following conversation.

[Audio] 호주식 발음 → 미국식 발음

M: Ms. Wheeler, I'm calling from Bernard Flooring. Unfortunately, we have to postpone your Tuesday appointment to have new carpet laid in your home. We're going to be understaffed for the next couple of days and won't be able to make it then. Thursday is the earliest we can come.

W: That's going to be inconvenient for me, as I'll be busy on that day. Could you possibly do the work on Wednesday instead?

M: No, we're fully booked on Wednesday as well. To make up for the inconvenience, though, I can take 15 percent off your final bill.

W: OK. I'll make time on Thursday then.

Questions 35-37 refer to the following conversation.

[Audio] 캐나다식 발음 → 영국식 발음

M: A group of investors will be stopping by the office in five days. While they're here, I want someone to give a presentation to them on our recent expansion into the South American market. Would you be willing to do that?

W: Normally, I would be. However, my team is working on another assignment, which is due in a few days. Unfortunately, I won't have enough time to take on both tasks before the investors arrive.

M: Oh, that's right! I forgot you're conducting research for a financial analysis. Well, the presentation is more pressing than the analysis, so please prioritize that. You should work on the other assignment later.

Questions 38-40 refer to the following conversation.

[Audio] 미국식 발음 → 호주식 발음

W: Hello. You've reached Lotus Restaurant. How can I help you?

M: Hi. My name is George Anderson, and I have a lunch reservation this Thursday at 12 P.M. I'd like to add two people. So, there will be eight instead of six.

W: Just a minute, please . . . Um, the only big tables we have available at that time are on the outside patio. Would you like me to book one for you?

M: Well . . . It's supposed to rain on Thursday.

W: Oh, I see. In that case, I suggest that you consider coming here at 1 P.M. instead of at noon. If that is acceptable, I can book you a table in the main dining area.

M: That's fine. Thank you.

Questions 41-43 refer to the following conversation.

[Audio] 캐나다식 발음 → 영국식 발음

M: It's Mitchell Joyce calling. Is the consumer research report for Vector Shoes ready yet? I'll be consulting with the company's director tomorrow, and I'd like to show it to him.

W: The report is nearly finished. I'm just waiting for some additional statistics from a colleague before I can finalize it. Everything will be completed by this afternoon.

M: Great. It would be best if you could bring a hard copy of the final report to my assistant. He'll pass it on to me when I return to the office.

W: OK. I'll get one to him no later than 3 o'clock.

Questions 44-46 refer to the following conversation.

[Audio] 미국식 발음 → 호주식 발음

W: Hello, Greg. Didn't you order the supplies that our resort needs for next month's Hotels & Accommodation Expo in Las Vegas?

M: Yes. Is something wrong?

W: Well, I can't find the pamphlets we were supposed to bring. I thought they were in the storage room, but I don't see them anywhere.

M: Oh, the pamphlets were sent to our Las Vegas branch. That will make things more convenient for us.

W: I see. How many did you send?

M: Around six boxes. But I intend to order six more to be printed. We'll attend another expo in Miami next month.

Questions 47-49 refer to the following conversation with three speakers.

[Audio] 캐나다식 발음 → 호주식 발음 → 미국식 발음

M1: Fred, we need to test the stage lighting. The play starts in less than two hours.

M2: I was just doing that. But the main spotlight doesn't seem to be working. I changed the bulb, but that didn't help.

M1: Hmm . . . The director will want to use that light. We need to figure something out.

W: Why don't I see if there is another spotlight in the storeroom? If there is one, you'll have enough time to install it before the audience members take their seats.

M2: That's a good idea, Michelle.

W: Okay. I'll do that now and report back in about 10 minutes.

Questions 50-52 refer to the following conversation.

[Audio] 영국식 발음 → 캐나다식 발음

W: Hi. I recently bought a protective cover for my laptop computer on your Web site. However, I'd like to exchange it. The one I purchased is too small.

M: So long as the item isn't damaged, we're happy to exchange it for you. However, you'll be charged for the extra shipping and handling fees related to your request.

W: That's fine. I'm also hoping you can help me figure out which case will fit my computer.

M: If you provide the brand name and model of your laptop, I can look up the proper item code. You can then use the code to search for the product on our Web site.

Questions 53-55 refer to the following conversation with three speakers.

3에 영국식 발음 → 호주식 발음 → 미국식 발음

W1: Please stand over here and raise your arms. I need to take one final measurement for your jacket.

M: Certainly. But, before I forget . . . how much will everything cost?

W1: Just one second. Hailey, can you check the work estimate?

W2: Sure. Hmm . . . About $75. However, if it takes longer than two hours to alter, it'll be slightly more.

M: I see. When will the suit be ready?

W1: I should be done altering it by next Tuesday.

M: That's actually convenient since I need to consult with a customer in this neighborhood then anyway.

W2: Great. Just note that we don't open until 11 A.M.

Questions 56-58 refer to the following conversation.

3에 캐나다식 발음 → 미국식 발음

M: This is Liam Gates calling from Ondine Bank. We are hosting our annual awards ceremony next month, and my associate strongly suggested using your company. I was wondering if we could meet this week to discuss the possibility of your business catering the event.

W: I would be happy to do that, Mr. Gates. Most of my afternoons this week are free.

M: What about tomorrow? Could you meet me here at our headquarters on Larson Avenue at two?

W: That's fine. But, before we meet, I suggest you take a look at our Web site. There are examples of menus we've prepared in the past as well as price lists. It should give you a better idea of what types of food we offer.

Questions 59-61 refer to the following conversation.

3에 캐나다식 발음 → 영국식 발음

M: I just had a meeting with our restaurant manager. He said that all the staff working in the dining area will have to wear uniforms starting next month. What do you think about that?

W: Why not? Employees in other establishments wear

them to look more presentable and organized. And think of the time it'll save us every morning. We won't have to figure out what to wear to work anymore.

M: You're probably right. It'll also be easier for customers to identify staff if we're all wearing the same type of clothing.

W: I just hope the uniforms aren't uncomfortable to wear.

Questions 62-64 refer to the following conversation and design.

3에 호주식 발음 → 미국식 발음

M: Hi, Ms. Wright. It's Garrett McKenzie. Did you take a look at the company sign examples I sent you yesterday?

W: Yes, I did. I would like to use one of the simpler designs, but could we try a variation on it?

M: Of course. What would you like me to do?

W: I'd like to put our logo below the Web site URL, at the bottom, instead of to the right of the company's name.

M: Oh, we can do that. I'll send you the rough design through e-mail when I'm done.

W: Thanks. Um, actually, could you just send it to all of my team at once? I'll send you a list of their e-mail addresses now.

Questions 65-67 refer to the following conversation and product manual.

3에 영국식 발음 → 캐나다식 발음

W: Hello. I'm calling to express my dissatisfaction with a tent I purchased from your sporting goods store yesterday.

M: OK. I can assist you with that. What seems to be the problem?

W: Well, neither of the two largest poles came in the box. I have the other poles and pegs but am unable to assemble the tent.

M: I apologize for the inconvenience, ma'am. We'll gladly provide you with the missing parts if you bring your receipt to our shop within 30 days.

W: All right. I'll do that this afternoon since my office is near the shopping center your store is in.

Questions 68-70 refer to the following conversation and map.

3에 호주식 발음 → 미국식 발음

M: Excuse me. I've got a package for one of the tenants of this apartment complex, but I can't find the building. Here is the address.

W: Let me see . . . Oh, that's the one between the playground and the flower garden. Just follow the path through the flower garden to get to it. Um, wasn't there a security guard at the entrance to give you directions?

M: There was, but I didn't think to ask. This complex is a lot bigger than I expected.

W: Yeah, it is quite large. And it is going to get even bigger. A building with another 100 units will be going up in front of the parking lot next January.

PART 4

Questions 71-73 refer to the following announcement.

[音] 영국식 발음

Welcome to the Stanbridge Museum of History. Drop by our information counter in the lobby to pick up a facility map and a brochure with details on our current exhibits. Also, don't forget to check out our newest display, *Art of the Ancient Egyptians*, located on the second floor in Hall D. This exhibit runs for this month only, with artifacts on loan from museums around the globe. And at the end of your visit at the museum, browse through our gift shop. As guests, you will qualify for 10 percent off any purchase if you present your admission ticket!

Questions 74-76 refer to the following announcement.

[音] 캐나다식 발음

Okay, everyone. Before we end today's meeting, I'd like to make a final announcement. I want to remind everyone that we are pushing through with our plan to move to the new office on August 1. That is just three weeks away, so make sure you are ready and have packed everything in boxes before the moving company comes. Now, I realize many of you were unhappy about leaving this office. And that is understandable as we've been here for many years. But, well . . . there are 500 staff members now. Besides, our new office is in a wonderful area. Westport has lots of quality restaurants, and it's easy to get to by bus and subway.

Questions 77-79 refer to the following telephone message.

[音] 미국식 발음

This is Gwen Stevens from Horizon Landscaping calling for Paul Carranza. We've come up with several proposals for the design of your building's courtyard. I would like to install a decorative fountain in the middle of the space. I also suggest planting a variety of flowers along the courtyard's main path. That will make the space feel very relaxing. If you don't care for that idea, however, I have sketches of other possible designs as well. Could you call me back and let me know what would be a good time for us to meet and go through the proposals? Thank you for this opportunity, and I look forward to getting started.

Questions 80-82 refer to the following introduction.

[音] 호주식 발음

Welcome to the annual Olympia Health Association meeting. It's surprising that so many of you made it despite the storm. I'm happy to say that we have a very special guest with us tonight—Dr. Mildred Jenkins. Not only was Dr. Jenkins the first female heart surgeon to set up a practice in Olympia, but she was also our association's first female president and the founder of our program to improve heart health among children in the city. However, I'm sure most of you already knew that. As for tonight, Dr. Jenkins will give us an update about her ongoing initiative to remove unhealthy snacks from local schools. Now, without further ado, let's welcome Dr. Jenkins to the stage.

Questions 83-85 refer to the following announcement.

[音] 캐나다식 발음

Could I have everyone's attention for a few moments? I just want to go over a couple of reminders before we start our shift. First, our order of new protective goggles has arrived. So, please pick up a pair before heading to the factory floor. Also, we have an inspection on Friday, so make sure to report any equipment problems to the technical department as soon as possible. That way, they will have sufficient time to make repairs before the inspection takes place. Finally, please ensure that your work areas are tidy and in order before you go home today.

Questions 86-88 refer to the following excerpt from a meeting.

[音] 미국식 발음

Hi, everyone. I have an update on the YT-90 Air Cleaner that we created the print advertisements for. The product has received positive reviews on technology Web sites. However, the sales department manager reported that fewer people than expected are buying it. To address this issue, we are going to start a new major project right away. Unfortunately, this means our company get-together will be canceled. The CEO wants to make sure that consumers are aware of the YT-90 Air Cleaner's many innovative features. To achieve this goal, we're going to design a brochure with detailed product information. It'll be handed out in stores where the air cleaner is sold.

Questions 89-91 refer to the following advertisement.

[音] 영국식 발음

Are you looking for a bargain on furniture? Look no further than Fair Value. Located in downtown Astoria, Fair Value stocks quality pre-owned merchandise for the office and home. Nowhere else will you find items like conference tables and sofas at such affordable prices. Not only that, but all paying customers receive instant membership to our online auction site at www.fairvalue.com. Come into Fair Value this holiday weekend, and we'll also include free delivery for purchases of $600 or more.

Questions 92–94 refer to the following talk.

⟨☌⟩ 캐나다식 발음

As most of you are aware, the provincial government has hired our firm to develop a new tourism campaign for British Columbia. It will target consumers in the US, Mexico, and Canada. We will emphasize how British Columbia can offer travelers a fairly priced, enjoyable holiday. We plan to launch the campaign this spring, so we need to get everything set up soon. Our team will be responsible for finding corporate sponsors. We plan to work in partnership with airlines, hotel chains, and other tourism-based businesses to develop a special promotional campaign. So, for our next meeting, you all need to come up with lists of potential companies that we should get in touch with.

Questions 95–97 refer to the following talk and graph.

⟨☌⟩ 호주식 발음

Thank you all for joining Synergy's trial session. As you know, we produce bookkeeping programs for small companies such as yours. Well, in February, we're replacing our best-selling program with a successor. Ledger Pro—the new application—builds upon the strengths of our top program and adds features that were requested in the customer experience surveys we conducted last quarter. For the test session, we'll update your systems to Ledger Pro, and you will simply continue to perform your bookkeeping duties as you have in the past. If you come across any unfamiliar features, just let someone from our firm know, and we'll walk you through them.

Questions 98–100 refer to the following telephone message and order form.

⟨☌⟩ 영국식 발음

Good morning. This is Glenda Brown from LMZ Investments. I need to change an order that I recently placed on your Web site. Christina Chine, the manager of our new office in Miami, just notified me that she will have a larger staff than planned. We have some extra desks that can be used, and we won't require additional cubicle partitions or file cabinets . . . but I need to double the number of seats. We'll need, uh, 30 in total. The accounting manager wants me to use a different company credit card to pay for the new charges, so please call me back for the number and expiration date. My contact details are included on the original order form. Thank you.

TEST 10 스크립트

• QR 코드로 바로가기

PART 1

1 캐나다식 발음
(A) The woman is closing a window.
(B) The woman is setting down some bags.
(C) The woman is adjusting her coat.
(D) The woman is leaving a store.

2 영국식 발음
(A) They are installing flooring in a room.
(B) Supplies are leaning against a wall.
(C) Some carpeting is being torn out.
(D) They are climbing a set of steps.

3 미국식 발음
(A) A man is taking a book from a shelf.
(B) Some papers have been placed on a table.
(C) Cups have been stacked up.
(D) Some people are looking at a screen.

4 캐나다식 발음
(A) A cabinet is being filled with items.
(B) A piece of furniture is being dusted.
(C) The woman is hanging up a clock.
(D) The woman is folding a hand towel.

5 영국식 발음
(A) Structures have been built near a hillside.
(B) Passengers are boarding vessels from the dock.
(C) A passenger boat is sailing out to sea.
(D) A flag has been attached to a pole.

6 호주식 발음
(A) A cord has been removed from a keyboard.
(B) The man is pointing at a monitor.
(C) A guitar has been set against the wall.
(D) The man is sitting in front of a window.

PART 2

7 영국식 발음 → 호주식 발음
Who represented our firm at the recent expo?
(A) It was held in Chicago.
(B) Mr. Dawkins will be going.
(C) The head of the marketing department.

8 캐나다식 발음 → 미국식 발음
You're going to the welcoming party for the new interns, right?
(A) Everyone from our team will be there.
(B) I'm glad it has been going well.
(C) I sent out invitations last week.

9 호주식 발음 → 미국식 발음
What problem are you having with the cash machine?
(A) We accept checks too.
(B) The maintenance person has one.
(C) My debit card was rejected.

10 캐나다식 발음 → 영국식 발음
Hasn't Ben decided on a vacation destination?
(A) No, we stayed in Brisbane.
(B) I don't believe so.
(C) A vacation package.

11 호주식 발음 → 영국식 발음
Jamie, would you schedule me an appointment with the director?
(A) Yes, let me draw you a map.
(B) Your reservation was canceled.
(C) I'll get on it right away.

12 미국식 발음 → 캐나다식 발음
You have this shirt also available in small, don't you?
(A) Actually, that size is sold out.
(B) I often visit this mall.
(C) The red dress is cheaper.

13 미국식 발음 → 호주식 발음
When will the acquisition be announced?
(A) Not for another week.
(B) The merger was very profitable.
(C) I start the position tomorrow.

14 캐나다식 발음 → 영국식 발음
Is someone sitting here, or can I take this chair?
(A) I've been there before.
(B) It will take about an hour.
(C) My friend is using it, I'm afraid.

15 호주식 발음 → 미국식 발음

Who's receiving the Employee of the Month Award?
(A) Later this evening.
(B) Mr. Kenichi, most likely.
(C) Just forward them to me.

16 캐나다식 발음 → 영국식 발음

Why don't you buy an extra monitor for your computer?
(A) I already bought tickets for that.
(B) I'd like that, but my budget is too tight.
(C) That sounds like a good bargain.

17 호주식 발음 → 미국식 발음

Did we get the results from last week's audit?
(A) You're right. It's pretty odd.
(B) Yes, it's occurring in the auditorium.
(C) We'll receive them later today.

18 캐나다식 발음 → 영국식 발음

When did Amit originally establish his business?
(A) The store opens at 8 A.M.
(B) A little over two years ago.
(C) Just around the corner.

19 미국식 발음 → 캐나다식 발음

Which of these briefcases should I buy?
(A) They're both very nice.
(B) Yes, to replace my old one.
(C) Thanks. I got them online.

20 영국식 발음 → 호주식 발음

Which applicant do you think we should hire?
(A) It depends on the interview results.
(B) Several people have applied for the position.
(C) The company is opening a new branch.

21 호주식 발음 → 미국식 발음

Everyone seemed to enjoy the gathering last night.
(A) At George's house in the country.
(B) A reservation for three nights.
(C) Yes, they had a good time.

22 캐나다식 발음 → 미국식 발음

Why don't we take a 10-minute coffee break?
(A) Can you wait half an hour?
(B) He has been coughing all day.
(C) About two days ago.

23 영국식 발음 → 호주식 발음

A customer accidentally left her purse at the register.
(A) You can sign up online.
(B) Place it under the counter for now.
(C) There are some on the display rack.

24 영국식 발음 → 캐나다식 발음

How did everything go at the real estate convention in Shanghai?
(A) Property values remain the same.
(B) I made some business connections.
(C) Near the downtown convention center.

25 미국식 발음 → 호주식 발음

Should we rearrange the layout of the shop?
(A) This is her favorite boutique.
(B) Yes, a few of them.
(C) I'd rather not.

26 캐나다식 발음 → 영국식 발음

Why aren't the salespeople at their desks?
(A) Let's have the sales team help.
(B) Some additional telemarketers.
(C) They are in the conference room.

27 호주식 발음 → 미국식 발음

Landscapers are going to plant rose bushes out front this morning.
(A) Why wasn't I informed sooner?
(B) Yesterday afternoon.
(C) The gardening course has a fee.

28 미국식 발음 → 호주식 발음

Haven't you already been accepted to a college?
(A) Here are your course materials.
(B) Yes, it's been filled out.
(C) Quite a few, actually.

29 영국식 발음 → 캐나다식 발음

Beginning next month, all personnel will be required to use security badges.
(A) We'd better notify the employees soon then.
(B) The president is obligated to attend.
(C) State safety regulations.

30 미국식 발음 → 캐나다식 발음

Aren't our subscription levels continuing to increase?
(A) You have to refill your prescription.
(B) According to the head accountant.
(C) I'm continuing to review applications.

31 호주식 발음 → 영국식 발음

What did the manufacturer do when you asked for a refund?
(A) One of the warehouses at the factory.
(B) They accommodated my request.
(C) We changed the return policy.

PART 3

Questions 32-34 refer to the following conversation.

영국식 발음 → 호주식 발음

W: I heard that you just returned from your business trip to Cape Town. How did it go?

M: Everything related to work went well, but the rest of my time there was a bit disappointing. It rained throughout my stay, so I didn't get a chance to walk around the city.

W: That's a shame. Cape Town has various public parks and some really beautiful monuments. I suppose you weren't able to see any of them.

M: No, I had to spend most of my free time in my hotel room. On the day before my departure, I watched a traditional dance at a nearby cultural center, though. It was very interesting.

Questions 35-37 refer to the following conversation.

캐나다식 발음 → 미국식 발음

M: This launch for our firm's GPS navigation device is going very well. It might be the most successful event that I've overseen since I started working as the manager of the product development team.

W: Yes, a lot of technology bloggers and industry figures have shown up. They all seem very impressed with the device. Hopefully, they'll bring positive attention to it as well as our firm.

M: I think they will. In fact, I just spoke with Emily Scott, a staff writer from *Everyday Science*. She intends to publish a favorable review about our product on her company's Web site.

Questions 38-40 refer to the following conversation with three speakers.

호주식 발음 → 캐나다식 발음 → 영국식 발음

M1: As you know, there's a lot of consumer demand for hiking boots these days. Our CEO thinks the company should release its own line.

M2: I agree. We need to capitalize on this trend.

W: But we mainly produce sneakers. None of our staff members has the necessary knowledge or skills to design a hiking boot.

M1: Hmm . . . Good point. Sam, do you have any ideas on what to do about this issue?

M2: I think the only option is to hire a designer who has experience with this type of footwear. I could create a rough draft of a job posting for the position now and then send it to you two for review.

W: OK. That would be helpful.

Questions 41-43 refer to the following conversation.

미국식 발음 → 호주식 발음

W: Good morning. I'm planning to take golf lessons, and I'd like to rent a set of clubs from your shop. I'll need them for three months, starting from today.

M: Not a problem. Our rental prices are quite competitive, and the fee includes damage insurance for the clubs. However, we recently modified our rental rules, so you'll have to rent them for at least six months, which is a bit too long for you, I think.

W: Hmm . . . I can practice with them after I complete the lessons.

M: All right. A piece of photo ID is required to rent our equipment, so I'll need to look at that first.

Questions 44-46 refer to the following conversation.

영국식 발음 → 캐나다식 발음

W: Sorry I'm a few minutes late, but it took me almost two hours to drive to the office today. Traffic on the freeway was extremely slow.

M: Really? I can't believe it took you so long. Why don't you just use public transportation? I'm sure it would be a lot faster than driving.

W: Well, the nearest subway or bus station from my apartment is 20 minutes on foot. With the cold weather here, I prefer not to walk. So, I usually end up taking my car.

M: Actually, the Transport Authority just changed its city bus routes. I think bus 402 now stops in your neighborhood, so that would be really convenient for you. I'll forward you a link to the city Web site for you to review.

Questions 47-49 refer to the following conversation.

캐나다식 발음 → 미국식 발음

M: Rochester Convention Center. How can I help you?

W: Good morning. I'm calling about the Westgate Auto Show on May 18. I know that tickets are $20 per person, but I will be attending with the other members of my auto club. Is it possible for us to get a group rate?

M: Yes. But you'll need to discuss it with Carol Humphrey who is in charge of group ticket sales. Her e-mail address is carol@conventionpro.com.

W: Great. We're really excited about the upcoming exhibit of antique cars.

M: We have some promotional material from the company that is organizing that event. Why don't I send it to you?

W: I picked up a brochure yesterday. But thanks.

Questions 50-52 refer to the following conversation with three speakers.

미국식 발음 → 호주식 발음 → 캐나다식 발음

W: Oh, no. One of our shoppers accidentally dropped a jar of pickles, and it shattered on the floor.

M1: I'll take care of that. But I just started working here, so I don't know where the mop is.

W: Hmm . . . Gustavo, can you show him where the mop is?

M2: Sure, I can. I'll show him where the storage with all the cleaning supplies is.

W: Thank you very much. Also, can you two please restock the cereal shelves after lunch? It needs to be done this afternoon.

M1: No problem. We'll let you know when we're finished.

Questions 53-55 refer to the following conversation.

미국식 발음 → 캐나다식 발음

W: A few of the convention attendees are curious whether video or audio clips of today's talks will be posted online. Do you know if that is going to happen?

M: Only some of them will be shared following the event. Is there a particular lecture that people are inquiring about?

W: Yes, a number of attendees have asked about Lillian Kraft's talk on investing in foreign markets. Many of them seem to have been quite impressed.

M: She is the keynote speaker, so video clips including her talk will definitely be uploaded to the Web site. You can inform anyone who inquires about it that they will be able to access them later on.

Questions 56-58 refer to the following conversation.

호주식 발음 → 영국식 발음

M: Felicity Gifford, who is one of the students coming to the library for today's job-search workshop, uses a wheelchair. We need to make sure she's able to comfortably pull her wheelchair up to a table.

W: Nick and I can take care of that since we're planning to shift some of the furniture around anyway. More people than anticipated registered for the class, so the tables and chairs must be rearranged to make better use of the space.

M: All right. Also, if a lot of people are coming, we should have one of our staff members welcome participants at the front door and help them find their seats.

Questions 59-61 refer to the following conversation.

미국식 발음 → 호주식 발음

W: I'm looking for someone to help me create a poster to increase awareness of our community

association. Another member told me that you are a graphic designer. But I thought that you work at a law firm.

M: Yes, I'm a legal assistant at Beale and Associates here in town. However, I do freelance graphic design to make extra money on the side.

W: Great. Well, we want to place the poster in cafes and other businesses in the neighborhood. Hopefully, it will draw in more people to our weekly meetings. Would you be willing to make it?

M: Of course! I'd be happy to volunteer my time to the association. I'll begin working on it this evening.

Questions 62-64 refer to the following conversation and table.

캐나다식 발음 → 영국식 발음

M: Thank you for calling EZ Home Cleaning. What can I assist you with today?

W: My uncle referred me to your company, and I'm interested in your services. I need my floors vacuumed, my furniture dusted, and my bathrooms cleaned.

M: We can do that for $70. If you'd like your windows cleaned as well, we have another package that costs $80.

W: That won't be necessary. Would you be able to send someone to my house this Saturday or Sunday?

M: Actually, we are fully booked for the weekend, but we can do it on Monday at 10:00 A.M. or Tuesday at 7:00 P.M.

W: Monday would work best for me.

Questions 65-67 refer to the following conversation and survey results.

호주식 발음 → 미국식 발음

M: Have you heard that one of our studio's movies made the top five on *New York Daily*'s reader poll?

W: Yes. The chief producer just e-mailed that news out to everyone. We placed just above *In and Out*! Everyone thought that movie was going to get the number one spot. I guess this year's increased marketing budget really paid off.

M: Right. We should promote this information as soon as possible.

W: Agreed. Mary said she would post a link to the reader's poll's results on our social media page later today.

Questions 68-70 refer to the following conversation and map.

캐나다식 발음 → 영국식 발음

M: Juliana, two new animals are being transferred to our zoo tomorrow.

W: The pandas—I heard. When will they get here?

M: About an hour before the zoo opens. Anyway, could you put some bamboo shoots in these buckets? That way, they'll have food when they arrive.

W: No problem.

M: And after that, please check whether the panda enclosure is clean. If not, we should wash it out this afternoon.

W: Do you mean the enclosure near the back exit on Lee Drive or the one near the sea life exhibit?

M: I'm talking about the one on Parker Lane.

PART 4

Questions 71-73 refer to the following announcement.

🎧 호주식 발음

Welcome to the annual South Hill Library Book Fair. Each autumn, we host a variety of special activities to encourage reading among local residents. In addition to offering a vast variety of both new and used books for sale, we are pleased to present a special event this year—an exhibition of rare first-edition books by early American authors. These publications are on loan from the University of Minneapolis and will be displayed in the lobby for the duration of the fair. And I would like to thank this year's corporate sponsor, Camdale Enterprises, for their financial support.

Questions 74-76 refer to the following radio broadcast.

🎧 캐나다식 발음

You're listening to WRP 99.9. The 20th annual Harrisburg Fireworks Fest is set to take place on Saturday evening. It will be held on the north end of Keaton Lake. The celebration, which has been made possible through funding by the municipal government, will feature an hour-long firework show. The city's hotel and restaurant industry are looking forward to the event, as thousands of people are expected to travel to Harrisburg over the weekend. Now, stay tuned for details about road congestion throughout the metro area.

Questions 77-79 refer to the following announcement.

🎧 영국식 발음

Before we explore the Chakra Wildlife Park, I want you to listen closely to the following instructions and information. First, food is not permitted inside the park. Second, photographs are allowed, but please do not use a flash because the light scares the animals. Third, do not exit the shuttle at any time during the tour. As a reminder, there will be an hour lunch break at the Jungle Café after we're done touring the African wildlife compound.

Once everyone has finished eating, we will resume the tour by continuing on to our Asian wildlife compound. OK, if you'll please follow me, we will begin our tour.

Questions 80-82 refer to the following advertisement.

🎧 미국식 발음

Are you looking for something fun to do this weekend? Then stop by Plaza Mall to celebrate the grand opening of our new food hall on Saturday, April 14! Located beside our indoor playground on the fifth floor, the food hall includes 17 restaurants serving a variety of dishes from all over the world. Still not sure if you should stop by? Singer Jacob Keeve will be on site this Saturday. He will be signing copies of his latest album on the ground floor. Visit our Web site for details about this event.

Questions 83-85 refer to the following telephone message.

🎧 호주식 발음

Hello, Kathryn. This is James Hartman from the editorial office. The human resources department just notified me that they've approved your leave request. However, your article on extreme sports activities must be finished before you complete your shift on Friday. This is very important, as the piece is going to be included in next month's magazine edition. Also, your team member, Joanne Marr, is going to take over responsibility for your other work while you're away. So, please share any notes or unfinished versions of next month's story that you have with her. Feel free to drop by my office if you have any questions. Otherwise, we'll talk again when you return.

Questions 86-88 refer to the following talk.

🎧 영국식 발음

It is my pleasure to welcome you all to the opening day of Keller University's scientific lecture series. We have invited a variety of scientific experts from the fields of biology, chemistry, and physics to elaborate on their most current studies and findings. I am sure you will find all four of today's talks very educational. I encourage everyone to pick up programs for today's event at the information booth near the main entrance. Also, we request that you wait until the conclusion of each lecture to ask questions. Each speaker will have an opportunity to address inquiries following his or her talk. Thank you, and I hope you enjoy the event.

Questions 89-91 refer to the following telephone message.

🎧 캐나다식 발음

Hi, this is Tim Kerensky from FV Auto Repair. We've been looking at your car, and we think we've identified the problem. It looks like the oil hasn't been changed in a long time, so it was clogging up the engine. We can perform an oil change for you right now at the sale price of just $40. If you don't change your oil every 10,000 kilometers or so, it causes a lot of problems. Please call us back and let us know if you want us to do that. The whole operation should take around 30 minutes.

Questions 92-94 refer to the following television broadcast.

🎧 미국식 발음

Good morning. I'm Sandra Choi with Channel 11 News. On Saturday, August 3, an organization called Our Natural Resources will be holding a five-kilometer run in Chicago. The goal of the event is to raise funds for the maintenance of public parks around the city. Organizers expect thousands of people to participate in the race and hope to generate nearly one million dollars. Online registration for the run will remain open until August 1, so there are still three weeks to sign up. Financial contributions are also being accepted from those who cannot attend the event but would like to offer support.

Questions 95-97 refer to the following recorded message and staff directory.

🎧 영국식 발음

Thank you for calling Fanli Technologies. To learn more about our home entertainment systems, please visit our Web site at www.fanlitech.com, where you will find product descriptions, manuals, and warranty information. If you know the extension of the person to whom you wish to speak, you may dial it at any time. To speak to one of our product management team, please dial 1099. To speak to a member of our corporate sales team, please dial 1220. To speak to someone in our accounting department about billing or payments, please dial 1330. For general inquiries, press 0 to be connected to the next available operator. If you are calling after business hours, please stay on the line to record a message. Thank you.

Questions 98-100 refer to the following report and consumer ratings.

🎧 캐나다식 발음

Now for our morning business update on WKSR Talk Radio. Oregon-based car manufacturer Aster attracted attention over the weekend when a letter it sent to shareholders was leaked to the press. The letter primarily addressed the company's ongoing financial struggles. But that's not all. In addition to detailing persistent quarterly losses, Aster CEO Giselle Bram outlined the company's plan for the future. To the surprise of many, the most poorly reviewed hatchback model is expected to be dropped from production this summer. Although Aster has yet to publicly respond to inquiries regarding the matter, experts who are familiar with the company believe the reports are likely to be true.

무료 토익·토스·오픽·지텔프 자료 제공
Hackers.co.kr

Answer Sheet

TEST 02

LISTENING (Part I~IV)

#	A	B	C	D	#	A	B	C	D	#	A	B	C	D	#	A	B	C	D	#	A	B	C	D
1	Ⓐ	Ⓑ	Ⓒ	Ⓓ	21	Ⓐ	Ⓑ	Ⓒ		41	Ⓐ	Ⓑ	Ⓒ	Ⓓ	61	Ⓐ	Ⓑ	Ⓒ	Ⓓ	81	Ⓐ	Ⓑ	Ⓒ	Ⓓ
2	Ⓐ	Ⓑ	Ⓒ	Ⓓ	22	Ⓐ	Ⓑ	Ⓒ		42	Ⓐ	Ⓑ	Ⓒ	Ⓓ	62	Ⓐ	Ⓑ	Ⓒ	Ⓓ	82	Ⓐ	Ⓑ	Ⓒ	Ⓓ
3	Ⓐ	Ⓑ	Ⓒ	Ⓓ	23	Ⓐ	Ⓑ	Ⓒ		43	Ⓐ	Ⓑ	Ⓒ	Ⓓ	63	Ⓐ	Ⓑ	Ⓒ	Ⓓ	83	Ⓐ	Ⓑ	Ⓒ	Ⓓ
4	Ⓐ	Ⓑ	Ⓒ	Ⓓ	24	Ⓐ	Ⓑ	Ⓒ		44	Ⓐ	Ⓑ	Ⓒ	Ⓓ	64	Ⓐ	Ⓑ	Ⓒ	Ⓓ	84	Ⓐ	Ⓑ	Ⓒ	Ⓓ
5	Ⓐ	Ⓑ	Ⓒ	Ⓓ	25	Ⓐ	Ⓑ	Ⓒ		45	Ⓐ	Ⓑ	Ⓒ	Ⓓ	65	Ⓐ	Ⓑ	Ⓒ	Ⓓ	85	Ⓐ	Ⓑ	Ⓒ	Ⓓ
6	Ⓐ	Ⓑ	Ⓒ	Ⓓ	26	Ⓐ	Ⓑ	Ⓒ		46	Ⓐ	Ⓑ	Ⓒ	Ⓓ	66	Ⓐ	Ⓑ	Ⓒ	Ⓓ	86	Ⓐ	Ⓑ	Ⓒ	Ⓓ
7	Ⓐ	Ⓑ	Ⓒ		27	Ⓐ	Ⓑ	Ⓒ		47	Ⓐ	Ⓑ	Ⓒ	Ⓓ	67	Ⓐ	Ⓑ	Ⓒ	Ⓓ	87	Ⓐ	Ⓑ	Ⓒ	Ⓓ
8	Ⓐ	Ⓑ	Ⓒ		28	Ⓐ	Ⓑ	Ⓒ		48	Ⓐ	Ⓑ	Ⓒ	Ⓓ	68	Ⓐ	Ⓑ	Ⓒ	Ⓓ	88	Ⓐ	Ⓑ	Ⓒ	Ⓓ
9	Ⓐ	Ⓑ	Ⓒ		29	Ⓐ	Ⓑ	Ⓒ		49	Ⓐ	Ⓑ	Ⓒ	Ⓓ	69	Ⓐ	Ⓑ	Ⓒ	Ⓓ	89	Ⓐ	Ⓑ	Ⓒ	Ⓓ
10	Ⓐ	Ⓑ	Ⓒ		30	Ⓐ	Ⓑ	Ⓒ	Ⓓ	50	Ⓐ	Ⓑ	Ⓒ	Ⓓ	70	Ⓐ	Ⓑ	Ⓒ	Ⓓ	90	Ⓐ	Ⓑ	Ⓒ	Ⓓ
11	Ⓐ	Ⓑ	Ⓒ		31	Ⓐ	Ⓑ	Ⓒ	Ⓓ	51	Ⓐ	Ⓑ	Ⓒ	Ⓓ	71	Ⓐ	Ⓑ	Ⓒ	Ⓓ	91	Ⓐ	Ⓑ	Ⓒ	Ⓓ
12	Ⓐ	Ⓑ	Ⓒ		32	Ⓐ	Ⓑ	Ⓒ	Ⓓ	52	Ⓐ	Ⓑ	Ⓒ	Ⓓ	72	Ⓐ	Ⓑ	Ⓒ	Ⓓ	92	Ⓐ	Ⓑ	Ⓒ	Ⓓ
13	Ⓐ	Ⓑ	Ⓒ		33	Ⓐ	Ⓑ	Ⓒ	Ⓓ	53	Ⓐ	Ⓑ	Ⓒ	Ⓓ	73	Ⓐ	Ⓑ	Ⓒ	Ⓓ	93	Ⓐ	Ⓑ	Ⓒ	Ⓓ
14	Ⓐ	Ⓑ	Ⓒ		34	Ⓐ	Ⓑ	Ⓒ	Ⓓ	54	Ⓐ	Ⓑ	Ⓒ	Ⓓ	74	Ⓐ	Ⓑ	Ⓒ	Ⓓ	94	Ⓐ	Ⓑ	Ⓒ	Ⓓ
15	Ⓐ	Ⓑ	Ⓒ		35	Ⓐ	Ⓑ	Ⓒ	Ⓓ	55	Ⓐ	Ⓑ	Ⓒ	Ⓓ	75	Ⓐ	Ⓑ	Ⓒ	Ⓓ	95	Ⓐ	Ⓑ	Ⓒ	Ⓓ
16	Ⓐ	Ⓑ	Ⓒ		36	Ⓐ	Ⓑ	Ⓒ	Ⓓ	56	Ⓐ	Ⓑ	Ⓒ	Ⓓ	76	Ⓐ	Ⓑ	Ⓒ	Ⓓ	96	Ⓐ	Ⓑ	Ⓒ	Ⓓ
17	Ⓐ	Ⓑ	Ⓒ		37	Ⓐ	Ⓑ	Ⓒ	Ⓓ	57	Ⓐ	Ⓑ	Ⓒ	Ⓓ	77	Ⓐ	Ⓑ	Ⓒ	Ⓓ	97	Ⓐ	Ⓑ	Ⓒ	Ⓓ
18	Ⓐ	Ⓑ	Ⓒ		38	Ⓐ	Ⓑ	Ⓒ	Ⓓ	58	Ⓐ	Ⓑ	Ⓒ	Ⓓ	78	Ⓐ	Ⓑ	Ⓒ	Ⓓ	98	Ⓐ	Ⓑ	Ⓒ	Ⓓ
19	Ⓐ	Ⓑ	Ⓒ		39	Ⓐ	Ⓑ	Ⓒ	Ⓓ	59	Ⓐ	Ⓑ	Ⓒ	Ⓓ	79	Ⓐ	Ⓑ	Ⓒ	Ⓓ	99	Ⓐ	Ⓑ	Ⓒ	Ⓓ
20	Ⓐ	Ⓑ	Ⓒ		40	Ⓐ	Ⓑ	Ⓒ	Ⓓ	60	Ⓐ	Ⓑ	Ⓒ	Ⓓ	80	Ⓐ	Ⓑ	Ⓒ	Ⓓ	100	Ⓐ	Ⓑ	Ⓒ	Ⓓ

TEST 02의 점수를 환산한 후 목표 달성기에 TEST 02의 점수를 표시합니다.
점수 환산표는 문제집 167페이지, 목표 달성기는 교재의 첫 장에 있습니다.

맞은 문제 개수: ___ /100

✂ 자르는 선

Answer Sheet

TEST 01

LISTENING (Part I~IV)

#	A	B	C	D	#	A	B	C	D	#	A	B	C	D	#	A	B	C	D	#	A	B	C	D
1	Ⓐ	Ⓑ	Ⓒ	Ⓓ	21	Ⓐ	Ⓑ	Ⓒ		41	Ⓐ	Ⓑ	Ⓒ	Ⓓ	61	Ⓐ	Ⓑ	Ⓒ	Ⓓ	81	Ⓐ	Ⓑ	Ⓒ	Ⓓ
2	Ⓐ	Ⓑ	Ⓒ	Ⓓ	22	Ⓐ	Ⓑ	Ⓒ		42	Ⓐ	Ⓑ	Ⓒ	Ⓓ	62	Ⓐ	Ⓑ	Ⓒ	Ⓓ	82	Ⓐ	Ⓑ	Ⓒ	Ⓓ
3	Ⓐ	Ⓑ	Ⓒ	Ⓓ	23	Ⓐ	Ⓑ	Ⓒ		43	Ⓐ	Ⓑ	Ⓒ	Ⓓ	63	Ⓐ	Ⓑ	Ⓒ	Ⓓ	83	Ⓐ	Ⓑ	Ⓒ	Ⓓ
4	Ⓐ	Ⓑ	Ⓒ	Ⓓ	24	Ⓐ	Ⓑ	Ⓒ		44	Ⓐ	Ⓑ	Ⓒ	Ⓓ	64	Ⓐ	Ⓑ	Ⓒ	Ⓓ	84	Ⓐ	Ⓑ	Ⓒ	Ⓓ
5	Ⓐ	Ⓑ	Ⓒ	Ⓓ	25	Ⓐ	Ⓑ	Ⓒ		45	Ⓐ	Ⓑ	Ⓒ	Ⓓ	65	Ⓐ	Ⓑ	Ⓒ	Ⓓ	85	Ⓐ	Ⓑ	Ⓒ	Ⓓ
6	Ⓐ	Ⓑ	Ⓒ	Ⓓ	26	Ⓐ	Ⓑ	Ⓒ		46	Ⓐ	Ⓑ	Ⓒ	Ⓓ	66	Ⓐ	Ⓑ	Ⓒ	Ⓓ	86	Ⓐ	Ⓑ	Ⓒ	Ⓓ
7	Ⓐ	Ⓑ	Ⓒ		27	Ⓐ	Ⓑ	Ⓒ		47	Ⓐ	Ⓑ	Ⓒ	Ⓓ	67	Ⓐ	Ⓑ	Ⓒ	Ⓓ	87	Ⓐ	Ⓑ	Ⓒ	Ⓓ
8	Ⓐ	Ⓑ	Ⓒ		28	Ⓐ	Ⓑ	Ⓒ		48	Ⓐ	Ⓑ	Ⓒ	Ⓓ	68	Ⓐ	Ⓑ	Ⓒ	Ⓓ	88	Ⓐ	Ⓑ	Ⓒ	Ⓓ
9	Ⓐ	Ⓑ	Ⓒ		29	Ⓐ	Ⓑ	Ⓒ		49	Ⓐ	Ⓑ	Ⓒ	Ⓓ	69	Ⓐ	Ⓑ	Ⓒ	Ⓓ	89	Ⓐ	Ⓑ	Ⓒ	Ⓓ
10	Ⓐ	Ⓑ	Ⓒ		30	Ⓐ	Ⓑ	Ⓒ	Ⓓ	50	Ⓐ	Ⓑ	Ⓒ	Ⓓ	70	Ⓐ	Ⓑ	Ⓒ	Ⓓ	90	Ⓐ	Ⓑ	Ⓒ	Ⓓ
11	Ⓐ	Ⓑ	Ⓒ		31	Ⓐ	Ⓑ	Ⓒ	Ⓓ	51	Ⓐ	Ⓑ	Ⓒ	Ⓓ	71	Ⓐ	Ⓑ	Ⓒ	Ⓓ	91	Ⓐ	Ⓑ	Ⓒ	Ⓓ
12	Ⓐ	Ⓑ	Ⓒ		32	Ⓐ	Ⓑ	Ⓒ	Ⓓ	52	Ⓐ	Ⓑ	Ⓒ	Ⓓ	72	Ⓐ	Ⓑ	Ⓒ	Ⓓ	92	Ⓐ	Ⓑ	Ⓒ	Ⓓ
13	Ⓐ	Ⓑ	Ⓒ		33	Ⓐ	Ⓑ	Ⓒ	Ⓓ	53	Ⓐ	Ⓑ	Ⓒ	Ⓓ	73	Ⓐ	Ⓑ	Ⓒ	Ⓓ	93	Ⓐ	Ⓑ	Ⓒ	Ⓓ
14	Ⓐ	Ⓑ	Ⓒ		34	Ⓐ	Ⓑ	Ⓒ	Ⓓ	54	Ⓐ	Ⓑ	Ⓒ	Ⓓ	74	Ⓐ	Ⓑ	Ⓒ	Ⓓ	94	Ⓐ	Ⓑ	Ⓒ	Ⓓ
15	Ⓐ	Ⓑ	Ⓒ		35	Ⓐ	Ⓑ	Ⓒ	Ⓓ	55	Ⓐ	Ⓑ	Ⓒ	Ⓓ	75	Ⓐ	Ⓑ	Ⓒ	Ⓓ	95	Ⓐ	Ⓑ	Ⓒ	Ⓓ
16	Ⓐ	Ⓑ	Ⓒ		36	Ⓐ	Ⓑ	Ⓒ	Ⓓ	56	Ⓐ	Ⓑ	Ⓒ	Ⓓ	76	Ⓐ	Ⓑ	Ⓒ	Ⓓ	96	Ⓐ	Ⓑ	Ⓒ	Ⓓ
17	Ⓐ	Ⓑ	Ⓒ		37	Ⓐ	Ⓑ	Ⓒ	Ⓓ	57	Ⓐ	Ⓑ	Ⓒ	Ⓓ	77	Ⓐ	Ⓑ	Ⓒ	Ⓓ	97	Ⓐ	Ⓑ	Ⓒ	Ⓓ
18	Ⓐ	Ⓑ	Ⓒ		38	Ⓐ	Ⓑ	Ⓒ	Ⓓ	58	Ⓐ	Ⓑ	Ⓒ	Ⓓ	78	Ⓐ	Ⓑ	Ⓒ	Ⓓ	98	Ⓐ	Ⓑ	Ⓒ	Ⓓ
19	Ⓐ	Ⓑ	Ⓒ		39	Ⓐ	Ⓑ	Ⓒ	Ⓓ	59	Ⓐ	Ⓑ	Ⓒ	Ⓓ	79	Ⓐ	Ⓑ	Ⓒ	Ⓓ	99	Ⓐ	Ⓑ	Ⓒ	Ⓓ
20	Ⓐ	Ⓑ	Ⓒ		40	Ⓐ	Ⓑ	Ⓒ	Ⓓ	60	Ⓐ	Ⓑ	Ⓒ	Ⓓ	80	Ⓐ	Ⓑ	Ⓒ	Ⓓ	100	Ⓐ	Ⓑ	Ⓒ	Ⓓ

TEST 01의 점수를 환산한 후 목표 달성기에 TEST 01의 점수를 표시합니다.
점수 환산표는 문제집 167페이지, 목표 달성기는 교재의 첫 장에 있습니다.

맞은 문제 개수: ___ /100

무료 토익·토스·오픽·지텔프 자료 제공
Hackers.co.kr

Answer Sheet

TEST 04

LISTENING (Part I~IV)

	A B C D		A B C D		A B C D		A B C D		A B C D
1	Ⓐ Ⓑ Ⓒ Ⓓ	21	Ⓐ Ⓑ Ⓒ Ⓓ	41	Ⓐ Ⓑ Ⓒ Ⓓ	61	Ⓐ Ⓑ Ⓒ Ⓓ	81	Ⓐ Ⓑ Ⓒ Ⓓ
2	Ⓐ Ⓑ Ⓒ Ⓓ	22	Ⓐ Ⓑ Ⓒ	42	Ⓐ Ⓑ Ⓒ Ⓓ	62	Ⓐ Ⓑ Ⓒ Ⓓ	82	Ⓐ Ⓑ Ⓒ Ⓓ
3	Ⓐ Ⓑ Ⓒ Ⓓ	23	Ⓐ Ⓑ Ⓒ	43	Ⓐ Ⓑ Ⓒ Ⓓ	63	Ⓐ Ⓑ Ⓒ Ⓓ	83	Ⓐ Ⓑ Ⓒ Ⓓ
4	Ⓐ Ⓑ Ⓒ Ⓓ	24	Ⓐ Ⓑ Ⓒ	44	Ⓐ Ⓑ Ⓒ Ⓓ	64	Ⓐ Ⓑ Ⓒ Ⓓ	84	Ⓐ Ⓑ Ⓒ Ⓓ
5	Ⓐ Ⓑ Ⓒ Ⓓ	25	Ⓐ Ⓑ Ⓒ	45	Ⓐ Ⓑ Ⓒ Ⓓ	65	Ⓐ Ⓑ Ⓒ Ⓓ	85	Ⓐ Ⓑ Ⓒ Ⓓ
6	Ⓐ Ⓑ Ⓒ Ⓓ	26	Ⓐ Ⓑ Ⓒ	46	Ⓐ Ⓑ Ⓒ Ⓓ	66	Ⓐ Ⓑ Ⓒ Ⓓ	86	Ⓐ Ⓑ Ⓒ Ⓓ
7	Ⓐ Ⓑ Ⓒ	27	Ⓐ Ⓑ Ⓒ	47	Ⓐ Ⓑ Ⓒ Ⓓ	67	Ⓐ Ⓑ Ⓒ Ⓓ	87	Ⓐ Ⓑ Ⓒ Ⓓ
8	Ⓐ Ⓑ Ⓒ	28	Ⓐ Ⓑ Ⓒ	48	Ⓐ Ⓑ Ⓒ Ⓓ	68	Ⓐ Ⓑ Ⓒ Ⓓ	88	Ⓐ Ⓑ Ⓒ Ⓓ
9	Ⓐ Ⓑ Ⓒ	29	Ⓐ Ⓑ Ⓒ	49	Ⓐ Ⓑ Ⓒ Ⓓ	69	Ⓐ Ⓑ Ⓒ Ⓓ	89	Ⓐ Ⓑ Ⓒ Ⓓ
10	Ⓐ Ⓑ Ⓒ	30	Ⓐ Ⓑ Ⓒ	50	Ⓐ Ⓑ Ⓒ Ⓓ	70	Ⓐ Ⓑ Ⓒ Ⓓ	90	Ⓐ Ⓑ Ⓒ Ⓓ
11	Ⓐ Ⓑ Ⓒ	31	Ⓐ Ⓑ Ⓒ	51	Ⓐ Ⓑ Ⓒ Ⓓ	71	Ⓐ Ⓑ Ⓒ Ⓓ	91	Ⓐ Ⓑ Ⓒ Ⓓ
12	Ⓐ Ⓑ Ⓒ	32	Ⓐ Ⓑ Ⓒ	52	Ⓐ Ⓑ Ⓒ Ⓓ	72	Ⓐ Ⓑ Ⓒ Ⓓ	92	Ⓐ Ⓑ Ⓒ Ⓓ
13	Ⓐ Ⓑ Ⓒ	33	Ⓐ Ⓑ Ⓒ	53	Ⓐ Ⓑ Ⓒ Ⓓ	73	Ⓐ Ⓑ Ⓒ Ⓓ	93	Ⓐ Ⓑ Ⓒ Ⓓ
14	Ⓐ Ⓑ Ⓒ	34	Ⓐ Ⓑ Ⓒ	54	Ⓐ Ⓑ Ⓒ Ⓓ	74	Ⓐ Ⓑ Ⓒ Ⓓ	94	Ⓐ Ⓑ Ⓒ Ⓓ
15	Ⓐ Ⓑ Ⓒ	35	Ⓐ Ⓑ Ⓒ	55	Ⓐ Ⓑ Ⓒ Ⓓ	75	Ⓐ Ⓑ Ⓒ Ⓓ	95	Ⓐ Ⓑ Ⓒ Ⓓ
16	Ⓐ Ⓑ Ⓒ	36	Ⓐ Ⓑ Ⓒ	56	Ⓐ Ⓑ Ⓒ Ⓓ	76	Ⓐ Ⓑ Ⓒ Ⓓ	96	Ⓐ Ⓑ Ⓒ Ⓓ
17	Ⓐ Ⓑ Ⓒ	37	Ⓐ Ⓑ Ⓒ	57	Ⓐ Ⓑ Ⓒ Ⓓ	77	Ⓐ Ⓑ Ⓒ Ⓓ	97	Ⓐ Ⓑ Ⓒ Ⓓ
18	Ⓐ Ⓑ Ⓒ	38	Ⓐ Ⓑ Ⓒ	58	Ⓐ Ⓑ Ⓒ Ⓓ	78	Ⓐ Ⓑ Ⓒ Ⓓ	98	Ⓐ Ⓑ Ⓒ Ⓓ
19	Ⓐ Ⓑ Ⓒ	39	Ⓐ Ⓑ Ⓒ	59	Ⓐ Ⓑ Ⓒ Ⓓ	79	Ⓐ Ⓑ Ⓒ Ⓓ	99	Ⓐ Ⓑ Ⓒ Ⓓ
20	Ⓐ Ⓑ Ⓒ	40	Ⓐ Ⓑ Ⓒ	60	Ⓐ Ⓑ Ⓒ Ⓓ	80	Ⓐ Ⓑ Ⓒ Ⓓ	100	Ⓐ Ⓑ Ⓒ Ⓓ

맞은 문제 개수: ____/100

TEST 04의 점수를 환산한 후 목표 달성기에 TEST 04의 점수를 표시합니다.
점수 환산표는 문제집 16페이지, 목표 달성기는 교재의 첫 장에 있습니다.

✂ 자르는 선

Answer Sheet

TEST 03

LISTENING (Part I~IV)

	A B C D		A B C D		A B C D		A B C D		A B C D
1	Ⓐ Ⓑ Ⓒ Ⓓ	21	Ⓐ Ⓑ Ⓒ Ⓓ	41	Ⓐ Ⓑ Ⓒ Ⓓ	61	Ⓐ Ⓑ Ⓒ Ⓓ	81	Ⓐ Ⓑ Ⓒ Ⓓ
2	Ⓐ Ⓑ Ⓒ Ⓓ	22	Ⓐ Ⓑ Ⓒ	42	Ⓐ Ⓑ Ⓒ Ⓓ	62	Ⓐ Ⓑ Ⓒ Ⓓ	82	Ⓐ Ⓑ Ⓒ Ⓓ
3	Ⓐ Ⓑ Ⓒ Ⓓ	23	Ⓐ Ⓑ Ⓒ	43	Ⓐ Ⓑ Ⓒ Ⓓ	63	Ⓐ Ⓑ Ⓒ Ⓓ	83	Ⓐ Ⓑ Ⓒ Ⓓ
4	Ⓐ Ⓑ Ⓒ Ⓓ	24	Ⓐ Ⓑ Ⓒ	44	Ⓐ Ⓑ Ⓒ Ⓓ	64	Ⓐ Ⓑ Ⓒ Ⓓ	84	Ⓐ Ⓑ Ⓒ Ⓓ
5	Ⓐ Ⓑ Ⓒ Ⓓ	25	Ⓐ Ⓑ Ⓒ	45	Ⓐ Ⓑ Ⓒ Ⓓ	65	Ⓐ Ⓑ Ⓒ Ⓓ	85	Ⓐ Ⓑ Ⓒ Ⓓ
6	Ⓐ Ⓑ Ⓒ Ⓓ	26	Ⓐ Ⓑ Ⓒ	46	Ⓐ Ⓑ Ⓒ Ⓓ	66	Ⓐ Ⓑ Ⓒ Ⓓ	86	Ⓐ Ⓑ Ⓒ Ⓓ
7	Ⓐ Ⓑ Ⓒ	27	Ⓐ Ⓑ Ⓒ	47	Ⓐ Ⓑ Ⓒ Ⓓ	67	Ⓐ Ⓑ Ⓒ Ⓓ	87	Ⓐ Ⓑ Ⓒ Ⓓ
8	Ⓐ Ⓑ Ⓒ	28	Ⓐ Ⓑ Ⓒ	48	Ⓐ Ⓑ Ⓒ Ⓓ	68	Ⓐ Ⓑ Ⓒ Ⓓ	88	Ⓐ Ⓑ Ⓒ Ⓓ
9	Ⓐ Ⓑ Ⓒ	29	Ⓐ Ⓑ Ⓒ	49	Ⓐ Ⓑ Ⓒ Ⓓ	69	Ⓐ Ⓑ Ⓒ Ⓓ	89	Ⓐ Ⓑ Ⓒ Ⓓ
10	Ⓐ Ⓑ Ⓒ	30	Ⓐ Ⓑ Ⓒ	50	Ⓐ Ⓑ Ⓒ Ⓓ	70	Ⓐ Ⓑ Ⓒ Ⓓ	90	Ⓐ Ⓑ Ⓒ Ⓓ
11	Ⓐ Ⓑ Ⓒ	31	Ⓐ Ⓑ Ⓒ	51	Ⓐ Ⓑ Ⓒ Ⓓ	71	Ⓐ Ⓑ Ⓒ Ⓓ	91	Ⓐ Ⓑ Ⓒ Ⓓ
12	Ⓐ Ⓑ Ⓒ	32	Ⓐ Ⓑ Ⓒ	52	Ⓐ Ⓑ Ⓒ Ⓓ	72	Ⓐ Ⓑ Ⓒ Ⓓ	92	Ⓐ Ⓑ Ⓒ Ⓓ
13	Ⓐ Ⓑ Ⓒ	33	Ⓐ Ⓑ Ⓒ	53	Ⓐ Ⓑ Ⓒ Ⓓ	73	Ⓐ Ⓑ Ⓒ Ⓓ	93	Ⓐ Ⓑ Ⓒ Ⓓ
14	Ⓐ Ⓑ Ⓒ	34	Ⓐ Ⓑ Ⓒ	54	Ⓐ Ⓑ Ⓒ Ⓓ	74	Ⓐ Ⓑ Ⓒ Ⓓ	94	Ⓐ Ⓑ Ⓒ Ⓓ
15	Ⓐ Ⓑ Ⓒ	35	Ⓐ Ⓑ Ⓒ	55	Ⓐ Ⓑ Ⓒ Ⓓ	75	Ⓐ Ⓑ Ⓒ Ⓓ	95	Ⓐ Ⓑ Ⓒ Ⓓ
16	Ⓐ Ⓑ Ⓒ	36	Ⓐ Ⓑ Ⓒ	56	Ⓐ Ⓑ Ⓒ Ⓓ	76	Ⓐ Ⓑ Ⓒ Ⓓ	96	Ⓐ Ⓑ Ⓒ Ⓓ
17	Ⓐ Ⓑ Ⓒ	37	Ⓐ Ⓑ Ⓒ	57	Ⓐ Ⓑ Ⓒ Ⓓ	77	Ⓐ Ⓑ Ⓒ Ⓓ	97	Ⓐ Ⓑ Ⓒ Ⓓ
18	Ⓐ Ⓑ Ⓒ	38	Ⓐ Ⓑ Ⓒ	58	Ⓐ Ⓑ Ⓒ Ⓓ	78	Ⓐ Ⓑ Ⓒ Ⓓ	98	Ⓐ Ⓑ Ⓒ Ⓓ
19	Ⓐ Ⓑ Ⓒ	39	Ⓐ Ⓑ Ⓒ	59	Ⓐ Ⓑ Ⓒ Ⓓ	79	Ⓐ Ⓑ Ⓒ Ⓓ	99	Ⓐ Ⓑ Ⓒ Ⓓ
20	Ⓐ Ⓑ Ⓒ	40	Ⓐ Ⓑ Ⓒ	60	Ⓐ Ⓑ Ⓒ Ⓓ	80	Ⓐ Ⓑ Ⓒ Ⓓ	100	Ⓐ Ⓑ Ⓒ Ⓓ

맞은 문제 개수: ____/100

TEST 03의 점수를 환산한 후 목표 달성기에 TEST 03의 점수를 표시합니다.
점수 환산표는 문제집 16페이지, 목표 달성기는 교재의 첫 장에 있습니다.

자르는 선

무료 토익·토스·오픽·지텔프 자료 제공
Hackers.co.kr

Answer Sheet

TEST 06

LISTENING (Part I~IV)

#					#					#					#					#				
1	Ⓐ Ⓑ Ⓒ Ⓓ				21	Ⓐ Ⓑ Ⓒ				41	Ⓐ Ⓑ Ⓒ Ⓓ				61	Ⓐ Ⓑ Ⓒ Ⓓ				81	Ⓐ Ⓑ Ⓒ Ⓓ
2	Ⓐ Ⓑ Ⓒ Ⓓ				22	Ⓐ Ⓑ Ⓒ				42	Ⓐ Ⓑ Ⓒ Ⓓ				62	Ⓐ Ⓑ Ⓒ Ⓓ				82	Ⓐ Ⓑ Ⓒ Ⓓ
3	Ⓐ Ⓑ Ⓒ Ⓓ				23	Ⓐ Ⓑ Ⓒ				43	Ⓐ Ⓑ Ⓒ Ⓓ				63	Ⓐ Ⓑ Ⓒ Ⓓ				83	Ⓐ Ⓑ Ⓒ Ⓓ
4	Ⓐ Ⓑ Ⓒ Ⓓ				24	Ⓐ Ⓑ Ⓒ				44	Ⓐ Ⓑ Ⓒ Ⓓ				64	Ⓐ Ⓑ Ⓒ Ⓓ				84	Ⓐ Ⓑ Ⓒ Ⓓ
5	Ⓐ Ⓑ Ⓒ Ⓓ				25	Ⓐ Ⓑ Ⓒ				45	Ⓐ Ⓑ Ⓒ Ⓓ				65	Ⓐ Ⓑ Ⓒ Ⓓ				85	Ⓐ Ⓑ Ⓒ Ⓓ
6	Ⓐ Ⓑ Ⓒ Ⓓ				26	Ⓐ Ⓑ Ⓒ				46	Ⓐ Ⓑ Ⓒ Ⓓ				66	Ⓐ Ⓑ Ⓒ Ⓓ				86	Ⓐ Ⓑ Ⓒ Ⓓ
7	Ⓐ Ⓑ Ⓒ				27	Ⓐ Ⓑ Ⓒ				47	Ⓐ Ⓑ Ⓒ Ⓓ				67	Ⓐ Ⓑ Ⓒ Ⓓ				87	Ⓐ Ⓑ Ⓒ Ⓓ
8	Ⓐ Ⓑ Ⓒ				28	Ⓐ Ⓑ Ⓒ				48	Ⓐ Ⓑ Ⓒ Ⓓ				68	Ⓐ Ⓑ Ⓒ Ⓓ				88	Ⓐ Ⓑ Ⓒ Ⓓ
9	Ⓐ Ⓑ Ⓒ				29	Ⓐ Ⓑ Ⓒ				49	Ⓐ Ⓑ Ⓒ Ⓓ				69	Ⓐ Ⓑ Ⓒ Ⓓ				89	Ⓐ Ⓑ Ⓒ Ⓓ
10	Ⓐ Ⓑ Ⓒ				30	Ⓐ Ⓑ Ⓒ Ⓓ				50	Ⓐ Ⓑ Ⓒ Ⓓ				70	Ⓐ Ⓑ Ⓒ Ⓓ				90	Ⓐ Ⓑ Ⓒ Ⓓ
11	Ⓐ Ⓑ Ⓒ				31	Ⓐ Ⓑ Ⓒ Ⓓ				51	Ⓐ Ⓑ Ⓒ Ⓓ				71	Ⓐ Ⓑ Ⓒ Ⓓ				91	Ⓐ Ⓑ Ⓒ Ⓓ
12	Ⓐ Ⓑ Ⓒ				32	Ⓐ Ⓑ Ⓒ Ⓓ				52	Ⓐ Ⓑ Ⓒ Ⓓ				72	Ⓐ Ⓑ Ⓒ Ⓓ				92	Ⓐ Ⓑ Ⓒ Ⓓ
13	Ⓐ Ⓑ Ⓒ				33	Ⓐ Ⓑ Ⓒ Ⓓ				53	Ⓐ Ⓑ Ⓒ Ⓓ				73	Ⓐ Ⓑ Ⓒ Ⓓ				93	Ⓐ Ⓑ Ⓒ Ⓓ
14	Ⓐ Ⓑ Ⓒ				34	Ⓐ Ⓑ Ⓒ Ⓓ				54	Ⓐ Ⓑ Ⓒ Ⓓ				74	Ⓐ Ⓑ Ⓒ Ⓓ				94	Ⓐ Ⓑ Ⓒ Ⓓ
15	Ⓐ Ⓑ Ⓒ				35	Ⓐ Ⓑ Ⓒ Ⓓ				55	Ⓐ Ⓑ Ⓒ Ⓓ				75	Ⓐ Ⓑ Ⓒ Ⓓ				95	Ⓐ Ⓑ Ⓒ Ⓓ
16	Ⓐ Ⓑ Ⓒ				36	Ⓐ Ⓑ Ⓒ Ⓓ				56	Ⓐ Ⓑ Ⓒ Ⓓ				76	Ⓐ Ⓑ Ⓒ Ⓓ				96	Ⓐ Ⓑ Ⓒ Ⓓ
17	Ⓐ Ⓑ Ⓒ				37	Ⓐ Ⓑ Ⓒ Ⓓ				57	Ⓐ Ⓑ Ⓒ Ⓓ				77	Ⓐ Ⓑ Ⓒ Ⓓ				97	Ⓐ Ⓑ Ⓒ Ⓓ
18	Ⓐ Ⓑ Ⓒ				38	Ⓐ Ⓑ Ⓒ Ⓓ				58	Ⓐ Ⓑ Ⓒ Ⓓ				78	Ⓐ Ⓑ Ⓒ Ⓓ				98	Ⓐ Ⓑ Ⓒ Ⓓ
19	Ⓐ Ⓑ Ⓒ				39	Ⓐ Ⓑ Ⓒ Ⓓ				59	Ⓐ Ⓑ Ⓒ Ⓓ				79	Ⓐ Ⓑ Ⓒ Ⓓ				99	Ⓐ Ⓑ Ⓒ Ⓓ
20	Ⓐ Ⓑ Ⓒ				40	Ⓐ Ⓑ Ⓒ Ⓓ				60	Ⓐ Ⓑ Ⓒ Ⓓ				80	Ⓐ Ⓑ Ⓒ Ⓓ				100	Ⓐ Ⓑ Ⓒ Ⓓ

맞은 문제 개수: ____ /100

TEST 06의 점수를 환산한 후 목표 달성기에 TEST 06의 점수를 표시합니다.
점수 환산표는 문제집 16페이지, 목표 달성기는 교재의 첫 장에 있습니다.

✂ 자르는 선

Answer Sheet

TEST 05

LISTENING (Part I~IV)

#					#					#					#					#				
1	Ⓐ Ⓑ Ⓒ Ⓓ				21	Ⓐ Ⓑ Ⓒ				41	Ⓐ Ⓑ Ⓒ Ⓓ				61	Ⓐ Ⓑ Ⓒ Ⓓ				81	Ⓐ Ⓑ Ⓒ Ⓓ
2	Ⓐ Ⓑ Ⓒ Ⓓ				22	Ⓐ Ⓑ Ⓒ				42	Ⓐ Ⓑ Ⓒ Ⓓ				62	Ⓐ Ⓑ Ⓒ Ⓓ				82	Ⓐ Ⓑ Ⓒ Ⓓ
3	Ⓐ Ⓑ Ⓒ Ⓓ				23	Ⓐ Ⓑ Ⓒ				43	Ⓐ Ⓑ Ⓒ Ⓓ				63	Ⓐ Ⓑ Ⓒ Ⓓ				83	Ⓐ Ⓑ Ⓒ Ⓓ
4	Ⓐ Ⓑ Ⓒ Ⓓ				24	Ⓐ Ⓑ Ⓒ				44	Ⓐ Ⓑ Ⓒ Ⓓ				64	Ⓐ Ⓑ Ⓒ Ⓓ				84	Ⓐ Ⓑ Ⓒ Ⓓ
5	Ⓐ Ⓑ Ⓒ Ⓓ				25	Ⓐ Ⓑ Ⓒ				45	Ⓐ Ⓑ Ⓒ Ⓓ				65	Ⓐ Ⓑ Ⓒ Ⓓ				85	Ⓐ Ⓑ Ⓒ Ⓓ
6	Ⓐ Ⓑ Ⓒ Ⓓ				26	Ⓐ Ⓑ Ⓒ				46	Ⓐ Ⓑ Ⓒ Ⓓ				66	Ⓐ Ⓑ Ⓒ Ⓓ				86	Ⓐ Ⓑ Ⓒ Ⓓ
7	Ⓐ Ⓑ Ⓒ				27	Ⓐ Ⓑ Ⓒ				47	Ⓐ Ⓑ Ⓒ Ⓓ				67	Ⓐ Ⓑ Ⓒ Ⓓ				87	Ⓐ Ⓑ Ⓒ Ⓓ
8	Ⓐ Ⓑ Ⓒ				28	Ⓐ Ⓑ Ⓒ				48	Ⓐ Ⓑ Ⓒ Ⓓ				68	Ⓐ Ⓑ Ⓒ Ⓓ				88	Ⓐ Ⓑ Ⓒ Ⓓ
9	Ⓐ Ⓑ Ⓒ				29	Ⓐ Ⓑ Ⓒ				49	Ⓐ Ⓑ Ⓒ Ⓓ				69	Ⓐ Ⓑ Ⓒ Ⓓ				89	Ⓐ Ⓑ Ⓒ Ⓓ
10	Ⓐ Ⓑ Ⓒ				30	Ⓐ Ⓑ Ⓒ Ⓓ				50	Ⓐ Ⓑ Ⓒ Ⓓ				70	Ⓐ Ⓑ Ⓒ Ⓓ				90	Ⓐ Ⓑ Ⓒ Ⓓ
11	Ⓐ Ⓑ Ⓒ				31	Ⓐ Ⓑ Ⓒ Ⓓ				51	Ⓐ Ⓑ Ⓒ Ⓓ				71	Ⓐ Ⓑ Ⓒ Ⓓ				91	Ⓐ Ⓑ Ⓒ Ⓓ
12	Ⓐ Ⓑ Ⓒ				32	Ⓐ Ⓑ Ⓒ Ⓓ				52	Ⓐ Ⓑ Ⓒ Ⓓ				72	Ⓐ Ⓑ Ⓒ Ⓓ				92	Ⓐ Ⓑ Ⓒ Ⓓ
13	Ⓐ Ⓑ Ⓒ				33	Ⓐ Ⓑ Ⓒ Ⓓ				53	Ⓐ Ⓑ Ⓒ Ⓓ				73	Ⓐ Ⓑ Ⓒ Ⓓ				93	Ⓐ Ⓑ Ⓒ Ⓓ
14	Ⓐ Ⓑ Ⓒ				34	Ⓐ Ⓑ Ⓒ Ⓓ				54	Ⓐ Ⓑ Ⓒ Ⓓ				74	Ⓐ Ⓑ Ⓒ Ⓓ				94	Ⓐ Ⓑ Ⓒ Ⓓ
15	Ⓐ Ⓑ Ⓒ				35	Ⓐ Ⓑ Ⓒ Ⓓ				55	Ⓐ Ⓑ Ⓒ Ⓓ				75	Ⓐ Ⓑ Ⓒ Ⓓ				95	Ⓐ Ⓑ Ⓒ Ⓓ
16	Ⓐ Ⓑ Ⓒ				36	Ⓐ Ⓑ Ⓒ Ⓓ				56	Ⓐ Ⓑ Ⓒ Ⓓ				76	Ⓐ Ⓑ Ⓒ Ⓓ				96	Ⓐ Ⓑ Ⓒ Ⓓ
17	Ⓐ Ⓑ Ⓒ				37	Ⓐ Ⓑ Ⓒ Ⓓ				57	Ⓐ Ⓑ Ⓒ Ⓓ				77	Ⓐ Ⓑ Ⓒ Ⓓ				97	Ⓐ Ⓑ Ⓒ Ⓓ
18	Ⓐ Ⓑ Ⓒ				38	Ⓐ Ⓑ Ⓒ Ⓓ				58	Ⓐ Ⓑ Ⓒ Ⓓ				78	Ⓐ Ⓑ Ⓒ Ⓓ				98	Ⓐ Ⓑ Ⓒ Ⓓ
19	Ⓐ Ⓑ Ⓒ				39	Ⓐ Ⓑ Ⓒ Ⓓ				59	Ⓐ Ⓑ Ⓒ Ⓓ				79	Ⓐ Ⓑ Ⓒ Ⓓ				99	Ⓐ Ⓑ Ⓒ Ⓓ
20	Ⓐ Ⓑ Ⓒ				40	Ⓐ Ⓑ Ⓒ Ⓓ				60	Ⓐ Ⓑ Ⓒ Ⓓ				80	Ⓐ Ⓑ Ⓒ Ⓓ				100	Ⓐ Ⓑ Ⓒ Ⓓ

맞은 문제 개수: ____ /100

TEST 05의 점수를 환산한 후 목표 달성기에 TEST 05의 점수를 표시합니다.
점수 환산표는 문제집 16페이지, 목표 달성기는 교재의 첫 장에 있습니다.

무료 토익·토스·오픽·지텔프 자료 제공
Hackers.co.kr

Answer Sheet

TEST 08

LISTENING (Part I~IV)

1	Ⓐ Ⓑ Ⓒ Ⓓ	21	Ⓐ Ⓑ Ⓒ	41	Ⓐ Ⓑ Ⓒ Ⓓ	61	Ⓐ Ⓑ Ⓒ Ⓓ	81	Ⓐ Ⓑ Ⓒ Ⓓ
2	Ⓐ Ⓑ Ⓒ Ⓓ	22	Ⓐ Ⓑ Ⓒ	42	Ⓐ Ⓑ Ⓒ Ⓓ	62	Ⓐ Ⓑ Ⓒ Ⓓ	82	Ⓐ Ⓑ Ⓒ Ⓓ
3	Ⓐ Ⓑ Ⓒ Ⓓ	23	Ⓐ Ⓑ Ⓒ	43	Ⓐ Ⓑ Ⓒ Ⓓ	63	Ⓐ Ⓑ Ⓒ Ⓓ	83	Ⓐ Ⓑ Ⓒ Ⓓ
4	Ⓐ Ⓑ Ⓒ Ⓓ	24	Ⓐ Ⓑ Ⓒ	44	Ⓐ Ⓑ Ⓒ Ⓓ	64	Ⓐ Ⓑ Ⓒ Ⓓ	84	Ⓐ Ⓑ Ⓒ Ⓓ
5	Ⓐ Ⓑ Ⓒ Ⓓ	25	Ⓐ Ⓑ Ⓒ	45	Ⓐ Ⓑ Ⓒ Ⓓ	65	Ⓐ Ⓑ Ⓒ Ⓓ	85	Ⓐ Ⓑ Ⓒ Ⓓ
6	Ⓐ Ⓑ Ⓒ Ⓓ	26	Ⓐ Ⓑ Ⓒ	46	Ⓐ Ⓑ Ⓒ Ⓓ	66	Ⓐ Ⓑ Ⓒ Ⓓ	86	Ⓐ Ⓑ Ⓒ Ⓓ
7	Ⓐ Ⓑ Ⓒ	27	Ⓐ Ⓑ Ⓒ	47	Ⓐ Ⓑ Ⓒ Ⓓ	67	Ⓐ Ⓑ Ⓒ Ⓓ	87	Ⓐ Ⓑ Ⓒ Ⓓ
8	Ⓐ Ⓑ Ⓒ	28	Ⓐ Ⓑ Ⓒ	48	Ⓐ Ⓑ Ⓒ Ⓓ	68	Ⓐ Ⓑ Ⓒ Ⓓ	88	Ⓐ Ⓑ Ⓒ Ⓓ
9	Ⓐ Ⓑ Ⓒ	29	Ⓐ Ⓑ Ⓒ	49	Ⓐ Ⓑ Ⓒ Ⓓ	69	Ⓐ Ⓑ Ⓒ Ⓓ	89	Ⓐ Ⓑ Ⓒ Ⓓ
10	Ⓐ Ⓑ Ⓒ	30	Ⓐ Ⓑ Ⓒ Ⓓ	50	Ⓐ Ⓑ Ⓒ Ⓓ	70	Ⓐ Ⓑ Ⓒ Ⓓ	90	Ⓐ Ⓑ Ⓒ Ⓓ
11	Ⓐ Ⓑ Ⓒ	31	Ⓐ Ⓑ Ⓒ Ⓓ	51	Ⓐ Ⓑ Ⓒ Ⓓ	71	Ⓐ Ⓑ Ⓒ Ⓓ	91	Ⓐ Ⓑ Ⓒ Ⓓ
12	Ⓐ Ⓑ Ⓒ	32	Ⓐ Ⓑ Ⓒ Ⓓ	52	Ⓐ Ⓑ Ⓒ Ⓓ	72	Ⓐ Ⓑ Ⓒ Ⓓ	92	Ⓐ Ⓑ Ⓒ Ⓓ
13	Ⓐ Ⓑ Ⓒ	33	Ⓐ Ⓑ Ⓒ Ⓓ	53	Ⓐ Ⓑ Ⓒ Ⓓ	73	Ⓐ Ⓑ Ⓒ Ⓓ	93	Ⓐ Ⓑ Ⓒ Ⓓ
14	Ⓐ Ⓑ Ⓒ	34	Ⓐ Ⓑ Ⓒ Ⓓ	54	Ⓐ Ⓑ Ⓒ Ⓓ	74	Ⓐ Ⓑ Ⓒ Ⓓ	94	Ⓐ Ⓑ Ⓒ Ⓓ
15	Ⓐ Ⓑ Ⓒ	35	Ⓐ Ⓑ Ⓒ Ⓓ	55	Ⓐ Ⓑ Ⓒ Ⓓ	75	Ⓐ Ⓑ Ⓒ Ⓓ	95	Ⓐ Ⓑ Ⓒ Ⓓ
16	Ⓐ Ⓑ Ⓒ	36	Ⓐ Ⓑ Ⓒ Ⓓ	56	Ⓐ Ⓑ Ⓒ Ⓓ	76	Ⓐ Ⓑ Ⓒ Ⓓ	96	Ⓐ Ⓑ Ⓒ Ⓓ
17	Ⓐ Ⓑ Ⓒ	37	Ⓐ Ⓑ Ⓒ Ⓓ	57	Ⓐ Ⓑ Ⓒ Ⓓ	77	Ⓐ Ⓑ Ⓒ Ⓓ	97	Ⓐ Ⓑ Ⓒ Ⓓ
18	Ⓐ Ⓑ Ⓒ	38	Ⓐ Ⓑ Ⓒ Ⓓ	58	Ⓐ Ⓑ Ⓒ Ⓓ	78	Ⓐ Ⓑ Ⓒ Ⓓ	98	Ⓐ Ⓑ Ⓒ Ⓓ
19	Ⓐ Ⓑ Ⓒ	39	Ⓐ Ⓑ Ⓒ Ⓓ	59	Ⓐ Ⓑ Ⓒ Ⓓ	79	Ⓐ Ⓑ Ⓒ Ⓓ	99	Ⓐ Ⓑ Ⓒ Ⓓ
20	Ⓐ Ⓑ Ⓒ	40	Ⓐ Ⓑ Ⓒ Ⓓ	60	Ⓐ Ⓑ Ⓒ Ⓓ	80	Ⓐ Ⓑ Ⓒ Ⓓ	100	Ⓐ Ⓑ Ⓒ Ⓓ

맞은 문제 개수: ___ / 100

TEST 08의 점수를 환산한 후 목표 달성기에 TEST 08의 점수를 표시합니다.
점수 환산표는 문제집 167페이지, 목표 달성기는 교재의 첫 장에 있습니다.

✄ 자르는 선

Answer Sheet

TEST 07

LISTENING (Part I~IV)

1	Ⓐ Ⓑ Ⓒ Ⓓ	21	Ⓐ Ⓑ Ⓒ	41	Ⓐ Ⓑ Ⓒ Ⓓ	61	Ⓐ Ⓑ Ⓒ Ⓓ	81	Ⓐ Ⓑ Ⓒ Ⓓ
2	Ⓐ Ⓑ Ⓒ Ⓓ	22	Ⓐ Ⓑ Ⓒ	42	Ⓐ Ⓑ Ⓒ Ⓓ	62	Ⓐ Ⓑ Ⓒ Ⓓ	82	Ⓐ Ⓑ Ⓒ Ⓓ
3	Ⓐ Ⓑ Ⓒ Ⓓ	23	Ⓐ Ⓑ Ⓒ	43	Ⓐ Ⓑ Ⓒ Ⓓ	63	Ⓐ Ⓑ Ⓒ Ⓓ	83	Ⓐ Ⓑ Ⓒ Ⓓ
4	Ⓐ Ⓑ Ⓒ Ⓓ	24	Ⓐ Ⓑ Ⓒ	44	Ⓐ Ⓑ Ⓒ Ⓓ	64	Ⓐ Ⓑ Ⓒ Ⓓ	84	Ⓐ Ⓑ Ⓒ Ⓓ
5	Ⓐ Ⓑ Ⓒ Ⓓ	25	Ⓐ Ⓑ Ⓒ	45	Ⓐ Ⓑ Ⓒ Ⓓ	65	Ⓐ Ⓑ Ⓒ Ⓓ	85	Ⓐ Ⓑ Ⓒ Ⓓ
6	Ⓐ Ⓑ Ⓒ Ⓓ	26	Ⓐ Ⓑ Ⓒ	46	Ⓐ Ⓑ Ⓒ Ⓓ	66	Ⓐ Ⓑ Ⓒ Ⓓ	86	Ⓐ Ⓑ Ⓒ Ⓓ
7	Ⓐ Ⓑ Ⓒ	27	Ⓐ Ⓑ Ⓒ	47	Ⓐ Ⓑ Ⓒ Ⓓ	67	Ⓐ Ⓑ Ⓒ Ⓓ	87	Ⓐ Ⓑ Ⓒ Ⓓ
8	Ⓐ Ⓑ Ⓒ	28	Ⓐ Ⓑ Ⓒ	48	Ⓐ Ⓑ Ⓒ Ⓓ	68	Ⓐ Ⓑ Ⓒ Ⓓ	88	Ⓐ Ⓑ Ⓒ Ⓓ
9	Ⓐ Ⓑ Ⓒ	29	Ⓐ Ⓑ Ⓒ	49	Ⓐ Ⓑ Ⓒ Ⓓ	69	Ⓐ Ⓑ Ⓒ Ⓓ	89	Ⓐ Ⓑ Ⓒ Ⓓ
10	Ⓐ Ⓑ Ⓒ	30	Ⓐ Ⓑ Ⓒ Ⓓ	50	Ⓐ Ⓑ Ⓒ Ⓓ	70	Ⓐ Ⓑ Ⓒ Ⓓ	90	Ⓐ Ⓑ Ⓒ Ⓓ
11	Ⓐ Ⓑ Ⓒ	31	Ⓐ Ⓑ Ⓒ Ⓓ	51	Ⓐ Ⓑ Ⓒ Ⓓ	71	Ⓐ Ⓑ Ⓒ Ⓓ	91	Ⓐ Ⓑ Ⓒ Ⓓ
12	Ⓐ Ⓑ Ⓒ	32	Ⓐ Ⓑ Ⓒ Ⓓ	52	Ⓐ Ⓑ Ⓒ Ⓓ	72	Ⓐ Ⓑ Ⓒ Ⓓ	92	Ⓐ Ⓑ Ⓒ Ⓓ
13	Ⓐ Ⓑ Ⓒ	33	Ⓐ Ⓑ Ⓒ Ⓓ	53	Ⓐ Ⓑ Ⓒ Ⓓ	73	Ⓐ Ⓑ Ⓒ Ⓓ	93	Ⓐ Ⓑ Ⓒ Ⓓ
14	Ⓐ Ⓑ Ⓒ	34	Ⓐ Ⓑ Ⓒ Ⓓ	54	Ⓐ Ⓑ Ⓒ Ⓓ	74	Ⓐ Ⓑ Ⓒ Ⓓ	94	Ⓐ Ⓑ Ⓒ Ⓓ
15	Ⓐ Ⓑ Ⓒ	35	Ⓐ Ⓑ Ⓒ Ⓓ	55	Ⓐ Ⓑ Ⓒ Ⓓ	75	Ⓐ Ⓑ Ⓒ Ⓓ	95	Ⓐ Ⓑ Ⓒ Ⓓ
16	Ⓐ Ⓑ Ⓒ	36	Ⓐ Ⓑ Ⓒ Ⓓ	56	Ⓐ Ⓑ Ⓒ Ⓓ	76	Ⓐ Ⓑ Ⓒ Ⓓ	96	Ⓐ Ⓑ Ⓒ Ⓓ
17	Ⓐ Ⓑ Ⓒ	37	Ⓐ Ⓑ Ⓒ Ⓓ	57	Ⓐ Ⓑ Ⓒ Ⓓ	77	Ⓐ Ⓑ Ⓒ Ⓓ	97	Ⓐ Ⓑ Ⓒ Ⓓ
18	Ⓐ Ⓑ Ⓒ	38	Ⓐ Ⓑ Ⓒ Ⓓ	58	Ⓐ Ⓑ Ⓒ Ⓓ	78	Ⓐ Ⓑ Ⓒ Ⓓ	98	Ⓐ Ⓑ Ⓒ Ⓓ
19	Ⓐ Ⓑ Ⓒ	39	Ⓐ Ⓑ Ⓒ Ⓓ	59	Ⓐ Ⓑ Ⓒ Ⓓ	79	Ⓐ Ⓑ Ⓒ Ⓓ	99	Ⓐ Ⓑ Ⓒ Ⓓ
20	Ⓐ Ⓑ Ⓒ	40	Ⓐ Ⓑ Ⓒ Ⓓ	60	Ⓐ Ⓑ Ⓒ Ⓓ	80	Ⓐ Ⓑ Ⓒ Ⓓ	100	Ⓐ Ⓑ Ⓒ Ⓓ

맞은 문제 개수: ___ / 100

TEST 07의 점수를 환산한 후 목표 달성기에 TEST 07의 점수를 표시합니다.
점수 환산표는 문제집 16페이지, 목표 달성기는 교재의 첫 장에 있습니다.

✄ 자르는 선

무료 토익·토스·오픽·지텔프 자료 제공
Hackers.co.kr

Answer Sheet

TEST 10

LISTENING (Part I~IV)

#	A	B	C	D	#	A	B	C	D	#	A	B	C	D	#	A	B	C	D	#	A	B	C	D
1	Ⓐ	Ⓑ	Ⓒ	Ⓓ	21	Ⓐ	Ⓑ	Ⓒ		41	Ⓐ	Ⓑ	Ⓒ	Ⓓ	61	Ⓐ	Ⓑ	Ⓒ	Ⓓ	81	Ⓐ	Ⓑ	Ⓒ	Ⓓ
2	Ⓐ	Ⓑ	Ⓒ	Ⓓ	22	Ⓐ	Ⓑ	Ⓒ		42	Ⓐ	Ⓑ	Ⓒ	Ⓓ	62	Ⓐ	Ⓑ	Ⓒ	Ⓓ	82	Ⓐ	Ⓑ	Ⓒ	Ⓓ
3	Ⓐ	Ⓑ	Ⓒ	Ⓓ	23	Ⓐ	Ⓑ	Ⓒ		43	Ⓐ	Ⓑ	Ⓒ	Ⓓ	63	Ⓐ	Ⓑ	Ⓒ	Ⓓ	83	Ⓐ	Ⓑ	Ⓒ	Ⓓ
4	Ⓐ	Ⓑ	Ⓒ	Ⓓ	24	Ⓐ	Ⓑ	Ⓒ		44	Ⓐ	Ⓑ	Ⓒ	Ⓓ	64	Ⓐ	Ⓑ	Ⓒ	Ⓓ	84	Ⓐ	Ⓑ	Ⓒ	Ⓓ
5	Ⓐ	Ⓑ	Ⓒ	Ⓓ	25	Ⓐ	Ⓑ	Ⓒ		45	Ⓐ	Ⓑ	Ⓒ	Ⓓ	65	Ⓐ	Ⓑ	Ⓒ	Ⓓ	85	Ⓐ	Ⓑ	Ⓒ	Ⓓ
6	Ⓐ	Ⓑ	Ⓒ	Ⓓ	26	Ⓐ	Ⓑ	Ⓒ		46	Ⓐ	Ⓑ	Ⓒ	Ⓓ	66	Ⓐ	Ⓑ	Ⓒ	Ⓓ	86	Ⓐ	Ⓑ	Ⓒ	Ⓓ
7	Ⓐ	Ⓑ	Ⓒ	Ⓓ	27	Ⓐ	Ⓑ	Ⓒ		47	Ⓐ	Ⓑ	Ⓒ	Ⓓ	67	Ⓐ	Ⓑ	Ⓒ	Ⓓ	87	Ⓐ	Ⓑ	Ⓒ	Ⓓ
8	Ⓐ	Ⓑ	Ⓒ	Ⓓ	28	Ⓐ	Ⓑ	Ⓒ		48	Ⓐ	Ⓑ	Ⓒ	Ⓓ	68	Ⓐ	Ⓑ	Ⓒ	Ⓓ	88	Ⓐ	Ⓑ	Ⓒ	Ⓓ
9	Ⓐ	Ⓑ	Ⓒ	Ⓓ	29	Ⓐ	Ⓑ	Ⓒ		49	Ⓐ	Ⓑ	Ⓒ	Ⓓ	69	Ⓐ	Ⓑ	Ⓒ	Ⓓ	89	Ⓐ	Ⓑ	Ⓒ	Ⓓ
10	Ⓐ	Ⓑ	Ⓒ	Ⓓ	30	Ⓐ	Ⓑ	Ⓒ		50	Ⓐ	Ⓑ	Ⓒ	Ⓓ	70	Ⓐ	Ⓑ	Ⓒ	Ⓓ	90	Ⓐ	Ⓑ	Ⓒ	Ⓓ
11	Ⓐ	Ⓑ	Ⓒ	Ⓓ	31	Ⓐ	Ⓑ	Ⓒ		51	Ⓐ	Ⓑ	Ⓒ	Ⓓ	71	Ⓐ	Ⓑ	Ⓒ	Ⓓ	91	Ⓐ	Ⓑ	Ⓒ	Ⓓ
12	Ⓐ	Ⓑ	Ⓒ	Ⓓ	32	Ⓐ	Ⓑ	Ⓒ		52	Ⓐ	Ⓑ	Ⓒ	Ⓓ	72	Ⓐ	Ⓑ	Ⓒ	Ⓓ	92	Ⓐ	Ⓑ	Ⓒ	Ⓓ
13	Ⓐ	Ⓑ	Ⓒ	Ⓓ	33	Ⓐ	Ⓑ	Ⓒ		53	Ⓐ	Ⓑ	Ⓒ	Ⓓ	73	Ⓐ	Ⓑ	Ⓒ	Ⓓ	93	Ⓐ	Ⓑ	Ⓒ	Ⓓ
14	Ⓐ	Ⓑ	Ⓒ	Ⓓ	34	Ⓐ	Ⓑ	Ⓒ		54	Ⓐ	Ⓑ	Ⓒ	Ⓓ	74	Ⓐ	Ⓑ	Ⓒ	Ⓓ	94	Ⓐ	Ⓑ	Ⓒ	Ⓓ
15	Ⓐ	Ⓑ	Ⓒ	Ⓓ	35	Ⓐ	Ⓑ	Ⓒ		55	Ⓐ	Ⓑ	Ⓒ	Ⓓ	75	Ⓐ	Ⓑ	Ⓒ	Ⓓ	95	Ⓐ	Ⓑ	Ⓒ	Ⓓ
16	Ⓐ	Ⓑ	Ⓒ	Ⓓ	36	Ⓐ	Ⓑ	Ⓒ		56	Ⓐ	Ⓑ	Ⓒ	Ⓓ	76	Ⓐ	Ⓑ	Ⓒ	Ⓓ	96	Ⓐ	Ⓑ	Ⓒ	Ⓓ
17	Ⓐ	Ⓑ	Ⓒ	Ⓓ	37	Ⓐ	Ⓑ	Ⓒ		57	Ⓐ	Ⓑ	Ⓒ	Ⓓ	77	Ⓐ	Ⓑ	Ⓒ	Ⓓ	97	Ⓐ	Ⓑ	Ⓒ	Ⓓ
18	Ⓐ	Ⓑ	Ⓒ	Ⓓ	38	Ⓐ	Ⓑ	Ⓒ		58	Ⓐ	Ⓑ	Ⓒ	Ⓓ	78	Ⓐ	Ⓑ	Ⓒ	Ⓓ	98	Ⓐ	Ⓑ	Ⓒ	Ⓓ
19	Ⓐ	Ⓑ	Ⓒ	Ⓓ	39	Ⓐ	Ⓑ	Ⓒ		59	Ⓐ	Ⓑ	Ⓒ	Ⓓ	79	Ⓐ	Ⓑ	Ⓒ	Ⓓ	99	Ⓐ	Ⓑ	Ⓒ	Ⓓ
20	Ⓐ	Ⓑ	Ⓒ	Ⓓ	40	Ⓐ	Ⓑ	Ⓒ		60	Ⓐ	Ⓑ	Ⓒ	Ⓓ	80	Ⓐ	Ⓑ	Ⓒ	Ⓓ	100	Ⓐ	Ⓑ	Ⓒ	Ⓓ

맞은 문제 개수: ___ /100

TEST 10의 점수를 환산한 후 목표 달성기에 TEST 10의 점수를 표시합니다.
점수 환산표는 문제집 167페이지, 목표 달성기는 교재의 첫 장에 있습니다.

✂ 자르는 선

Answer Sheet

TEST 09

LISTENING (Part I~IV)

#	A	B	C	D	#	A	B	C	D	#	A	B	C	D	#	A	B	C	D	#	A	B	C	D
1	Ⓐ	Ⓑ	Ⓒ	Ⓓ	21	Ⓐ	Ⓑ	Ⓒ		41	Ⓐ	Ⓑ	Ⓒ	Ⓓ	61	Ⓐ	Ⓑ	Ⓒ	Ⓓ	81	Ⓐ	Ⓑ	Ⓒ	Ⓓ
2	Ⓐ	Ⓑ	Ⓒ	Ⓓ	22	Ⓐ	Ⓑ	Ⓒ		42	Ⓐ	Ⓑ	Ⓒ	Ⓓ	62	Ⓐ	Ⓑ	Ⓒ	Ⓓ	82	Ⓐ	Ⓑ	Ⓒ	Ⓓ
3	Ⓐ	Ⓑ	Ⓒ	Ⓓ	23	Ⓐ	Ⓑ	Ⓒ		43	Ⓐ	Ⓑ	Ⓒ	Ⓓ	63	Ⓐ	Ⓑ	Ⓒ	Ⓓ	83	Ⓐ	Ⓑ	Ⓒ	Ⓓ
4	Ⓐ	Ⓑ	Ⓒ	Ⓓ	24	Ⓐ	Ⓑ	Ⓒ		44	Ⓐ	Ⓑ	Ⓒ	Ⓓ	64	Ⓐ	Ⓑ	Ⓒ	Ⓓ	84	Ⓐ	Ⓑ	Ⓒ	Ⓓ
5	Ⓐ	Ⓑ	Ⓒ	Ⓓ	25	Ⓐ	Ⓑ	Ⓒ		45	Ⓐ	Ⓑ	Ⓒ	Ⓓ	65	Ⓐ	Ⓑ	Ⓒ	Ⓓ	85	Ⓐ	Ⓑ	Ⓒ	Ⓓ
6	Ⓐ	Ⓑ	Ⓒ	Ⓓ	26	Ⓐ	Ⓑ	Ⓒ		46	Ⓐ	Ⓑ	Ⓒ	Ⓓ	66	Ⓐ	Ⓑ	Ⓒ	Ⓓ	86	Ⓐ	Ⓑ	Ⓒ	Ⓓ
7	Ⓐ	Ⓑ	Ⓒ	Ⓓ	27	Ⓐ	Ⓑ	Ⓒ		47	Ⓐ	Ⓑ	Ⓒ	Ⓓ	67	Ⓐ	Ⓑ	Ⓒ	Ⓓ	87	Ⓐ	Ⓑ	Ⓒ	Ⓓ
8	Ⓐ	Ⓑ	Ⓒ	Ⓓ	28	Ⓐ	Ⓑ	Ⓒ		48	Ⓐ	Ⓑ	Ⓒ	Ⓓ	68	Ⓐ	Ⓑ	Ⓒ	Ⓓ	88	Ⓐ	Ⓑ	Ⓒ	Ⓓ
9	Ⓐ	Ⓑ	Ⓒ	Ⓓ	29	Ⓐ	Ⓑ	Ⓒ		49	Ⓐ	Ⓑ	Ⓒ	Ⓓ	69	Ⓐ	Ⓑ	Ⓒ	Ⓓ	89	Ⓐ	Ⓑ	Ⓒ	Ⓓ
10	Ⓐ	Ⓑ	Ⓒ	Ⓓ	30	Ⓐ	Ⓑ	Ⓒ	Ⓓ	50	Ⓐ	Ⓑ	Ⓒ	Ⓓ	70	Ⓐ	Ⓑ	Ⓒ	Ⓓ	90	Ⓐ	Ⓑ	Ⓒ	Ⓓ
11	Ⓐ	Ⓑ	Ⓒ	Ⓓ	31	Ⓐ	Ⓑ	Ⓒ	Ⓓ	51	Ⓐ	Ⓑ	Ⓒ	Ⓓ	71	Ⓐ	Ⓑ	Ⓒ	Ⓓ	91	Ⓐ	Ⓑ	Ⓒ	Ⓓ
12	Ⓐ	Ⓑ	Ⓒ	Ⓓ	32	Ⓐ	Ⓑ	Ⓒ	Ⓓ	52	Ⓐ	Ⓑ	Ⓒ	Ⓓ	72	Ⓐ	Ⓑ	Ⓒ	Ⓓ	92	Ⓐ	Ⓑ	Ⓒ	Ⓓ
13	Ⓐ	Ⓑ	Ⓒ	Ⓓ	33	Ⓐ	Ⓑ	Ⓒ	Ⓓ	53	Ⓐ	Ⓑ	Ⓒ	Ⓓ	73	Ⓐ	Ⓑ	Ⓒ	Ⓓ	93	Ⓐ	Ⓑ	Ⓒ	Ⓓ
14	Ⓐ	Ⓑ	Ⓒ	Ⓓ	34	Ⓐ	Ⓑ	Ⓒ	Ⓓ	54	Ⓐ	Ⓑ	Ⓒ	Ⓓ	74	Ⓐ	Ⓑ	Ⓒ	Ⓓ	94	Ⓐ	Ⓑ	Ⓒ	Ⓓ
15	Ⓐ	Ⓑ	Ⓒ	Ⓓ	35	Ⓐ	Ⓑ	Ⓒ	Ⓓ	55	Ⓐ	Ⓑ	Ⓒ	Ⓓ	75	Ⓐ	Ⓑ	Ⓒ	Ⓓ	95	Ⓐ	Ⓑ	Ⓒ	Ⓓ
16	Ⓐ	Ⓑ	Ⓒ	Ⓓ	36	Ⓐ	Ⓑ	Ⓒ	Ⓓ	56	Ⓐ	Ⓑ	Ⓒ	Ⓓ	76	Ⓐ	Ⓑ	Ⓒ	Ⓓ	96	Ⓐ	Ⓑ	Ⓒ	Ⓓ
17	Ⓐ	Ⓑ	Ⓒ	Ⓓ	37	Ⓐ	Ⓑ	Ⓒ	Ⓓ	57	Ⓐ	Ⓑ	Ⓒ	Ⓓ	77	Ⓐ	Ⓑ	Ⓒ	Ⓓ	97	Ⓐ	Ⓑ	Ⓒ	Ⓓ
18	Ⓐ	Ⓑ	Ⓒ	Ⓓ	38	Ⓐ	Ⓑ	Ⓒ	Ⓓ	58	Ⓐ	Ⓑ	Ⓒ	Ⓓ	78	Ⓐ	Ⓑ	Ⓒ	Ⓓ	98	Ⓐ	Ⓑ	Ⓒ	Ⓓ
19	Ⓐ	Ⓑ	Ⓒ	Ⓓ	39	Ⓐ	Ⓑ	Ⓒ	Ⓓ	59	Ⓐ	Ⓑ	Ⓒ	Ⓓ	79	Ⓐ	Ⓑ	Ⓒ	Ⓓ	99	Ⓐ	Ⓑ	Ⓒ	Ⓓ
20	Ⓐ	Ⓑ	Ⓒ	Ⓓ	40	Ⓐ	Ⓑ	Ⓒ	Ⓓ	60	Ⓐ	Ⓑ	Ⓒ	Ⓓ	80	Ⓐ	Ⓑ	Ⓒ	Ⓓ	100	Ⓐ	Ⓑ	Ⓒ	Ⓓ

맞은 문제 개수: ___ /100

TEST 09의 점수를 환산한 후 목표 달성기에 TEST 09의 점수를 표시합니다.
점수 환산표는 문제집 167페이지, 목표 달성기는 교재의 첫 장에 있습니다.

무료 토익·토스·오픽·지텔프 자료 제공
Hackers.co.kr

MEMO

MEMO

최신 기출유형으로 실전 완벽 마무리

해커스 토익 LC

실전 1000제 2 LISTENING 문제집

개정 3판 5쇄 발행 2024년 11월 4일

개정 3판 1쇄 발행 2023년 1월 2일

지은이	해커스 어학연구소
펴낸곳	㈜해커스 어학연구소
펴낸이	해커스 어학연구소 출판팀

주소	서울특별시 서초구 강남대로61길 23 ㈜해커스 어학연구소
고객센터	02-537-5000
교재 관련 문의	publishing@hackers.com
동영상강의	HackersIngang.com

ISBN	978-89-6542-539-7 (13740)
Serial Number	03-05-01

외국어인강 1위, 해커스인강
HackersIngang.com

해커스인강

· 해커스 토익 스타강사의 **본 교재 인강**
· 단기 리스닝 점수 향상을 위한 **무료 받아쓰기&쉐도잉 프로그램**
· 최신 출제경향이 반영된 **무료 온라인 실전모의고사**
· 들으면서 외우는 **무료 단어암기장 및 단어암기 MP3**
· 빠르고 편리하게 채점하는 **무료 정답녹음 MP3**

영어 전문 포털, 해커스토익
Hackers.co.kr

해커스토익

· 본 교재 **무료 지문 및 문제 해석**
· **무료 매월 적중예상특강 및 실시간 토익시험 정답확인/해설강의**
· 매일 실전 RC/LC 문제 및 토익 기출보카 TEST, 토익기출 100단어 등 다양한 무료 학습 콘텐츠

5천 개가 넘는
해커스토익 무료 자료!

대한민국에서 공짜로 토익 공부하고 싶으면

해커스영어 Hackers.co.kr ▾   검색

RC 정수진   **RC 이상길**

강의도 무료

베스트셀러 1위 토익 강의 150강 무료 서비스,
누적 시청 1,900만 돌파!

문제도 무료

토익 RC/LC 풀기, 모의토익 등
실전토익 대비 문제 3,730제 무료!

LC 한승태   **RC 김동영**

최신 특강도 무료

2,400만뷰 스타강사의
압도적 적중예상특강 매달 업데이트!

공부법도 무료

**토익 고득점 달성팁, 비법노트,
점수대별 공부법 무료 확인**

가장 빠른 정답까지!

615만이 선택한 해커스 토익 정답!
시험 직후 가장 빠른 정답 확인

*미션 달성 시

더 많은 토익무료자료
보기 ▶